Delere Press
The Screaming Series

This paperback edition first published in 2017 by Delere Press LLP, as part of The Screaming Series.

The (Im)Possibility of Literature as the Possibility of Ethics © Nemanja Mitrović

First published in 2017 by Delere Press LLP
www.delerepress.com
Delere Press LLP Reg No. T11LL1061K

All rights reserved

ISBN 978-981-11-0533-3
Layout by Yanyun Chen

THE (IM)POSSIBILITY OF LITERATURE AS THE POSSIBILITY OF ETHICS

NEMANJA MITROVIĆ

FOR MY FRIENDS

ACKNOWLEDGEMENTS

This book is a reworked version of my doctoral dissertation which was defended at the University of Aberdeen in the spring of 2014. I would like to thank my supervisor and friend, Professor Christopher Fynsk, for his help and support. His guidance and infinite patience made this dissertation possible. A special gratitude goes to my friend Svetlana Gavrilović for the influence that she had on my life. I would like to thank Sanja Kunjadić and Karlo Pellegrinelli for our joyous conversations that gave me strength to complete this study. Finally, I do not want to forget Julia Hölzl, Greg Herman, and William B. Anderson - our adventures served as the infinite source of inspiration for this book.

THE (IM)POSSIBILITY OF LITERATURE AS THE POSSIBILITY OF ETHICS

FORWARD

From Belgrade comes a captivating critical voice of the most surprising and disarming candor. We have in the pages before us the work of a devoted researcher of impeccable scholarly and philosophical preparation. At the same time, they cannot hide an irrepressible love for the topic in question—the literary—and an evident penchant for play. The honest critic who speaks here is thus also something of a showman who cannot resist staging the impossible problems with which he is at grips, and cannot resist an open reflection on this very staging and the mystery that reforms at every step. Yes, a serious, obviously trustworthy student of literature, this Nemanja Mitrović, posing textual questions of dizzying difficulty in a forthright manner, and seeking answers in the most diligent way with ample and always generous appeal to other scholarly support. But also a canny philologist who delights in playing at the foldings of textual disclosure, an unconcealment that is also a constant regeneration of what fascinates: the "impenetrable strangeness" that haunts and impels the literary endeavour.

One might ask: who finally prevails here, the workman or the showman? And what are we to make of the result?

There is display, to be sure, but nothing self-satisfied or in any way distracting or obscuring (were Mitrović a magician, he would always be explaining his tricks). At the same time, there is mastery of craft, but no endeavour to demonstrate and secure a critical hold, even in the construction of the frames that set the staging by which the exposition proceeds. Delight in hermeneutic discovery (sometimes hard-won), and a distinctive form of presentation (*Darstellung*) that *engages*, even *performs* the questions at hand—these are what distinguish Mitrović's efforts.

In such an undertaking, however, there are no "correct" answers in the traditional, "scientific" sense. Here, the effort to bring answers must cede always to the imperative of disclosure, and truth (in the sense of an adequation between description and object) must show its aletheic shadow. Probity, in this field, will be judged by an insistent answerability, a willing exposure. I do not doubt the reader will conclude that we have to do in these pages with an eminently honest philology, the work of a thinking that grows only more determined and responsible as the mysteries before it thicken. And the reader's trust can only be enhanced in entering the final pages in which Mitrović seeks to draw the aletheic play he documents into the light of ethics—not because his words are reassuring in their appeal to the established value represented by this field of inquiry, but rather because this writer is willing to argue for something he cannot fully establish, and will not hide his awareness of the tentative character of his thesis.

We may *share* the concern he expresses, in fact. Where, exactly, is he going with this question of ethics, or has he in fact touched upon a dimension of the literary that recasts some of our most fundamental presuppositions about the conditions of the ethical relation? Mitrović will satisfy the reader with his answers, I believe, but all readers will hope for more instalments to come. At the same time, the reader will leave with more than sympathy for the presenter who has won our affection, even our identification, through an earnest demonstration that never fails to expose its machinations and its questions in the critical equivalent of a literary work's reflexive disclosure of its abysses.

It is my sincere hope that every reader will *allow* themselves this identification by attending to the voice and the gestures that will prompt it, for they will enjoy the volume all the more. For the native reader of English, this presence will appear as much in an occasional strangeness in locution as in the use of the first-person pronouns and the many indications of staging. But this presence is easily forgotten once the reader begins to entertain an argument and a spectacle of a singularly original and challenging character. I do not want to rehearse this argument, since Mitrović will do this quite sufficiently himself (again, there is nothing hidden here—the method is overt). But I will touch briefly on its movement in order to clarify my meaning in speaking of a deepening mystery.

The volume initially offers itself to the trained reader, by its very title, as an exercise in deconstruction. And indeed it contains a veritable lesson in deconstructive principles as it performs its encounter with works that cannot but entrap with their conceits the reader who is hesitant to release the handholds of methodology and traditional assumptions regarding reference and intentionality--like the hapless Dejan Ilić who is caught in the snares of Sreten Ugričić's *Infinitive* (not quite Derrida's Searle, but no less humorously trammelled by his common-sense assumptions), or those troubled sleuths attempting to deal with the mystery of a fake biography (in the case of Hildesheimer's *Marbot*). But this pedagogical exercise is only preparatory with respect to the movement of reflection devoted to a structure of literary reference whereby an absent or fictional ur-text (*The Axiological Infinitive* of *Infinitive*) can take on a function comparable to that of the real event that haunts the narrative of Alain Fournier's novel, *The Lost Estate*. Here, Mitrović's critical analysis becomes properly a thought of the literary that requires a re-evaluation of the meaning of truth, as I have already noted. But Mitrović does not rest content with a Heideggerian account of the concealment that occurs in the literary work (though he offers, along the way, a precious indication of the manner in which Heidegger's notion of "createdness" can capture the text's always enigmatic manner of indicating its relation to its own "(im)possibility"). To account for the persistent enigma of the literary, its singular manner of "sheltering an absence in presence" through its performative constitution of what it cannot present, he is impelled to push forward into Blanchot's literary thought and a more abyssal, more radical understanding of the absence in question. Here, Mitrović's thinking about the literary seems to find its home—or rather the exile that always draws him onward. His comfort with this text is manifested in a beautiful grasp of the importance of the myth of Orpheus and Eurydice for Blanchot's thinking and practice.

There is a passage in Blanchot's *The Infinite Conversation* in which Blanchot appears to show a certain anguish about the inescapable *simulation* "proper" to the literary endeavour, despite the gravity of what is at stake in it. This comes in a moment of apparent self-reflection regarding one of the dialogues in the volume; though "self-reflection" is more properly understood in terms of the becoming other in and by the experience of reading and writing that is carefully attended to by Mitrović as he approaches the question of ethics and its conditions of possibility. The one who speaks is the apparent "author" of the dialogue:

> *I listen in my turn to these two voices, being neither close to the one, nor close to the other; being, nevertheless, one of them and being the other only insofar as I am not me— and thus, from the one to the other, interrupting myself in a manner that dissimulates (simulates only) the decisive interruption. How can one pretend to receive the enigmatic force that comes from the interruption that becomes infinite relation in speech, and that we betray with our insufficient means?*[1]

There is no certainty guiding the response to what is nonetheless felt as an exigency by the writer; one cannot pretend to knowledge in this sphere, and yet the exigency of testimony remains, as Blanchot insists throughout his later work. One can only "pretend" in the ludic sense of the term (by a dissimulation that "simulates only"), though the interruption that *ex-poses* the subject as they lend themselves to its enigmatic force in an "infinite relation" is no less real for this fact. This exigency is in fact of an ethical order, as we learn in the *The Step Not Beyond* in a narrative passage that touches upon the writer's responsibility to the other and in which the narrator questions recourse to the metaphor of play for the literary act, even under the form of Mallarmé's reference to "this mad game of writing."[2] How can one pretend to knowledge in this domain, and how can one shirk one's responsibility once it is encountered, even if the means are little better than pretense? This is the ground of Mitrović's claim in his title, and his tenuous (but quite compelling) argument concerning the proximity of Blanchot's literary thought to the ethical thinking of Emmanuel Levinas. It is in fact quite clear where Mitrović is going in his last pages, even if these steps can do little more than open a question of vast proportions. I won't seek to explore the question further here, but I would like to underscore that it is precisely Mitrović's probity that drives him to this final turn in his analysis. Having played demonstratively at structures that will appear frivolous to some readers, it is incumbent upon him to recognize what has occurred for him (to him) in this "mere" philological exercise—namely a form of exposure that opens the question of the ethical. His effort to hold to an irreducible obscurity or enigma in the literary "thing" has not represented some deconstructive stubbornness or arrogance before the requirements of good sense or a more seated literary science (a narratology, for example). It has been a fidelity to an "irreducible strangeness" that attends the human experience of the other, and first of all in the ethical relation. As I noted above, one knows that other instalments will have to come, but one also knows that this performance has offered far more than a play of mirrors. It has touched on the most fundamental questions bearing on the nature of the literary engagement with language.

Christopher Fynsk

---

1 Maurice Blanchot, *The Infinite Conversation*, trans. Susan Hanson (Minneapolis: University of Minnesota Press, 1986), 72.
2 Maurice Blanchot, *The Step Not Beyond*, trans. Lycette Nelson (Albany: State University of New York Press, 1973), 62.

CHAPTER ONE:
THE (IM)POSSIBILITY OF *INFINITIVE*

Like all totalities, language is the referent of a descriptive phrase, a referent whose reality cannot be established for want of an ostensive phrase (the phrase descriptive of the whole is a phrase of the Idea, in the Kantian sense. One can in fact describe *Language is this and that,* but not show, *And this is language.* The totality is not presentable.

Jean-François Lyotard, *The Differend: Phrases in Dispute*

The *sans* of the *sans*-theme and the *sans*-text must be marked, without being either present or absent, in the thing to which it does not belong and which is no longer quite a thing, which one can no longer name, which is not, once charged with the mark, a material support or form of what is to be found neither here nor there, and which one might indicate, given a certain displacement, by the name of text or trace.

Jacques Derrida, *The Truth in Painting*

It is always most interesting when the theoretical work starts with a story, and thus we will begin with the fourth chapter of the book named *Infinitive*: "The Shape of a Snowflake."[1] During the US Open Women's Final, which was played in 1992, the author of *Infinitive* claims to have noticed one puzzling thing. Among the commercials that surrounded the Central Court one was completely new and unknown to him: the simple word *INFINITIVE* written in white italic letters on a blue surface. He asked his sporting friends about that new commercial, but nobody knew anything about it. This is not the end, because the author spotted another strange thing, a discreet symbol on the t-shirts of Monica Seleš and Steffi Graf. During the slow-motion replays and close-ups he managed to see that this symbol had a shape of a snowflake. It was clearly not the AIDS awareness red ribbon or red poppy, a familiar emblem of Remembrance Day - it was a simple snowflake. "But, if the meaning of a red ribbon is AIDS awareness, if this ribbon is a sign of something more important, then a snowflake also signifies something similar" – that was the author's line of thinking. His curiosity only increased when he started to notice this symbol in different places: other tennis and football players were seen wearing it and the author also noticed it on Prince's guitar when he watched a VHS recording of his Tokyo concert.

Since he lived in wartime Serbia he was unable to discover the meaning of this symbol by himself and he decided to make a desperate move – he wrote a letter to Monica Seleš. This was a long letter: the author congratulated Seleš on her successes, he offered some advice about the improvement of her serving technique, but he also posed two questions. The first question was a rhetorical one: "For which country will she play in the upcoming Olympic Games, for Yugoslavia or for the USA?"

The second question was about the snowflake: "What is the meaning of a snowflake symbol on her t-shirts?" Surprisingly, after a couple of weeks, the reply arrived. In this letter Monica Seleš, or (more likely) someone from her PR office, eluded the first question about the participation in the Olympic Games, but provided a straight answer about the meaning of a snowflake. The letter said that "the snowflake signifies infinitive-awareness, the awareness that tolerance is the only way of preserving that sublime value which determines all other values." This answer also contained a reference: "You can read more about it in: Stewart W. Greenchurch, *The Axiological Infinitive*, Cambridge University Press, Boston, 1990."

The author somehow managed to find the book in question and, after he read it, his *Infinitive* was born. *Infinitive* is a book about *The Axiological Infinitive*. It begins with a short biography of Stewart W. Greenchurch and with a list of his published works. At the very beginning of Sreten Ugričić's *Infinitive,* we have a photograph of Greenchurch's *The Axiological Infinitive* and, at the end, we have a photograph of Stewart W. Greenchurch himself. Ugričić's *Infinitive* has fifteen chapters and it is the examination of Greenchurch's *magnum opus* from numerous perspectives. Essentially, the task of Sreten Ugričić's monograph is to explain the basic idea of Greenchurch's theory (the axiological infinitive) and to show how this idea is connected with narratology, history and ethics. Also, this book contains several translations from English. At the Cornell University Library (Rare and Manuscript Collections), Sreten Ugričić discovered Thomas Pynchon's letter to Stewart W. Greenchurch and the famous translator Srđan Vujica translated it into Serbian (Chapter 10 of *Infinitive*). Also, Greenchurch's interview with *Time Magazine* (no. 1866, 24. December 1991) is included in Ugričić's monograph (Chapter 11 *of Infinitive*). Sreten Ugričić translated two theoretical texts of Stewart Greenchurch and they are also present in his monograph. The first one is the chapter from Greenchurch's book *Narrative, Performative, Infinitive* that is entitled "A Story Before All Stories"(Chapter 13 of *Infinitive*). The second one comes from Greenchurch's book *Incognito* and its name is "I Promise That I Will Prove That I Exist" (Chapter 14 of *Infinitive*). One of the important parts of *Infinitive* is also the chapter "They Said About *The Axiological Infinitive*" that presents commentaries of famous philosophers (e.g. Jacques Derrida, Jean-François Lyotard, Jürgen Habermas), artists (e.g. Umberto Eco, John Fowles, Joseph Brodsky) and pop-culture icons (e.g. David Bowie, Björk, Michael Stipe) about the work of Stewart W. Greenchurch. Since *Infinitive* is a monograph, a book about another book, then my first task is to present some basic theses of *The Axiological Infinitive*.

The Axiological Infinitive, we learn, is the final and most important book of the famous American philosopher Stewart W. Greenchurch. This is also a very large book (over 1800 pages) and its three volumes were published by the Cambridge University Press between 1980 and 1991. One of Greenchurch's most important theses is that the main term from the title (*infinitive*) resists any attempt at definition: to be more precise, it cannot be conceptualized. We all have some kind of values and this means that we all have some intuitive grasp of infinitive, because infinitive makes values possible. Infinitive is the most universal value and to define it means to lose it. The inherent paradox of the infinitive prevents its definition.

In *Rhetoric* (Book I, Chapter 9) Aristotle claims: "Now *kalon* describes whatever, through being chosen itself, is praiseworthy or whatever, through being good [*agathon*], is pleasant because it is good. If this, then, is the *kalon*, then virtue is necessarily *kalon*; for it is praiseworthy because of being good [*agathon*]."[2] Nevertheless, there are some values that cannot be praised. Eudoxus of Cnidus was one of the first people who draw our attention to these kinds of values. The first volume of Greenchurch's work thus begins with the analysis of the 10th book of *The Nicomachean Ethics*, namely with Eudoxus's paradox.

Eudoxus was a mathematician, astronomer, a notable member of Plato's academy and a friend of Aristotle's son Nicomachus. The argument of Eudoxus is often described as hedonistic and it goes like this: of all things that are good, happiness is the crowning good because it cannot be praised. Why can we not praise this crowning good? The answer is: something can be praised only in relation to something else; reference must always exist in a praise. In short, this is Eudoxus's paradox and, as you can see, it is very simple and consists in the following: the highest value is the only principle and the criterion of evaluation. Where is the paradox in this statement? It arises from the fact that the source of values, the highest criterion of evaluation or the final evaluative instance cannot be evaluated. The evaluative cannot be evaluated because it evaluates everything else. Why? The reason for this is quite obvious and it is connected with the problem of reference: we can evaluate the highest evaluative instance only with some higher instance and this would mean that our presumed highest evaluative instance is not the highest. There can be only one highest value. So, at the origin of values lies a value that cannot be defined and therefore it cannot be either praised or criticized. Greenchurch's name for this value is *the infinitive*.

Having finished the analysis of Eudoxus's paradox, Greenchurch gives his readers another example to clarify things further. This example is a Zen story about the student who constantly bothered his master with the following questions: "What is the most valuable thing in the world? What is the highest value above all values? What is the highest good?" One day the master gave his response: "The dead cat." The student was puzzled by this response and he asked: "Why is that? Why is the dead cat the most valuable thing in the world?" The master's final response was: "The dead cat gives value to everything else, because no one can say its value."

The infinitive does not have value like other values – it is less value and more the condition for the appearance of values. The story about the dead cat clearly illustrates the paradoxality of the infinitive: the highest value shows itself as valueless. When something is invaluable it means that we cannot determine (and consequently define) its value. This is the basis of Greenchurch's claim that if *The Axiological Infinitive* were a book about mathematics its name would have been *The Zero*, because zero is the only number that is not a number.

Let us consider another illustration of Greenchurch's main term. The infinitive is very similar to the hidebehind animal from Borges's *The Book of Imaginary Beings*.[3] A hidebehind is a mythical creature that a human may spot in the corner of their eye, but which disappears upon further inspection, because it is always hiding behind something. Nobody is able to describe exactly what a hidebehind looks like because, by definition, nobody has ever seen one clearly. When an observer attempts to look directly at it, the creature hides again behind an object or the observer and therefore cannot be directly seen. Therefore, the next important question is: what hides the infinitive?

The answer to this question lies in Greenchurch's explanation of the definitive. The definitive (or definitive value) is the evaluated instance, some concrete and historical value, a measure and a definition of the infinitive. The definitive is a value that can be legitimately praised or criticized, and it signifies the withdrawal of infinitive: the definitive is the ebb of infinitive. Greenchurch uses Anaxagoras's fragment 21a : "…what appears is a vision of the unseen"[4] or "…appearances are a sight of the unseen"[5], to explain the relationship between infinitive and definitive. He transports this fragment from the context of ontology into the sphere of axiology and claims that *unseen (or invisible)* is infinitive and that *what appears* is definitive. To define, to form a definitive, means to curtain the infinitive. So, the logic of definitive can be simply described as: *cover the invisible*! Definitive determines and defines with the exact criterion of measurement, but this precise definition masks, covers, and consequently misses, something immeasurable.

The emergence of confidence in precise definitions signals the forgetfulness of the infinitive. The cause of this forgetfulness is the basic human need for certainty. The definitive covers the infinitive: assuaged by the certainty of the definitive people forget that something invisible exists. This need for certainty produces axiological *hybris*; people start to believe that the highest value can be visible and measurable. But, if the definitive hides the infinitive, how do we even know that the infinitive exists? We can take the example of any given axiological structure: if we just try to overcome the highest value we will have to deal with Eudoxus's paradox. At this very moment the infinitive appears, but this appearance does not mean that we can point our finger at it. In this case, what we have is the appearance of disappearance. The infinitive shows itself only when it remains undisclosed and unexplained. This kind of self-showing cannot be reconciled with our need for certainty.

People do not understand the infinitive because they have forgotten about it. At this point, it can be useful to introduce the analogy with Sigmund Freud's *Interpretation of Dreams*.[6] Freud claims that dream-forgetting is in the service of resistance and that the forgotten fragments of our dreams (or our early childhood) are usually the most important ones. It is the same with the infinitive: the most important thing for us, the highest value, is, at the same time, the most inaccessible to our consciousness. To illustrate this thesis Greenchurch quotes Tom Waits and his song "Time": "... and the things you can't remember tell the things you can't forget."

A definition of the infinitive can only be described as *hybris*, since it is a substitution of evaluative by evaluated. However, Greenchurch proposes an interesting alternative to this axiological *hybris*. He claims that some works of art are able to constitute a group of definitives that can take the role of the infinitive. Not all works of art are like that, not all of them can be meta-definitive. These works of art that can be described as meta-definitive (masterpieces of art) are beautiful because they are infinitive; in short, they are definitives that can be interpreted as infinitive. Things that are said in these works cannot be rephrased or told differently. Masterpieces of art, meta-definitives, can be rephrased or imitated only as tautology. The prime example of this is the story of Jorge Luis Borges "Pierre Menard, Author of the *Quixote*."[7]

We can now return to the snowflake from the beginning. Why is the snowflake a symbol of the infinitive? One particular snowflake cannot be identical with another one: the concrete shape of a snowflake can be understood as a definitive of something infinitive. The infinitive crystal of a snowflake is something that cannot be seen, no matter how hard we try and no matter which microscope we use – science and technique are helpless in this situation. What we will see is a new snowflake, which is similar, but somehow always different from the previous one and from all past and future snowflakes. It seems like every snowflake, in its own authentic way, tries to copy some perfect, unreal and absent pattern or criterion. In this attempt every snowflake is equally imperfect in comparison with this endlessly absent pattern. The example of a snowflake tells us that some things exist only as infinitely absent – and these things are the most important ones.

In short terms, I have tried to sketch not just the outline of Greenchurch's *The Axiological Infinitive*, but also of Sreten Ugričić's *Infinitive*. We must not forget that the form of *Infinitive* is the monograph, that it is built around another book. But, the problem lies in the fact that this other book and its author, Stewart W. Greenchurch, do not exist – or, to be more precise, they exist only on the pages of Ugričić's *Infinitive*. The photograph of *The Axiological Infinitive* from the beginning of *Infinitive* is fake; it was constructed in Photoshop. The photograph of Stewart Greenchurch is actually the photograph of Cleanth Brooks. *Infinitive* is full of fake quotations; the chapter "They Said About *The Axiological Infinitive*" is the prime example of this fabrication. Sreten Ugričić sometimes just tweaks the existing statements of real persons to suit his purposes and sometimes he completely invents their statements about the work of Stewart Greenchurch. Through the course of his book Ugričić pretends that he quotes from *The Axiological Infinitive* and he also pretends that he translates other theoretical texts of Stewart Greenchurch. Ugričić also claims that Jerome David Salinger sent his unpublished story "Bringing No Presents, Just Pasts" to Stewart Greenchurch that had an enormous influence on the American philosopher. This story is also present on the pages of *Infinitive*, but it does not belong to Jerome David Salinger. It is a story written by Sreten Ugričić which he published in one of his previous texts. Also, epigraphs to numerous chapters of *Infinitive* that are attributed to different philosophers and artists (e.g. Friedrich Nietzsche, Dionysius the Areopagite, Fyodor Dostoyevsky) are again Ugričić's inventions written in the style of these artists or philosophers. The last pages of *Infinitive* are devoted to the excerpts from the reviews of this book and all these reviews are completely fabricated.

Of course, this masking of narrative as a critical discourse is not something new. For example, inspired by Carlyle's *Sartor Resartus* Jorge Luis Borges wrote several stories using this technique ("The Approach to Al-Mu'tasim", "Tlön, Uqbar, Orbis Tertius", "An Examination of the Work of Herbert Quain", "Pierre Menard, Author of the *Quixote*"). He liked to write notes about imaginary books and to present bogus information about these books to his readers (with date and place of publication, the name of the publisher, quotations from other critics, etc.) But, although this is very interesting, the important question is: what is the meaning of these imaginary works? Is this technique just a hoax or irresponsible invention? In his "Autobiographical Essay" Borges claims:

> My next story, "The Approach to Al-Mu'tasim" written in 1935, is both a hoax *and* a pseudo-essay. It purported to be a review of a book published originally in Bombay

three years earlier. I endowed its fake second edition with a real publisher, Victor Gollanz, and a preface by a real writer, Dorothy L. Sayers. But the author and the book are entirely my own invention. I gave the plot and details of some chapters - borrowing from Kipling and working in the twelfth-century Persian mystic Farid ud-Din Attar – and then carefully pointed out its shortcomings. The story appeared the next year in a volume of my essays, *Historia de la eternidad* (*A History of Eternity*), buried at the back of the book together with an article on the "Art of Insult." Those who read "The Approach to Al-Mu'tasim" took it at face value, and one of my friends even ordered a copy from London. It was not until 1942 that I openly published it as a short story in my first story collection *El jardin de senderos que se bifurcan* (*The Garden of Branching Paths*). Perhaps I have been unfair to this story; it now seems to me to foreshadow and even to set the pattern for those tales that were somehow awaiting me, and upon which my reputation as a storyteller was to be based.[8]

Emir Rodriguez Monegal claims that the importance of "The Approach to Al-Mu'tasim", "Tlön, Uqbar, Orbis Tertius", "An Examination of the Work of Herbert Quain", "Pierre Menard, Author of the *Quixote*" lies in the fact that all these stories deal with a certain concept of what fiction is. However, something even bigger is at stake in these stories (and in *Infinitive*, as well), something more than just an understanding and practice of fiction. This nothingness at the centre of the existing works of Jorge Luis Borges and Sreten Ugričić cannot be easily discarded as irresponsible imagination. The search for the meaning of these invisible works can lead to the problem of "literarity" in general. To put it succinctly, this absence, this nothingness around which *Infinitive* and some stories of Jorge Luis Borges are built tells us something very important about literature itself. It tells us something about the (im)possibility of literature. In this work I will try to provide some answers to this problem of literature's (im)possibility through a dialogue with the works of Martin Heidegger and Maurice Blanchot. But, before I start to move in this direction, I first have to explain what I will not do.

First, or at least at the very beginning, I will have to try to avoid *Infinitive's* trap of endless mirroring. I say "at least at the very beginning" because this endless mirroring is an important characteristic of *Infinitive* and therefore it will be addressed in the third chapter of this study. However, some other characteristics of Ugričić's work will need to be described first. We must notice that Sreten Ugričić's book is about the invisible philosopher and his invisible work. Hence, the relationship between the book of Stewart Greenchurch and Ugričić's book is similar to the relationship between infinitive and (meta) definitive. Is my reading of *Infinitive* going to become just another definitive of the invisible theory of Stewart Greenchurch? In this study, I am not going to accept or to treat this possibility of endless mirroring as irresponsible textual playfulness. But, I will also not try to break off from the circular argumentation of *Infinitive*. My aim is to try to read the invisible; to be more precise, to let the invisibility show itself precisely as invisibility. Because of that, my main question will be: what makes *Infinitive* (im)possible?

Second, although some similarities exist, *The Axiological Infinitive* is not the MacGuffin. In his interview with François Truffaut, Alfred Hitchcock says about the MacGuffin:

> Truffaut: Isn't the MacGuffin the pretext for the plot?Hitchcock: Well, it's the device, the gimmick, if you will, or the paper that the spies are after. I'll tell you about it. Most of Kipling's stories, as you know, were set in India,

and they dealt with the fighting between the natives and the British on the Afghanistan border. Many of them were spy stories, and they were concerned with the efforts to steal the secret plans out of a fortress. The theft of a secret document was the original MacGuffin. So the 'MacGuffin' is the term that we use to cover all that sort of thing: to steal plans or documents or discover a secret. It doesn't matter what it is. And the logicians are wrong in trying to figure out the truth of a MacGuffin, since it's beside the point. The only thing that really matters is that in the picture the plans, documents, or secrets must seem of vital importance to the characters. To me, the narrator, they're of no importance whatsoever. You may be wondering where the term originated. It might be a Scottish name, taken from a story about two men in a train. One man says, "What's that package up there in the baggage rack?" And the other answers, "Oh that's a MacGuffin." The first one asks, "What's a MacGuffin?" "Well," the other man says, "it's an apparatus for trapping lions in the Scottish Highlands." The first man says, "But there are no lions in the Scottish Highlands," and the other one answers, "Well then, that's no MacGuffin!" So you see that a MacGuffin is actually nothing at all.[9]

In *The Sublime Object of Ideology* Slavoj Žižek equates the MacGuffin with *objet petit a* and claims that its sole role is to set the story in motion.[10] Its only significance lies in the fact that it has some significance for the characters in the story and that these characters are willing to do almost anything to possess it. But, psychoanalytic analysis and the understanding of MacGuffin in general do not quite offer the answer to the crucial question: why is this nothingness that lies under the guise of MacGuffin so powerful? In the world of narrative the MacGuffin is never empty, it is never nothing. For example, in Hitchcock's movies the MacGuffin is always something (glove, necklace, uranium, lighter, etc.); it is never nothing. MacGuffin functions because it always has reference and only its meta-interpretation can show us the logic of endless substitutions. On the other hand, it is clear that *Infinitive* does not have a reference: *Infinitive*'s reference is *The Axiological Infinitive*, which is precisely nothing in itself. I am especially interested (or maybe I can say drawn to) this nothingness which lies at the core of *Infinitive*. Consequently, some of the questions that I will try to answer are: What is nothingness? Why is this nothingness important? What is the meaning of this nothingness?

Third, I will not try to access *Infinitive* either from the position of common sense, or armed with presuppositions of literary theory. I decline to do this because these approaches operate on the shared assumption that there is some present-at-hand literary object which can be described or analyzed. In the first two chapters of my work, I will show the problems with this basic assumption. Too much of contemporary literary theory rests upon the representationalist view of language, and also too much of purported deconstructive literary theory can be described as the inverted image of this positivistic approach. If we bear this impasse in mind then the important questions must be asked: is literature an expression of experiences or an expression of some general cultural processes? Does the language of literature obey the rules of formal logic? Is language just a tool or means of self-expression and communication?

In this chapter, I will try to offer provisional answers to some of these questions. The answers will be offered through a dialogue with Dejan Ilić's reading of *Infinitive*, which can be found in the texts "There Are Three Eudoxus, the First One Is Ours"[11] and "The 'Miraculous' Performative."[12] Dejan Ilić is a Serbian critic and publisher, so far the only person who has tried to write about *Infinitive*. However, his reading rests upon some basic presuppositions of common sense. I will try to disturb this familiar mode of questioning and to offer some alternatives to this view of literature. Ilić's readings of *Infinitive* are the example of something that can be called *a common sense reductiveness*. In these interpretations Ilić equates thinking and common sense, but this move is fundamentally problematic. Common sense is not thinking, and it cannot function as a substitute for thinking. Thinking challenges common sense and its views about meaning, writing, and literature. Dejan Ilić (and many similar critics) never bothered to learn the lesson from Martin Heidegger's "The Nature of Language": "It therefore might be helpful to us to rid ourselves of the habit of always hearing only what we already understand."[13] My opinion is that *Infinitive* is, before everything else, an enigma. In order for the enigma to show itself precisely as an enigma current pseudo-concepts of common sense and so called literary theory must first be set aside.

The texts of Dejan Ilić sparked a discussion between him and Sreten Ugričić about the genre of *Infinitive*.[14] My aim is not to add another contribution to this discussion (although I will offer a possible view on the genre of *Infinitive*), but to pinpoint the limitations of Dejan Ilić's perspective. Also, I will argue that the basis of these limitations is the understanding of truth as correspondence. This understanding of truth will prove to be the basic block for Ilić's attempts to interpret *Infinitive*.

The noticeable feature of Dejan Ilić's text "The 'Miraculous' Performative" is impatience, because it wants to translate *Infinitive* into a definitive. One of the paradigmatic articulations of this impatience can be found at the very beginning of "The 'Miraculous' Performative":

> I am ready to agree with those who claim that to understand some text means to understand what the author wanted to say. And, furthermore, that language gives the author the options to actualize and to record with words what he wants to say, and that the reader is capable of understanding what the author wrote. Starting from this position, as I did before, I wrote about Sreten Ugričić's book *Infinitive*.[15]

The first real problem is already before us: what is language? Dejan Ilić takes for granted two things: the referential function of language and the role of the author. According to this usual account, language serves as a means for achieving understanding. In this conception, language is understood as written (or oral) expression of what needs to be communicated. The starting point of Ilić's text is the understanding of a writer as someone who aims to express what troubles him. According to this understanding, the author's aim is to present the reflection of himself in the work of art. Dejan Ilić's text desires everyday truth; to be more precise, it demands the sense that can be extracted from the work. This desire is the well-known characteristic of the common conception of language - the view that language is just a transparent medium for the exchange of ideas. From this perspective, language has three components: *words* transmit *concepts* that refer to *things*. The clear implication of this perspective is desire for the transparency of words, desire for perfect understanding and desire for ideal communication. Can we really think about literature from this perspective?

In their famous essay on *the intentional fallacy*, W.K. Wimsatt and M.C. Beardsley question the widespread opinion about the governing role of the author's intention in the interpretation of literary works. They argue that the intention is understood as the cause of a work; it is the plan or the design of the author for the construction of his work.[16] The intentional fallacy "is a confusion between the poem and its origins . . . It begins by trying to derive the standard of criticism from the psychological causes of the poem and ends in biography and relativism."[17] It is important to note that W.K. Wimsatt and M.C. Beardsley do not deny the existence of the author's intention, they argue that this intention does not provide the criterion for judging (and evaluating) some literary work.

In our case, another problem stems from the fact that *Infinitive* is writing and writing stays even after the person that writes has departed. This possibility of absence is something that is structural to writing; it is possible to read what was written even in the radical absence (death) of its author. This is the even more radical claim than the one about intentional fallacy and it is formulated by Jacques Derrida in his essay "Signature Event Context." In this essay, Derrida claims that writing must remain readable despite the absolute disappearance of any receiver, determined in general, and that a writing which is not structurally readable beyond the death of its addressee is not writing. Derrida says that "to write is to produce a mark that will constitute a sort of machine which is productive in turn, and which my future disappearance will not, in principle, hinder in its functioning, offering things and itself to be read and to be rewritten."[18] This means that writing must continue to be readable even when the author no longer answers for what he has written, because he is temporarily absent, dead or because he did not mean what he wrote. This is a dangerous feature of writing and precisely what Plato condemns in his work. This strange (and dangerous) quality of writing is something that he recognized and elaborated in the famous Thamous-Theuth story.[19]

In his reply to Derrida, John Searle poses some questions that are very similar to the ones that Dejan Ilić pose to Sreten Ugričić: "Do the special features of writing determine that there is some break with the author's intentions in particular or with intentionality in general in the forms of communication that occur in writing? Does the fact that writing can continue to function in the absence of the writer, the intended receiver, or the context of production show that writing is not a vehicle of intentionality?"[20] In order to provide the answer to these questions, Searle uses the example of a sentence written by an author who is obviously dead: "On the twentieth of September 1793 I set out on a journey from London to Oxford."[21] John Searle will claim that the fact that the author of this sentence is dead has no bearing to the understanding of what he meant to say. This leads him to the conclusion that is very similar to Dejan Ilić's claim that I mentioned previously.[22] In his reply to Derrida, Searle says:

> To the extent that the author says what he means the text is the expression of his intentions. It is always possible that he may not have said what he meant or that the text may have become corrupt in some way; but exactly parallel considerations apply to spoken discourse. The situation as regards intentionality is exactly the same for the written word as it is for the spoken: understanding the utterance consists in recognizing the illocutionary intentions of the author and these intentions may be more or less perfectly realized by the words uttered, whether written or spoken.[23]

In his elaborate answer to John Searle, "Limited Inc a b c...", Jacques Derrida claims that Searle's example "On the twentieth of September 1793 I set out on a journey from London to Oxford." only appears to be simple. It merely seems simple because in this example it is presumed that the person who says "I" and who speaks about himself "best satisfy the idealizing hypothesis of 'saying what he means.'"[24] "On the twentieth of September 1793 I set out on a journey from London to Oxford" is clearly the utterance made in the first person, but who is the "I" of this utterance? Derrida points to the fact that "the functioning of the I, as is well known, is no less iterable or replaceable than any other word. And in any case, whatever singularity it might possess is not of a kind to guarantee any adequation between saying and meaning."[25] Also, Searle does not take into account the transformative possibilities of the context. Derrida argues that it can be useful to compare this sentence with the one that was found in Nietzsche's notes: "I forgot my umbrella."[26] What is the context of this sentence? Consequently, what is the context of Searle's sentence about the trip London to Oxford? When we pose this question about the context infinite possibilities begin to open. Are these sentences citations? Beginning of a literary work? Some secret code? A message to someone? The meaning of these two sentences will depend upon their position in the particular context.[27]

Another problem is also clearly visible from Dejan Ilić's claim: "I am ready to agree with the ones who claim that to understand some text means to understand what the author wanted to say." This sentence implies that the writer is the origin of the literary work. This is an obvious simplification, because circular motion is understood as a straightforward line. The origin of the literary work is the writer, but only his work makes him the writer.[28] This is an important claim from Maurice Blanchot's "Literature and the Right to Death"[29] that deserves to be elaborated.

At the beginning of his text, Blanchot explores the contradiction of a writer. In order for the writer to write he needs talent, but only writing can prove his talent. This is a contradiction that actually describes the (im)possibility of literature. Blanchot says: "This difficulty illuminates, from the outset, the anomaly which is the essence of literary activity and which the writer both must and must not overcome."[30] The writer can become who he is only through his work. Before his work, he is simply nothing, but, if we bear in mind the already described contradiction, how can the work exist? This is precisely the question that concerns me in the case of *Infinitive*. Blanchot claims:

> "An individual," says Hegel, "cannot know what he [really] is until he has made himself a reality through action. However, this seems to imply that he cannot determine the End of his action until he has carried it out; but, at the same time, since he is a conscious individual, he must have the action in front of him beforehand as entirely his own, i.e. as an End." Now, the same is true for each new work, because everything begins again from nothing. And the same is also true when he creates a work part by part: if he does not see his work before him as a project already completed formed, how can he make it the conscious end of his conscious acts? But if the work is already present in its entirety in his mind and if this presence is the essence of the work (taking the words for the time being to be inessential), why would he realize it any further? Either: as an interior project it is everything it will ever be, and from that moment the writer knows everything about it that he can learn, and so will leave it to lie there in its twilight, without translating it into words, without writing it - but then he won't ever write: and he won't be a writer. Or: realizing that the work cannot be planned, but only carried out, that it has value, truth and reality only through the words that unfold it in time and inscribe it in space, he will begin to write,

> but starting from nothing and with nothing in mind - like a nothingness working in nothingness, to borrow an expression of Hegel's.[31]

It is clear that Blanchot does not offer a straightforward solution. The crucial contradiction is not solved, but preserved. Precisely the impossibility of its solution creates the possibility of the work's existence. This (im)possibility is one of the reasons why we cannot claim that the work is a simple shell for the author's ideas. In the texts of Dejan Ilić it is suggested that the author's intention stands as the final word, as the guarantee of the truth, but, luckily things are not that simple. For example, it is also possible to define the goal of productive thinking in a completely opposite way; we may try to discover not the author's intention, but what lies unsaid and unthought at the basis of what the author says and thinks.

Various reasons are already offered (and more will be offered in the next pages of this work) that put into doubt the standard conception which claims that the author is, at the same time, the master of language and the anchor of meaning. It is true, he produces work, but what is that work that is produced? How is the work of art produced? Is this process of production similar to the production of equipment? A piece of equipment (for example, a stove) is also something that is produced. What are the differences (and similarities) between a work of art and a piece of equipment? These are all important questions, and I will come back to them in depth in the second chapter of this study (where I will offer a perspective on Heidegger's understanding of truth and some important points from "The Origin of the Work of Art"). However, we need to start somewhere. This is why I would like to offer a preliminary exploration of the most important question of them all: what is the work of art? This is the question that

Blanchot shares with Heidegger and the prominent question from Heidegger's "The Origin of the Work of Art". For now, I will focus solely on one aspect of Blanchot's response from "Literature and the Right to Death".

In this essay Blanchot writes about the production of the simple object and connects this production with the question: When a man works, what does he do? The answer is: with his work he creates an object that is a realization of a plan that was unreal before the creation. For example, my project is to get warm and I will produce a stove. The produced object then changes my reality: the idea of warmth is nothing in itself, just an empty ideal, but I changed the state of things with the production of the object, and, in turn, I am also changed. What is the difference between a literary work and a simple object (like a stove)? The simple object does not refer to itself, it does not ask the question about its own origin, it just serves its purpose.

What does one actually do when one writes? Blanchot claims that the writer produces the work by transforming natural and human reality. Before the beginning of the writing, there was certainly an idea, but the difference between the realized work and that idea is the same as the difference between the idea of warmth and the realized stove. A literary work of art is an unforeseen and interesting innovation: even its maker cannot fully understand it, and he certainly cannot control its consequences. Also, it is impossible for the author to remain the same after his work is finished – in the presence of something other, he becomes other.

At the first glance, it seems that the work is basically the same kind of thing as all other things in the world. The work is finished and after that other people are interested in it. But, at that point, as Blanchot describes, the work begins to disappear for its author. The value of the work comes from its comparison with other works. The work is original if it does not resemble them, and its understanding is based on the reading of other works that came before it. The writer exists in his work, but the work exists only if it is published and thus made public. But, this also means that when the work is published it starts to disappear for its author (the readers start to create their own work) and the author becomes alienated from the very thing he created. Of course, this does not mean that the reader is more important than the author or that he has all the answers. The reader desires something unknown, something different and alien to him – but, at the same time, something that can transform him and that he can transform into himself. The work really disappears, but this disappearance is the basis of its appearance:

> My books (which do not know that I exist)
> are as much a part of me as is this face,
> the temples gone to grey and the eyes grey,
> the face I vainly look for in the mirror,
> tracing its outline with a concave hand.
> Not without understandable bitterness,
> I feel now that the quintessential words
> expressing me are in those very pages
> which do not know me, not in those I have written.
> It is better so. The voices of the dead
> will speak of me forever...[32]

So, if we take into consideration Blanchot's arguments, then a writer can be defined in several different ways at the same time: a writer without a name (pure absence), a writer who is identical with his work (and a guarantee of its meaning), a writer as a reader, and a reader as a writer, a writer who is a result and a function of the work, etc. When we try to define him once and for all (and consequently to rigidify him) we are presented with a problem: According to Blanchot, the problem is "that a writer is not only several people in one, but each stage of himself denies all the others, demands everything for itself alone and does not tolerate any conciliation or compromise."[33]

In "The 'Miraculous' Performative" Dejan Ilić asks:

> When he says that every reading is legitimate does Sreten Ugričić really mean that? Maybe his text „About Himself" supports the opposite thesis: not every reading is a legitimate one. Does the text „About Himself" express the wish of Sreten Ugričić for the accurate reading of his book, the wish for a reader who can accurately understand what the author wanted to say? Do the explanations of the *Infinitive*'s author contradict his statement that every reading is equally logical and justifiable, and that every reading is based on the text?[34]

But, if we remember that *a writer is not only several people in one, but each stage of himself denies all the others*, then the reaction of Sreten Ugričić in his text "About Himself" is completely understandable. This constant change of characters marks the impossibility of Dejan Ilić's task and makes the rigidification of a writer impossible. The work itself demands a writer's response to several absolute and completely different commands at the same time, and this means that we can turn Ilić's argument around. Let us suppose a hypothetical situation: Dejan Ilić wrote a text in which he claims that *Infinitive* is an excellent work of literature. But, the result of this text would probably be the same: the discussion with Sreten Ugričić. Only, in this hypothetical case, he would be discussing the genre of *Infinitive* with the philosopher whose name is Sreten Ugričić, and this philosopher would probably have tried to prove that the nature of his book is philosophical.[35]

In my opinion, this idea that *a writer is not only several people in one, but each stage of himself denies all the others* is very valuable and I would like to try to connect it with "Pierre Menard, Author of the *Quixote*."[36] "Pierre Menard, Author of the *Quixote*" is a story about reading, precisely a story about the complex relationship between reading and writing.[37] In this story, Menard's reading becomes writing, and Borges himself, when he attributes the authorship of his stories to some imaginary artists, presents his writing as a reading. The task that Menard has chosen to fulfill is not difficult, only impossible: "My undertaking is not difficult, essentially... I should only have to be immortal to carry it out."[38] One of the roles of this impossible task is to show us the way toward a new poetics which can be based on the activity of anachronistic reading. The basic idea of this poetics is that the meaning of books is not fixed by the time of their making or by the author's intention – the meaning of the books is always in front of them, not behind them. The meaning is context-bound, but the context is boundless; the context is non-saturable and because of that it is transformative. In his essay "The Wall and the Books" Borges writes:

> Generalizing, we might infer that *all* forms have their virtue in themselves and not in an imagined "content." This would support the theory of Benedetto Croce; by 1877, Pater had already stated that all the arts aspire to resemble music, which is nothing but form. Music, states of happiness, mythology, faces worn by time, certain twilights and certain places all want to tell us something, or have told us something we shouldn't have lost, or are about to tell us something; this imminence of a revelation as yet unproduced is, perhaps, the aesthetic fact.[39]

"This imminence of a revelation as yet unproduced" is important because it opens the work toward futurity. Dejan Ilić claims that the meaning of work lies in the past (in the author's intention), but Borges tells us that something completely opposite is the case. The meaning of books is always in front of them, not behind them. Dejan Ilić believes in the possibility of the ultimate meaning and Borges (together with Derrida) argues that meaning is always dependent on context and is something that exceeds any determinable context. Context always shifts and changes and because of that we cannot achieve the ultimate meaning.

The story of Pierre Menard addresses this issue and parodies the ultimate goal of romantic hermeneutic: *to understand an author better than he understood himself*. Schleiermacher argues that understanding does not simply come from reading the text, but also involves knowledge of the historical context of the text which is combined with the psychology of the author. Unfortunately, as time goes by, as the literary text strays further and further from its point of origin, its meaning becomes complicated. Schleiermacher is concerned with the problem of allegorical interpretation, because this kind of interpretation assumes that the author of a text intended something other than what is literally expressed. This is a method of interpretation which is used when there is a big gulf between the present context and the context in which the text was created, and, also, in cases when the intention of the author is unknown to us. Schleiermacher is the opponent of allegorical interpretation, and he claims that the goal of hermeneutics must be the foundation of the text's original meaning. How can we do this? Schleiermacher's answer was the *hermeneutic circle (Zirkel im Verstehen)* which is conceived in terms of the mutual relationship between the text as a whole and its individual parts. The relationship between text and its tradition is very important and, because of that, the study of history becomes an indispensable tool in the process of interpretation.

"Pierre Menard, Author of the *Quixote*" plays with this idea when it tells us about the tasks Menard set for himself: proficiency in Spanish language (Menard is French), return to Catholicism, fighting against the Moor or Turk, forgetting the history of Europe from 1602 to 1918. However, the main clue is philological fragment no. 2005, by Novalis: "Nur dann zeig ich, dass ich einen Schriftsteller verstanden habe, wenn ich in seinem Geiste handeln kann, wenn ich ihn, ohne seine Individualität zu schmälern, übersetzen, *und* mannigfach verändern kann."[40] In accordance with this fragment Menard had decided not to write *Don Quixote* as Miguel de Cervantes, but as Pierre Menard, and he wrote the ninth, thirty-eighth and one part of the twenty-second chapter of *Don Quixote*. This short overview of the story which I presented points to its complexity, and now I would like to focus my attention on the ninth chapter of *Don Quixote* (and of Menard's *Invisible Work*), because this chapter not only further elaborates the problem of the authorship, but also clarifies a strange sentence from "Prologue" in which Miguel de Cervantes claims: "But although I seem like Don Quixote's father, I am his stepfather..."[41]

Chapter IX begins as the continuation of the previous one; as a narration of the battle between Don Quixote and the Bacque. Suddenly, the narration stops just as Don Quixote is about to strike the final blow. Cervantes turns to his readers and tells them that the historical account, which served as his source, ends at this point: "...and at this critical point the delightful history stopped short and was left truncated, without any indication from its author about where the missing section might be found."[42]

Cervantes then explains how he found the missing part of the story at a fair in the city of Toledo:

> One day when I was in the main shopping street in Toledo, a lad appeared, on his way to sell some old notebooks and loose sheets of paper to a silk merchant; and since I'll read anything, even scraps of paper lying in the gutter, this leaning of mine led me to pick up one of the notebooks that the lad had for sale, and I saw it was written in characters that I recognized as Arabic. Although I knew that much, I couldn't read them. And so I looked around to see if there was some Spanish-speaking Moor in the street, and it wasn't very hard to find one, because even if I'd been looking for a translator from another better and older language, I should have found him, too. In short, chance provided me with a man who, when I told him what I wanted and put the book in his hands, opened it in the middle and after reading a little began to laugh. I asked him why, and he replied that he was laughing at something written in the margin of the book by way of annotation. I told him to tell me what it was and, still laughing, he replied: 'As I said this is written here in the margin: "This woman Dulcinea del Toboso, so often mentioned in this book, is said to have been a dabber hand at salting pork than any than any other woman in La Mancha."'[43]

The title that binds all these notebooks together is *History of Don Quixote de la Mancha, Written by Cide Hamete Benengeli, an Arab Historian.* After he bought all the papers and notebooks, Cervantes asked Morisco (converted Catholic inhabitant of Spain with a Muslim heritage) to translate the writing into Castillian for him. In a little more than a month and a half, the translation was completed. Cervantes continues and claims that, from this point on, his story about Don Quixote, is a redacted translation of Cide Hamete Benengeli's work. It is also important to note that Cervantes states some reservation about the truthfulness of this history and of the translation that followed it: "If there is any objection to be made about the truthfulness of this history, it can only be that its author was an Arab, and it's a well-known feature of Arabs that they're all liars; but since they're such enemies of ours it's to be supposed that he fell short of the truth rather than exaggerating it."[44]

In the ninth chapter of *Don Quixote* (and of Menard's *Invisible Work*), the authorship problem is clearly stated. In this chapter, what we have is not only a multiplication of authors, but also a multiplication of the presumed original. After he discovered Benengeli's notebooks Cervantes (author) became a reader. This situation, as we will see, reappears in *Infinitive*. In order to come back to Sreten Ugričić's work, we should pose the following questions: what is the meaning of this multiplication of authors and what does it mean when the author masks himself as a reader, when he speaks about writing from the position of reading?

As I previously noted in the reference to Derrida, the very act of writing detaches the author from himself; writing is something that must be readable even beyond the death of its author. Because of this feature, writing can be characterized as a splitting, a strange differing and deferring of presence and identity. Jacques Derrida emphasized this characteristic of writing in his passage about a simple shopping list:

> The shopping "list for myself" would be neither producible nor utilizable, it would not be what it is nor could it even exist, were it not for it to function, from the very beginning, in the absence of sender and of receiver: that is, of *determinate, actually present* senders and receivers. And *in fact* the list cannot function unless

these conditions are met. *At the very moment* "I" make a shopping list, I know (I use 'knowing' here as a convenient term to designate the relations that I necessarily entertain with the object being constructed) that it will only be a list if it implies my absence, if it already detaches itself from me in order to function beyond my "present" act and if it is utilizable at another time, in the absence of my being-present-now, even if this absence is the simple "absence of memory" that the list is meant to make up for, shortly, in a moment, but one which is already the following moment, the absence of the now of writing, of the writer maintaining, grasping with one hand his ballpoint pen. Yet no matter how fine this point may be, it is like the *stigmè* of every mark, already split. The sender of the shopping list is not the same as the receiver, even if they bear the same name and are endowed with the identity of a single ego. Indeed, were this self-identity or self-presence as certain as all that, the very idea of a shopping list would be rather superfluous or at least the product of a curious compulsion.[45]

From Dejan Ilić's perspective of common sense the author is the centre/the origin of a literary work and the creator of its meaning. In short, he is the guarantee for the stability of meaning. At the first glance, it seems that an author precedes his work and that he is posited outside of it. This perspective transposes the author's empirical characteristics into some kind of omniscient, theological figure; in his essence, the author becomes an almost God-like origin of all meaning. He is, at the time, a basis for the explanation of the work; a principle of unity of writing; he neutralizes the contradictions that may arise in a different texts produced during the period of several years, etc. On the basis of this, Michel Foucault[46] claims that an author is figure endowed with multiple functions: he is posited inside the literary work as its organizing principle and an anchor of meaning, but also outside the work. For example, his name can be used for the classification of work; it can serve to characterize the work's mode of being:

> ...the fact that the discourse has an author's name, that one can say "this was written by so-and-so" or "so-and-so is its author," shows that this discourse is not ordinary everyday speech that merely comes and goes, not something that is immediately consumable. On the contrary, it is a speech that must be received in a certain mode and that, in a given culture, must receive a certain status... The author's name manifests the appearance of a certain discursive set and indicates the status of this discourse within a society and a culture.[47]

The author is multiplied into several functions and this multiplication is made possible by the differing and deferring of the presence and identity that are inherent in the very act of writing.

The author is not something that can be taken for granted; he or she is always constructed and Foucault therefore speaks about *the author function*. He states that, in our time, literary discourses can be accepted only when they are endowed with the author function. When we encounter a fictional text our first questions are: who wrote it, when, and with what intention? If, by any chance, the text is anonymous then we try to discover its author. This construction of an author is not the spontaneous attribution of a discourse to an individual. It is a complex operation which varies according to periods and types of discourses.

Foucault argues that the manner in which literary criticism defines the author is derived from the very same method that Christian exegesis employed when it tried to prove the value of the text by the author's saintliness. In *De viris illustribus* (*On Illustrious Men*) Saint Jerome proposes four criteria according to which modern criticism brings the author into play:

> 1) **A constant level of value.** If among several books of the same author one is substandard in the relationship with others than it must be excluded from the list of author's works.
> 2) **Conceptual and theoretical coherence.** A work which contradicts other works attributed to the same author must also be excluded.
> 3) **Stylistic unity.** A work written in a different style which is not ordinarily found in the writer's production must be excluded.
> 4) **The author as a historical figure.** Passages with statements and events that occurred after the author's death must be regarded as interpolated texts.

The problems with Saint Jerome's criterion are evident from a literary point of view:

> 1) **A constant level of value.** It is clear that the level of value can vary in the works of the same author, but several authors can also achieve the same level of value in collaborative works.
> 2) **Conceptual and theoretical coherence.** There can be different types of coherence; coherence in theoretical text and coherence in the work of art is not the same thing. Also, Borges in his story tells us that Pierre Menard wrote an invective against Paul Valéry, and that this invective is the exact opposite of his true opinion of Valéry. This means that the theoretical and political views of the author are sometimes not identical with the theoretical

and political views that can be found in the work of the same author. From the criterion of conceptual and theoretical coherence this statement of Marcel Duchamp can only be incomprehensible: "I have forced myself to contradict myself in order to avoid conforming to my own taste."[48]

3) **Stylistic unity**. It is a well-known fact that a single work of art can contain a variety of styles and that these styles can be mixed and juxtaposed. For example, in *Ulysses,* episode 14 takes place in the maternity ward hospital and it is told through parodies of English prose style (Bunyan, Defoe, Sterne, Dickens, Carlyle, etc.) before concluding in a nearly incomprehensible slang;

4.) **The author as a historical figure**. Deliberate anachronisms can be easily found in literary works; the history presented in the artwork and the history of the author can be totally different. Also, anachronism can obtain an aesthetic role. The final passage of Borges's story tells us how Pierre Menard enriched the art of reading/writing with his new technique of the deliberate anachronism and erroneous attribution.

Because of all these problems, Foucault urges us to bear in mind that things are far more complicated then they appear in the common approach to the author's intention. It can also be argued that the author function is not a simple reconstitution from a text given as a passive material. This is why Foucault claims:

> Everyone knows that, in a novel narrated in the first person, neither the first-person pronoun nor the present indicative refers exactly either to the writer or to the moment in which he writes, but rather to an alter ego whose distance from the author varies, often changing

> in the course of the work. It would be just as wrong to equate the author with the real writer as to equate him with the fictitious speaker; the author function is carried out and operates in the scission itself, in this division and this distance.[49]

The author function does not refer simply to a real individual, because it can give rise simultaneously to several selves, to several subjects – it is a position that can be occupied by different classes of individuals. In short, the author function arises from the difference, and splitting, between the author and the narrator signified in the text.

If we consult the biographical data, we will see that *Infinitive* is a book written by Sreten Ugričić, which is published in Belgrade in 1997. We also discover that its writer is born in 1961 and that he graduated in philosophy at the Philosophical Faculty in Belgrade. He also worked as a director of the National Library of Serbia. If we presume that all this is true, we can ask: what is the exact relationship between this man and *Infinitive*?[50] Maybe, some time ago, he just decided to write *Infinitive* and to transcribe his ideas into that book? We understand that it cannot be that simple. Or, maybe, his ideas became real only after the act of writing? Giorgio Agamben follows Foucault's text "What is an Author?" and he tries to answer this question:

> Does this mean that the place of thought and feeling *is* in the poem itself, in the signs that make up the text? How could a passion, a thought be contained in a piece of paper? By definition, feelings and thoughts require a subject to experience and think them. In order for them to become present, someone must take up the book and read. This individual will occupy the empty place in the poem left by the author; he will repeat the same inexpressive

gesture the author used to testify to his absence in the work. The place of the poem - or, rather, its taking place - is therefore neither in the text nor in the author (nor in the reader): it is in the gesture through which the author and reader put themselves into play in the text and, at the same time, are infinitely withdrawn from it. The author is only the witness or guarantor of his own absence in the work in which he is put into play, and the reader can only provide this testimony once again, making himself in turn the guarantor of the inexhaustible game in which he plays at missing himself. Just as, according to Averroes, thought is unique and separate from the individuals who use their imaginations and fantasies to join with it from time to time, so do the author and the reader enter into a relationship with the work only on the condition that they remain unexpressed in it. And yet the text has no other light than the opaque one that radiates from the testimony of this absence.[51]

Bearing all this in mind, let us go back to the first and to the last sentence of *Infinitive*. The importance of these two sentences from *Infinitive* is emphasized in the text "There Are Three Eudoxus, the First One Is Ours."[52] The first sentence is: "It is possible to read this monograph as a novel about a theoretical book."[53] The last sentence of *Infinitive* is: "It is possible (least wrong) to read this monograph as a novel; a mimetic and realist novel about an idea."[54] Dejan Ilić does not read these sentences as a part of a text that is named *Infinitive*, but they are attributed to Sreten Ugričić. In his text, Dejan Ilić poses the following question: why does the author insist that his book can (and should) be read as a novel? He then replies that this insistence is the obvious evidence of the **Author**'s fear that **his** book will not be read according to **his** intention. Ilić himself insists on the role of the author, he claims that the author is the guarantee of meaning: "...if the reader does not intend merely to read, but also to understand something, then it is clear that the author's remarks can be decisive in our attempt to understand something. On the other hand, instructions and remarks are not enough, the text itself (on which edges these remarks exist and to which they pertain) needs to confirm their validity and soundness."[55] The text of Dejan Ilić puts the equality sign between reading and understanding and, in accordance with it, depreciates "mere reading." It is important to notice that this kind of interpretation uses the logic of identity, but, at the same time, does not exclude the referring of a text to itself. To be more precise, the logic of the above-mentioned argument works in the following way: if *Infinitive* is a novel then the sentences "It is possible to read this monograph as a novel..." and "It is possible (least wrong) to read this monograph as a novel..." have to point to something inside *Infinitive*, some essence, some being that can be identified as a novel, or, to put it more generally, as literature. However, I will attempt to show that the basic feature of literature is precisely its non-coincidence with itself.

Another important paragraph from the text of Dejan Ilić refers to the problem of genre:

> Sreten Ugričić claims that I put the books in the drawers. This is not true. The books that I have are standing on the shelves. But, it is true that I have the tendency to agree with the premise that an accurate decision about the genre of some text can prove to be crucial for its understanding. It is understandable that this does not mean that I am ready to defend a claim that we can decide the genre of any given text. It is obvious that the borderline cases exist. We can formulate the sentence that some text does not belong to any genre or the sentence that a text is on a borderline of several similar genres, but if we want our sentences to be meaningful then it is necessary to have

at least a vague knowledge about what genre is and what kinds of genres exist.[56]

At the first glance, this seems like a refinement of Dejan Ilić's argumentation. However, this is just another example of the logic of correspondence, and the words *accurate* and *genre* are treated as something unproblematic and easily understandable. In his first text "There Are Three Eudoxus, the First One Is Ours", Dejan Ilić focuses on the figure of author and he claims that in the author's intention lies the key for the understanding of the work. According to him, if we want to understand the work correctly, our understanding has to correspond with the author's intention. In "The 'Miraculous' Performative", he focuses on the problem of genre, but again with the help of the logic of correspondence. He says that he is not "ready to defend a claim that we can decide the genre of any given text", but "that an accurate decision about the genre of some text can prove to be crucial for its understanding." We can presume that his argument is more refined than the one about the author, because it allows the existence of borderline cases. However, in the last sentence he says that "it is necessary to have at least a vague knowledge about what genre is and what kinds of genres exist" and this is the place where he returns to the logic of correspondence. The borderline cases are just exceptions that prove the rule. Although the borderline cases exist, we need to know what genre is in order to detect them. What we need to possess in advance is the notion about the essence of genre which will correspond with the actual examples of genres. But, the real question is: can we use the logic of correspondence in our thinking about literature?[57] In this case, Dejan Ilić first introduces and then tries to eliminate a necessary moment of undecidability that underlies every decision about some genre.

Where is the border between different genres? Can we easily identify the line where one genre crosses into another? What is the role of repetition and citation in this process of genre identification? What marks are the distinctive ones (decisive for the classification of literary works) and what are the unimportant? Can we doubt the authority that classifies or is this authority beyond any doubt? Everything would be easy if we could just draw the line between citation and non-citation. John Langshaw Austin tried to draw that line when he excluded parasitical or empty utterances (used by the actors on stage or in some poem) from his analysis of performatives. In his text "Signature, Event, Context", Derrida asks: can it be true that what J. L. Austin excluded as "non-serious" is just a modification of a general citationality without which even a successful performative would not exist? Derrida poses the following question:

> Could a performative utterance succeed if its formulation did not repeat a "coded" or iterable utterance, or in other words, if the formula I pronounce in order to open a meeting, launch a ship or a marriage were not identifiable in some way as a "citation"?[58]

All these problems lead to a crucial question: does literature exist? Or, how is literature possible? Can we identify the distinctive mark that classifies some work as literature? In his text "The Law of Genre" Derrida deals with these questions.[59] When we try to classify some work what we need is a decision. This decision will have to translate a certain internal division into external opposition – basically what we need is a judgment. But, before this decision a moment of undecidability is necessary. Maybe this moment of undecidability does not last long, just a blink of an eye, but it makes the decision possible – without undecidability we would have only automatic responses. In the heart of our decision about something, for example about a genre of some work, there is always a possibility that things could have turned out differently, because genres are already and irreversibly mixed.

The classification of some text must be based on some distinctive mark of that text. On the basis of this distinctive mark, a text is defined as a crime story, realist novel or symbolist poetry. In any case, what we need is a system for the classification and the above-mentioned distinctive feature of a text is necessary for our decision about the genre. But, this distinctive characteristic functions like a label on a can, or like a doorkeeper in Kafka's story "Before the Law": something that is outside the law decides about the belonging to some genre.[60] This supplementary and distinctive trait (a mark of belonging) does not pertain to any genre or class – the mark of belonging actually does not belong. To put it simply, what we have is a certain kind of participation without belonging.

This distinctive mark can be re-marked in the work itself that we need to classify. Derrida claims that this possibility of re-marking is not present only in literary works. This also happens, for example, when text in the newspaper characterizes itself as newspaper's text. This possibility of re-marking is always present. It does not constitute some text as literature, but it creates another possibility – a possibility for the text to become literature. *Infinitive* speaks about Stewart Greenchurch's book, but this book exists only on the pages of *Infinitive*. The texts of Dejan Ilić suggest that the law of genre is pure and consequently "that an accurate decision about the genre of some text can prove to be crucial for its understanding."[61] But, a text does not properly belong to any genre. There is no such thing as a genreless text, but every text participates in one or several genres and this is a participation without belonging. Literature is interested in itself, literature turns to itself, but this is not a *simple reflection, some formalism* or *literature about literature* – literature is interested in its own origin and the main question it raises is the question of its foundation as literature.

In "The Song of the Sirens" Maurice Blanchot writes that Ahab only encounters Moby Dick in Herman Melville's novel, but we can also say that such an encounter is what enables Melville to write his book.[62] What we have here is an unavoidable paradox, because any act of foundation is based on its own prior absence. This why Leslie Hill claims that every act of foundation is preceded by an absence of foundation – a foundation is built on a bottomless abyss and this abyss is the only reliable foundation.[63] *Infinitive* starts as an encounter with *The Axiological Infinitive* and we read about the encounter with the book that was never written. Also, in the final chapter of *Infinitive* we have the words of Stewart Greenchurch: "I promise that I will prove that I exist."[64] These words move the end of *Infinitive* into the future, but this future is actually a return to Greenchurch's book. This is the reason why the beginning of *Infinitive* testifies to the absence of beginning and the end about the endlessness of language. "It is possible to read this monograph as a novel…" and "It is possible (least wrong) to read this monograph as a novel…"; the end that is the beginning and the beginning that is the end testify to the unattainability of infinitive (or *Infinitive*). Sometimes it looks like the infinitive is at the reach of a hand, but then it becomes dissolved by endless repetition, by the impossibility of the end or the beginning. But, this absence and this unattainability are not meaningless and Dejan Ilić's pursuit for *Infinitive*'s limit can be pursued to the point of limitlessness:

But where has art led us? To a time before the world, before the beginning. It has cast us out of our power to begin and to end; it has turned us toward the outside where there is no intimacy, no place to rest. It has led us into the infinite migration of error. For we seek art's essence, and it lies where the non-true admits of nothing essential. We appeal to art's sovereignty: it ruins the kingdom. It ruins the origin by returning to it the errant immensity of directionless eternity. The work says the word *beginning* from a starting point - art - which is complicit with the futility of starting over. The work declares being - and says choice, mastery, form - by announcing art which says the fatality of being, says passivity and formless prolixity. At the very moment of the choice art still holds us back in a primordial Yes and No. There, before any beginning, the sombre ebb and flow of dissimulation rumbles.[65]

Let us go back to Ilić's texts about *Infinitive*, or, to be more precise, to his statements about Stewart Greenchurch's role in *Infinitive*. He claims that Stewart Greenchurch is a completely marginal and unimportant character and that only the philosophical statements of Sreten Ugričić (that are unfortunately attributed to Stewart Greenchurch) have the crucial importance for the understanding of *Infinitive*:

> ...what did Sreten Ugričić want to achieve with his partial fictionalization of the philosophical discourse? How much did the half-fictionalized character of Stewart Greenchurch contribute to the cogency of the philosophical statements that were presented to the reader? Is it possible that the mostly consistent thoughts of the author would have been more cogent if they were presented in somewhat traditional form? Did the author, by turning the attention of his readers in the wrong way, make the understanding of his work deliberately harder for his readers?

> ... I think that most of the statements written in *Infinitive* are not disputable. Also, I think that they can be reformulated, their content can be expressed in a different way. This leads me to a following conclusion: the content of these statements does not depend upon a way in which these statements were expressed. To put it differently, in literary work its form plays a crucial role in its understanding (and in the interpretation of its content), but in *Infinitive* this relation does not have that crucial importance.[66]

A similar opinion is repeated in the "The 'Miraculous' Performative":

> I wrote that the logical validity of the statements that can be found in *Infinitive* does not depend upon the person who formulated them. Sreten Ugričić correctly understood that I think that, without any consequences for the validity, he could have formulated these statements. Also, I would like to add: he and anybody else. (The validity of, for example, some theorem, does not depend upon the person who formulated or proved that theorem, but on the logical validity of its formulation.)[67]

Dejan Ilić searches for the meaning of *Infinitive* and he believes that the core of Ugričić's work can be found and brought to the daylight. This search excludes Stewart Greenchurch, the author of *The Axiological Infinitive,* because he is unimportant – he is the unnecessary supplement that breaks the free flow of sense and consequently makes the understanding more difficult. Do the terms "unnecessary ornament" or "decoration" offer an adequate description of Stewart Greenchurch's role in *Infinitive*? Do Stewart Greenchurch and his invisible work really blur the meaning of *Infinitive*?

On the one hand, we can follow Ilić and claim that *The Axiological Infinitive* and its author are unnecessary additions to something (in this case Ugričić's main idea or his theoretical position) that is already full and sufficient in itself. But, how can something be added to what is already full and sufficient in itself? On the other hand, *The Axiological Infinitive* (a dangerous supplement) can be a substitution for something that is essentially lacking. *Infinitive* and *The Axiological Infinitive* are entangled in a strange logic of the supplement and this logic transforms our sense of the completeness of the whole.

In his analysis, Dejan Ilić follows the logic of the definitive and he covers the invisible with his insistence on common sense. But, Stewart Greenchurch and his *Invisible Work* disrupt the "natural" order of things. Ilić thinks that Stewart Greenchurch is the unnecessary supplement, added to something that is whole, but the reason for this addition lies in the fact that there is some lack which needs to be supplemented – there is no *Infinitive* without Stewart Greenchurch and *The Axiological Infinitive*, although *The Axiological Infinitive* and its author exist only on the pages of *Infinitive*. It is important to see that *Infinitive* and *The Axiological Infinitive* are not one and the same. Sreten Ugričić's book is about the invisible philosopher and his invisible work and the relationship between the book of Stewart Greenchurch and Ugričić's book is similar to the relationship between the infinitive and meta-definitive. Because of that, we can say that the work of Stewart Greenchurch, the internal indeterminacy of *Infinitive*, functions as *parergon: The Axiological Infinitive* is not a work (*ergon*), but, at the same time, it is not something outside of a work – Stewart Greenchurch and his work have the same role, and that role is the deconstruction of this opposition between inside and outside. *The Axiological Infinitive* makes the paradox of *Infinitive* visible. Since *Infinitive* is a monograph (a book about another book) *The Axiological Infinitive*, at the same time, makes this monograph possible and impossible. In short, *The Axiological Infinitive* is the (im)possibility of *Infinitive*.

Why do the texts of Dejan Ilić overlook this role of *The Axiological Infinitive* (and the paradox of *Infinitive*)? We can say that the main reason is impatience, because Ilić desires definitive meaning and he is unable to accept the depth of inexhaustible absence. This is the reason why *Infinitive* disappoints him – for him, this work is not literature. In his *Blue Octavo Notebooks* Kafka writes about impatience and describes it as a crucial mistake: "There are two main human sins from which all the others derive: impatience and indolence. Because of impatience, they were banished from Paradise. Because of indolence, they do not return. Perhaps there is only one main sin, impatience. Because of impatience, they were driven out, because of impatience, they do not return."[68] Blanchot adds:

> Klamm is by no means invisible. The land surveyor wants to see him, and he sees him. The Castle, supreme goal, is by no means out of sight. As an image, it is constantly at his disposal. Naturally when you look at them closely, these figures are disappointing. The Castle is only a cluster of village huts; Klamm, a big heavy man seated in front of a desk. There is nothing here that isn't very ordinary and ugly. But this is the land surveyor's good luck - the truth, the deceptive honesty of these images: they are not seductive in themselves, they possess nothing to justify the fascinated interest people take in them. Thus they remind us that they are not the true goal. In this insignificance, however, the other truth lets itself

> be forgotten. And the other truth is that these images are, all the same, images of the goal; they partake of its glow, of its ineffable value, and not to attach oneself to them is already to turn away from the essential.
>
> We could summarize this situation as follows: it is impatience which makes the goal inaccessible by substituting for it the proximity of an intermediary figure. It is impatience that destroys the way toward the goal by preventing us from recognizing in the intermediary the figure of the immediate.[69]

Dejan Ilić claims: "I am ready to agree with the ones who claim that to understand some text means to understand what the author wanted to say. And furthermore that language gives the author the options to actualize and to record with words what he wants to say and that the reader is capable to understand what the author wrote. Starting from this position, as I did before, I wrote about Sreten Ugričić's book Infinitive."[70] In this statement, literature is understood as *mimēsis* and the critic insists that *Infinitive* is just a shell for some unknown and crucial idea of Sreten Ugričić; the task of *Infinitive* is simply to illustrate that idea. But, *Infinitive* does not represent anything, it just testifies about the book which exists only on its pages. The representation of *The Axiological Infinitive* is its creation, and this creation represents *The Axiological Infinitive* as something that is infinitely absent. *Infinitive* is the monograph about Stewart Greenchurch and *The Axiological Infinitive*, the double of *The Axiological Infinitive*, but nothing comes before that double. Thus we might adapt Mallarmé and claim that "*Infinitive* illustrates but the idea, not any actual action, in a hymen (out of which flows Dream), tainted with vice yet sacred, between desire and fulfillment, perpetration and remembrance: here anticipating, there recalling, in the future in the past, **under the false appearance of a present**. That is how *Infinitive* operates, whose act is confined to a perpetual allusion without breaking the ice or the mirror: he thus sets up the medium, a pure medium, of fiction."[71] This is how *Infinitive* breaks with the system of representation; this work does not produce, or reveal, any kind of presence, it creates "an empty space, a medium between matter and nothingness, without belonging to either the one or to the other."[72]

Dejan Ilić is a negligent reader, he knows the story about Eudox, but he forgot the one about Gnaeus Pompeius, who was also known as Pompey the Great, and this story is also mentioned in the work of Stewart Greenchurch. After Pompey conquered Jerusalem, he rushed to enter into the inner sanctuary of the Tabernacle, the most sacred site - *Kodesh Hakodashim*, the place where the presence of God dwells. He wanted to see the object of Jewish devotion, to see and to touch the basis and the essence of their faith. But, this visit left him bitterly disappointed and, at the end, he felt cheated – the room, from which he expected so much, was completely empty.

CHAPTER TWO:
TRUTH AND ABSENCE

> There is an active, productive way of reading which produces text and reader and thus transports us. Then there is a passive kind of reading which betrays the text while appearing to submit to it, by giving the illusion that the text exists objectively, fully sovereignly: as one whole. Finally, there is the reading that is no longer passive, but is passivity's reading. It is without pleasure, without joy; it escapes both comprehension and desire. It is like nocturnal vigil, that 'inspiring' insomnia when, all having said, 'Saying' is heard, and the testimony of the last witness is pronounced.
>
> Maurice Blanchot, *The Writing of the Disaster*

The strange case of Andrew Marbot

Let's begin with another story which can provide a different perspective on the problems presented in the first chapter. Sir Andrew Thomas Marbot was born on 4 April, 1801, as the first son of Sir Francis Marbot and Lady Catherine (daughter of Lord Claverton). Since his father's interests were limited to horse riding and hunting, the main influence on young Marbot came from the maternal side. His grandfather was a well educated and intellectual man; he also had an excellent library and a small (but very valuable) collection of paintings at his home – Redmond Manor. Also, Lord Claverton brought Father Gerardus van Rossum from Rome and the educated Jesuit became the chaplain of Marbot Hall and, most importantly, the tutor of young Andrew.

In his biography of Andrew Marbot, Wolfgang Hildesheimer claims that Andrew had a short, but dynamic and colorful life.[73] Even as a child he was curious and full of spirit, but also constantly in contact with famous artists and intellectuals of his time; Hildesheimer's text records meetings and sometimes even friendships with Henry Raeburn, William Turner, Sir David Bruster, Thomas De Quincey, and William Wordsworth. These artists and intellectuals were frequent visitors of Lord Claverton at Redmond Manor.

The meetings and conversations with the above mentioned people certainly gave some impetus to Marbot's developing interest in art, but they did not play the crucial part. One particular painting, from the collection of his grandfather, Tintoretto's *The Origin of the Milky Way*, triggered his passion for art, but also an incestuous relationship with his mother. Wolfgang Hildesheimer writes about that incident in his book:

After his grandfather had tried to explain the subject of the painting to him in so far as he understood it, and no doubt avoiding anything improper, but had evidently not succeeded to Andrew's satisfaction, he one day asked his mother, then twenty-five years old, to explain it again, and above all, since she was visibly of the same sex as Juno in the painting, to show to him the corresponding parts of her body which made their appearance with such surprising frankness in Juno. His mother refused his request, but not at all indignantly; she laughed and took the child in her arms so that he was able to discover "this mysterious territory" for himself, "not with his eyes, but feeling with his body." It was his first conscious memory, and the most wonderful. Here he was, in beauty softly embedded, "feeling with all his senses a previously unknown territory which he was to explore and conquer later."

This observation, probably made in 1820, when he had just begun his notes, the second of its kind since Sophocles quotation [*You should not fear your mother's bed!/So many mortal men have, in their dreams/Slept with their mother!*], is the start of a kind of secret diary, kept sporadically and often only in the form of keywords, in which Marbot makes an attempt at detachment by putting himself into the third person singular, as if his intention were to make fiction of his experience.[74]

This relationship was doomed from the beginning and in 1825 Andrew Marbot decided to leave his homeland (and his mother) for good. He briefly visited Weimar to see great Johann Wolfgang von Goethe, and there he had a short-lived affair with his daughter-in-law Ottilie. The following year he was in Rome where he was introduced to Giacomo Leopardi and they talked on the topic of suicide. Marbot's last home was a small Italian city, Urbino, and there he lived with Anna Maria Baiardi before his enigmatic disappearance in the February of 1830.

One morning Marbot left his house for the last time. His disappearance was noticed in the evening, but his friends thought that he decided to spend the night at the house of Anna Maria Baiardi's relatives. When he did not return, and when his horse came back without him, they had a clear sign that something is wrong. Systematic search was organized and they did not find even the smallest trace of Marbot – he vanished from the face of the Earth, and he was never found. After a week, his family in England was notified and he was presumed dead. Marbot's biographer assumes that he committed suicide and he states that Anna Maria Baiardi discovered the unmistakable evidence which supports this assumption. One of the two pistols from Marbot's duelling kit was never found. Marbot left no last messages and his last entry in the notebooks is a quotation from *King Lear* (the last words of the fool in Shakespeare's play):

> "'and I shall go to bed at noon.' Admittedly it is not yet noon, but why wait until the sun stands at its zenith? It is not *my* sun."[75]

After Marbot's disappearance Anna Maria Baiardi sent his writings to Lady Catherine. In order to protect the reputation of her family, she censored her son's manuscripts with the help of Father Gerardus van Rossum. The work of Andrew Marbot is not big and there are many unfinished texts, but his notes were published by John Murray in 1834; Gerard Ross was listed as the editor of these notes. The title of the book was *Art and Life*. In 1839, this book appeared in Germany under the title *Die Kunst und das Leben* and the translator was Heinrich Wilhelm Schultz. It is clear that Gerard Ross is actually Father Gerard van Rossum and Hildesheimer states that, although flawed and over-simplified, *Art and Life* is a very important work. Without Father Gerard we would know nothing of Andrew Marbot. It is worth noting that, in 1888, Frederic Hadley-Chase published a biography *Sir Andrew Marbot* which was based on the material from *Art and Life* and on some letters of Andrew Marbot.

Father Gerardus van Rossum died in 1847 and Marbot's manuscripts passed to his brother. Adrian van Rossum, the brother's nephew preserved these manuscripts and Franz van Rossum, the last descendant of the van Rossum family and the reviewer of Hildesheimer's Mozart in 1979, gave Marbot's manuscripts to the author of *Marbot: A Biography*. With the help of modern quartz lamp Hildesheimer finally managed to decipher Marbot's censored secret journal. Among other things, this new material brought to daylight Marbot's illicit passion for his mother.

Andrew Marbot was not an artist, he was a critic, but, at the same time, much more than some ordinary critic. His aesthetic theory is based on the understanding that works of art are unique and irreproducible. He was sceptical toward contemporary art critics and philosophers who wrote about art without the personal knowledge of the original works. In short, for Marbot, the copy is always lesser work than the original and the observation deduced from the reproductions can lead to errors. In his writings about art, Marbot claims that the original has the ability to communicate a unique message, and that this message is based on the personality of the artist. According to Hildesheimer, Marbot was forgotten because his work was too novel and radical for his time. He also claims that Marbot was a Freudian *avant la lettre*, because he searched for the psychological reasons behind artistic creation.

As the readers of my previous chapter will surely guess, *Marbot: A Biography* shares one important feature with Sreten Ugričić's *Infinitive*. *Infinitive* is a monograph about a non-existent book, and Hildesheimer's work is a biography of a non-existent person. Dorrit Cohn describes Hildesheimer's book as "the life story of an imaginary person presented in the guise of a historical biography, a guise that the author evidently intended to be recognized and admired for what it is: a masterful disguise."[76]

Nevertheless, this genre innovation and *masterful disguise* produced interesting effects. Käte Hamburger draws our attention[77] to the text of Johannes Kleinstück, "Sündiger englischer Aristokrat" (*Die Welt*, 14 October 1981). François Bondy, translator of Ionesco's books in German, was amazed how easily Kleinstück believed in Hildesheimer's deception, but the truth is maybe a little bit different. It is possible that this review was very subtle and that its author ironically accepted the existence of Marbot. The example from the *London Review of Books* is even more interesting.[78] J.P. Stern, presumably like Johannes Kleinstück, reviewed Hildesheimer's book as if Marbot was a real historical figure. But, unlike Kleinstück, he left several hints in his text which suggested that the author of the review was aware of Marbot's non-existence. In the later issue of the journal Wolfgang Hildesheimer's short letter was published:

> SIR: To my dismay, I find that the reviewer of my latest book, *Marbot*, has missed the point of the book: namely, the fact that the hero of this biography has never existed. He is purely fictitious and has no model in cultural history (nor, for that matter, in history). The quotations from his writings, his letters, the letters of Lady Catherine, his diaries etc. are *my own* and so are the English translations. The illustrations of his family

portraits depict a certain Baron Schwiter, Mrs Robert Scott Moncrieff, a Herr von Boist etc. There is no Marbot Hall, neither in Northumberland nor anywhere else, nor is there Redford. On the other hand, all persons except the Marbot family, Father van Rossum and Anna Maria Baiardi *have* existed, including Sir David Brewster, the inventor of the kaleidoscope. Marbot's non-existence might easily have been found out by looking him up in the *Encyclopedia Britannica*, in Goethe's *Gespräche mit Eckermann*, the Letters of Ottilie von Goethe, or Schopenhauer and Mendelssohn-Bartholdy, the diaries of Delacroix, Berlioz, Count Platen and Lady Charlotte Bury, the writings of de Quincey, Boisserée, Bunsen, Ruskin and others, the biographies of Byron, Rumohr, etc. You will look for him in vain. In my view, it speaks for the book that the reviewer has taken Marbot's existence for granted. In fact, he could have existed. My book might have begun as a joke – I don't remember – but it became increasingly more serious. One does not work four years on a joke.[79]

The editor of the *London Review* replied succinctly:

It speaks for the reviewer that the author of the book should take for granted an assumption, on the reviewer's part, of Marbot's existence.[80]

These two examples of *trompe l'oeil* clearly show that *Marbot: A Biography*, like *Infinitive*, poses some important questions about the nature of fiction and, consequently, about literature in general. May biography resort to fiction? Is it permitted to blur the differences between fiction and fact? What is the relationship between literature and historiography? And, most importantly, what is the relationship between truth and literature? In this chapter I will try to offer some responses to the above mentioned questions, but, before I do that, I would like to focus on three, from my perspective, exemplary responses to *Marbot* that came from the field of literary theory. These responses came from Jean-Marie Schaeffer,[81] Käte Hamburger,[82] and Dorrit Cohn.[83]

In his short analysis, Jean-Marie Schaeffer emphasizes the reception of Marbot and he claims that readers accepted the text not as fictional, but as factual; they were convinced that *Marbot* is a real biography.[84] Schaeffer claims that this is an important problem and he analyses the means which Hildesheimer used to create his deception.

1.) According to Schaeffer, *Marbot* is clearly inspired by Hildesheimer's previous work, by his biography of Wolfgang Amadeus Mozart. The text of *Marbot* possesses many structural similarities with the biography of Mozart – Hildesheimer perfectly mimics the seriousness of his previous biographical study. These two books are also visually similar; in both cases the front cover shows the portrait of the person presented in the book. Also, before the publication of *Marbot*, Hildesheimer tried to incorporate his character in the present day consciousness. He spoke about Andrew Marbot in his public lectures and appearances. Because of all this, Schaeffer claims that a certain *context of authority* was already established and this context played a big part in the deception that *Marbot* supposedly created. The most important part of this context was Hildesheimer's previous work - his biography of Wolfgang Amadeus Mozart. Since Hildesheimer previously wrote a biography of a real person, it was supposed that his new biography will be about a real person too.

This is all true, but some important things that subvert the supposed authority are omitted. Hildesheimer's biography of Mozart was a controversial book that was rejected by the academic community. In his text "In No-man's-land beyond Biography: Dr Cake, Mozart and Other Cases", Richard Littlejohns explains why Mozart experts rejected Hildesheimer's biography:

> In his unorthodox and controversial book *Mozart* (Frankfurt: Suhrkamp, 1977) Hildesheimer ditched not only the conventions of hagiographic biography but also any claim to authorial omniscience and objectivity. Instead he offered a series of personal reflections, sometimes brilliant but sometimes idiosyncratic, on Mozart's life and work, often digressing, and only loosely following the chronological course of Mozart's career. Facing the enigmas of Mozart's life and character bluntly, he did not offer pseudo-authoritative solutions, but instead speculated openly and did not hesitate to employ creative reconstruction. In particular he fished in psychologically muddy waters, seeking explanations for both Mozart's genius and his aberrations in his primitive sexuality and in an undiscarded infantility which expressed itself most obviously in scatology. Genius, so Hildesheimer dared to argue, was not infrequently to be found in individuals whose personal lives were characterized by egocentricity and venality, or by distastefully morbid and deviant behaviour.[85]

This brings us back to the authorship problem that I elaborated in the previous chapter. In short, the question is: who is Wolfgang Hildesheimer? Schaeffer replies: he is the biographer of Mozart and, subsequently, the author of *Marbot*. However, he is not an ordinary biographer but the person who clearly introduced fictionality into biography. Also, Norman Mailer and Truman Capote are novelists and *The Armies of the Night* and *In Cold Blood* are novels. They are non-fiction novels, but novels nevertheless. The case of Hildesheimer is even more complicated. Schaeffer is right, Wolfgang Hildesheimer is the biographer of Mozart, but, at the same time he is also the writer of radio plays and a well-known novelist (before *Marbot*, he wrote two novels *Tynset* and *Masante*). Who is the author of Marbot? Wolfgang Hildesheimer, the biographer or Wolfgang Hildesheimer, the novelist?

2.) There are several *paratextual elements* in Hildesheimer's book, but the most obvious one is its subtitle – *A Biography*. The paintings and photographs in the middle of the book can be considered as the second paratextual element: Andrew Marbot's portrait by Eugene Delacroix, Lady Catherine and Sir Francis Marbot's portraits by Henry Raeburn, Lord Claverton's portrait by Anton Graff, the photographs of Marbot Hall and Redmond Manor, and the etching of Anna Maria Baiardi by an unknown artist. The further research discovered that these are the hijacked portraits of other persons, but the names of the painters are correct. The same goes for two photographs, which are not from Northumberland, but from Norfolk. The third paratextual element is the index of names at the end of the book. On the one hand, the role of this index is to mimic the structure of a serious biographical study. On the other hand, it suggests that something is not quite right with this biography. The most important names are missing from the index: Andrew Marbot, his parents and grandfather, Father Gerald, etc. are excluded from the index. Invented and fictitious names are not present in the index.

The role of paratext in *Marbot* is more complicated for Dorrit Cohn than for Jean-Marie Schaefer. She emphasizes the double function of paratextual elements, while Schaeffer claims that their function is simply to deceive. Dorrit Cohn writes:

Did Hildesheimer want his readers to be caught in his game? Not if we judge from his protests against Stern's (as he mistakenly believed gullible) review, quoted at the beginning of this discussion. Nor if we believe another even clearer postpublication pronouncement: "If some of my readers and critics were duped, I can only assure them that the fault isn't mine. Granted that my intention was to bestow life on Marbot; but it wasn't to commit a fraud." He immediately concedes, however, "that my demonstrations of the fictional nature [of the work] was perhaps too hidden and too weak." This "demonstration", he now explains, consisted of two paratextual items: a single phrase in the first sentence of the (German) book-jacket text, which reads: "Sir Andrew Marbot, the hero of this biography, is as it were woven into the cultural history of the early nineteenth century" (my translation); and the omission from his *index nomini* of all Marbot family member's names. What Hildesheimer does *not* mention here (or in any other place) is another paratextual item that easily outweighs the discreet and less than decisive signals he mentions: the subtitle *Eine Biographie* (*A Biography*) featured on the title page. This is surely the factor most immediately responsible for the fact that some readers and even some early reviewers were misled.[86]

Generic subtitles often play a decisive role in the reception and categorization of literary works. They are obvious signs of author's intentions and they can be also understood as kind of contractual agreement on the author's part. If we bear in mind this convention then we can easily understand why Schaeffer claims that *Marbot* is a deception. But, the subtitle *A Biography* can also be a part of the main text itself:

> Another way of conceptualizing the ambiguity attending Hildesheimer's title page would be to say that it overtly

frames *Marbot* as a biography – with the term *framing* here used in Erwing Goffman's sense of contextualizing – but that this overt frame is surrounded by another *covert* frame that, once it is discovered, transforms this biography (including its title page) into a novel.[87]

3.) According to Schaeffer, one of the main problems of *Marbot* is *the problem of narration*. In his book, Schaeffer uses the language of narratology and names this problem - *the problem of formal mimesis*. He states that the narrator of *Marbot* is never the *I-narrator* (*Ich-Erzähler*), for example, like Serenus Zeitblom in *Doctor Faustus*. In *Marbot*, the narrator is never a character in the story (like, for example, Serenus Zeitblom), but he is always in the position of a biographer. He never uses internal focalization, and he always narrates about Andrew Marbot from the outside. According to Schaffer, this is a part of Hildesheimer's deception. He conceals the fictionality of his work and seemingly posits the narrator outside the life story of Andrew Marbot. In *Marbot*, the narrator always wears the mask of a biographer. Through the whole narrative the narrator tries to maintain this perspective on Andrew Marbot in order to achieve the illusion of objectivity. However, the beginning of the book is especially interesting because it starts as a dramatization of a certain encounter. The book begins *in medias res*, with the meeting of young Marbot and Johann Wolfgang von Goethe, and with their conversation about mythology and tradition. But, immediately after the dramatization of this conversation, the narrator states the sources which he used for the reconstruction of this meeting: the letter of Prussian Privy Councillor Schultz and the famous Eckerman's *Conversations with Goethe* (December 1825). Some quotations in *Marbot* are simply true. This is the case with the ones that do not speak explicitly about Andrew Marbot. The ones that explicitly speak about Marbot are, of course, completely invented. However, sometimes we have a combination of factual and fictional; sometimes the actual sentences from some work are combined with the invented ones. The same technique is used in Sreten Ugričić's *Infinitive*.

Jean-Marie Schaeffer mentions Dorrit Cohn who carefully and meticulously analyzed the problem of narration in *Marbot*. Schaeffer and Cohn agree that Hildesheimer is never an omniscient narrator. Sometimes, he interprets Marbot's actions and writings from psychological perspective as though he is trying to decipher Marbot's mind in the manner of modern psychobiographers. But, this discourse and the conclusions derived from it are always modalized with the following expressions: *so it seems, there is much to support this, I am uncertain if,* etc. Dorrit Cohn writes:

> By now my insistence on the *Marbot* narrator's antiomniscient stance must have brought into view what I view as the deep chasm that separates the biographer's enterprise from the novelist's. To deepen this perspective further still, imagine for a moment the unimaginable: what the fictional lives of memorable characters would be like if their authors had treated them in the manner Hildesheimer treats Marbot – the lives, say, of Stephen Dedalus, Raskolnikov, Isabel Archer, Emma Bovary, Aschenbach. Without episodes packed with their gestures and words, without moments of lonely self-communion minutely tracing spiritual and emotional conflicts, these characters would no doubt never have come to life or become engraved in our reading memories… In sum, had Mann renounced the novelist's privilege of making his protagonist's mind transparent to his reader's eyes, there would be no *Death in Venice*.[88]

4.) The last problem is *the intrusion of fiction into the real and historical world*. Hildesheimer's book records Marbot's meetings with different historical figures. I have already mentioned his conversation with Goethe and I will give more examples: during the first 19 years of his life Andrew Marbot met Henry Raeburn and Sir David Brewster (inventor of the kaleidoscope) and he visited Thomas De Quincey and William Wordsworth. In 1822, he spoke with Arthur Schopenhauer in Florence, and in 1826, the Prussian Ambassador introduced him to Giacomo Leopardi in Rome.

One possible perspective on this problem emphasizes *Marbot*'s traditionality. The similarities of Hildesheimer's work with the common biography are obvious, but *Marbot* also has some similarities with the traditional historical novel. From this perspective the chasm that separates "fake biography" and the typical historical novel is not as clearly defined as Schaeffer thinks; it seems that they share some important similarities. In the typical 19th century historical novel, historical persons are relegated to secondary roles. This is also the case in *Marbot*. The role of these persons is to validate or authenticate the fictional world by their presence, to close the gap between fiction and history. This is also successfully achieved in Hildesheimer's work (according to Schaeffer, maybe even too successfully). But, we have to bear in mind that, at the same time, all historical novels violate ontological boundaries. The usual case is the claim to trans-world identity between historical characters in the projected worlds of novels and the historical figures from the real world. Traditional historical novels try to hide these violations; they avoid contradictions between their representation of historical figures and the respected lives of these figures in the real world. It is clear that *Marbot* is inspired by the traditional structure of biography and historical novel, but, at the same time, this inspiration leads to an interesting result – it leads to the clear violation of ontological boundaries and to successful blurring of difference between truth and fiction.[89]

Another possible perspective emphasizes the novelty of *Marbot* and its starting point is precisely this violation of ontological boundaries. This intrusion of fiction into the real world is connected with Hildesheimer's manner of narration. Dorrit Cohn writes that Marbot is the exact inversion of the type of fictional biography exemplified, for example, in Herman Broch's *The Death of Virgil*. In this work, fictional discourse narrates the life of a historical figure, while in *Marbot* non-fictional, to be more precise – historiographic, discourse narrates the life of a fictional figure. Because of that, Hildesheimer's *Mozart* can be called *historical biography*; Mann's *Death in Venice* - *fictional biography*; Broch's *The Death of Virgil* - *fictionalized historical biography*; and *Marbot* - *historicized fictional biography*.[90]

With respect to the problem of narration, we can also employ Steven Connor's observations on the poetics of modernism, and thus form the third possible answer to the problem.[91] Connor states that the poetics of modernism operated according to principles of scenography. The most important question was who "sees" and how – this means that the question of narrative voice is displaced into questions of point of view. This is the reason why one of the most important figures in the poetics of modernism is the figure of "unreliable narrator". In contrast to this, in the works of Hildesheimer and Ugričić, we are unable to encode the identity of the narrative voice; this voice has no personality. We cannot even claim if this narrative voice is either reliable or unreliable; we can only be witnesses of its strange impersonality. In this case, Blanchot's reference to the myth of Orpheus can be instructive, because the song of Orpheus underlies the paradox of *Infinitive* and *Marbot*. Blanchot claims:

> It is in his song that Orpheus really descends to the Underworld - which we translate by adding that he descends to it through the power of his singing. But this song, already instrumental, signifies an alteration in the institution of narration. To tell a story is a mysterious thing. The mysterious "he" of the epic institution very quickly splits: the "he" becomes the impersonal coherency of a *story* (in the full and magical sense of this word). The *story* stands alone, performed in the thought of a demiurge; and since it exists on its own there is nothing left to do but to tell it.[92]

Jean-Marie Schaeffer uses narratology in order to address the problems of Hildesheimer's *Marbot*. According to him, the answer is very simple: Hildesheimer over-emphasized the mimetic component of his work and thus, albeit involuntarily, created a deception. He writes that the reception of *Marbot* proves that this book cannot function as fiction. To be more precise, Hildesheimer's book is not a fiction, but a work that failed to reach the status of fiction. The conclusion is: fiction (in this case - *Marbot*) that does not function as fiction is a simple deception. This conclusion shows that Jean-Marie Schaeffer and Dejan Ilić stand on the same positions; Ilić also thinks that we cannot read *Infinitive* as the work of fiction, because the text itself does not allow that kind of reading. Unlike Schaeffer, he does not claim that *Infinitive* is a hoax or deception. For him, *Infinitive* is a theoretical work. But, it is possible that he does not claim exactly the same thing as Schaeffer because he is deceived. He thinks that *Infinitive* is a theoretical work – maybe he is successfully deceived into believing that the monograph about a non-existent book belongs to theoretical discourse. In his interpretation, the story about a systematically developed theoretical position became exactly the text of that theory.[93] Dejan Ilić read a book *about* Stewart Greenchurch's theory and he became convinced that he read the text of that theory. In similar fashion, we can presume that, in the hands of inexperienced readers, *Marbot*, the simulation of biography, became the real biography. Unlike Ilić, Jean-Marie Schaeffer is not deceived; he knows that *Marbot* is not a biography, but he claims that this book has the ability to deceive – people will think that this is a real biography. So, for both theoreticians, deception is a very important term and it is connected with the genre of discourse. If we decide to write biography, we should write it about some person who is, for some reason, important to us or to humanity in general. But we must fulfill one necessary condition – we must write about a person who existed or who exists. The same goes for the monograph – existence is crucial. Why? Because it is connected with truth, or, to be more precise, with the truth that is understood as correspondence. But, why is truth so dependent on language? And, are the texts such as *Marbot* and *Infinitive* completely divorced from truth? I will leave these questions for now, and I will focus on Käte Hamburger's and Dorrit Cohn's readings of Marbot. This may help us to illuminate the above mentioned questions even further.

If we now proceed to Käte Hamburger's text we will notice something important. At the very beginning of her study, in the first paragraph, Hamburger states that *Marbot* is an unusual, unconventional and extraordinary work. Her opinion is that the press was fully aware of the fictional nature of *Marbot*, because of authorial comments that preceded and followed the work. For her, the unconventionality of this book becomes obvious if we try to put ourselves in the position of a reader 50 or 100 years from now. The question is: if the authorial comments are missing, what will this future reader think of *Marbot*? Is he going to think that *Marbot* is a real biography? The question is posed, but the answer is not given in Käte Hamburger's text. But, she thinks that our inability to answer is a serious problem. Maybe, but, then again, maybe not. Any book is exposed to the passing of time and all signs can change their meaning with time. The change of context brings a change of meaning and the desire for saturable or exhaustively determinable context is just wishful thinking. Käte Hamburger's emphasis on the above mentioned question reveals this desire for a stable identity. It is a desire for a certain identity (and also for a meaning) that can be determined once and for all. At the same time, this is also the basic weakness of narratology. Something important is missed in narratology's attempt to map the open and sometimes even self-contradictory process of narrative. The basic feature of narratology, we might say, is an (unsuccessful) attempt to map and fix the narration in some abstracted form. The promise of narratology is very simple – once we grasp the grammar of the work we will also achieve its understanding. But, Jean-Marie Schaeffer and Käte Hamburger analyzed *Marbot* in this way, and they only managed to hit the wall; it did not bring them any closer to the understanding of what this work is. At the end of her text, Käte Hamburger admits that she has a problem with *Marbot*. She follows Schaeffer's line of thinking, but she also claims that *Marbot* is a theoretical paradox:

> Precisely what this work does is to turn the reality into fiction rather than fiction into reality. Here truth is not to be understood in the vague sense of some inward, higher, deeper, or artistic truth, but rather, in Goethe's words as "the truth of reality". The problem is that the real individuals do not, as in historical novel, become fictional, but that they consciously remain real. This is also the case for Sir Andrew Marbot, as long as the

reader believes that he is a historical figure and that the biographer is following "the tracks of a forgotten man". If its fictionality comes to light, however, then the fiction does not become truth; rather, it acquires a hint of illusion, of deception. The invented character Marbot does not, as has been claimed, become an artistic figure in the sense of Thomas Mann's Doctor Faustus, the composer Adrian Leverkühn. In Mann's work another fictional character, the Leverkühn biographer Serenus Zeitblom, steps between the author and its creation; *Doctor Faustus* is a first-person narrative. When in 1929 Leverkühn composes the cantata "*Dr. Fausti Weheklag*" using the twelve-tone technique of his contemporary Schönberg, this account by Zeitblom, himself a character in the novel, does not perplex us in the same way as does the pronouncement by the biographer Hildesheimer that Marbot anticipated libidinal theory. As soon as we recognize Marbot as a fictional (that is, invented) character, such a claim, in my opinion, dissolves into thin air, and what remains are only the author's views of art and the art of interpretation – whether intended seriously or parodistically, or both at once, incarnated in a fictional figure. The point is that this is a fictional character who is not portrayed as fictional, recognizable as such; he is instead presented as a real person. Herein lie the problematics and stumbling blocks of the book *Marbot: A Biography*, a book one might also term a theoretical paradox.[94]

Dorrit Cohn's answer is somewhat different. She addresses the question of the genre of *Marbot*, and, like Käte Hamburger, she claims that critics quickly saw through Hildesheimer's mock-historiographic travesty. For her, *Marbot* (a historicized fictional biography), is a generic anomaly, a one-of-a-kind experiment and possibly a sole specimen of its species. Unlike Schaeffer, she thinks that *Marbot* is fiction, to be more precise – a new genre of fiction. I think that the problem is far too complicated to be solved in this way. Like *Infinitive*, or "Tlön, Uqbar, Orbis Tertius", *Marbot* subverts determined concepts of what fiction is and what it is not. How is this achieved?

In the introduction to his book on Mozart, Hildesheimer speaks about the serious problems he faced. Biographers, just as modern day historians, have a lot of resources at their disposal – libraries and archive centers are well equipped and the past can be surveyed without much difficulties. But, Hildesheimer warns that the biographer has to be aware of a simple fact: he will never be able to discover the full truth about his chosen historical character. Hildesheimer claims that, in the case of Mozart, he was always faced with *the impenetrable strangeness* of his subject. This *impenetrable strangeness* is the origin of his book on Andrew Marbot. If we bear in mind that parody always challenges and subverts what it mimics, then we can say that *Marbot* is a very successful and deliberate parody of the classical historical biography. What is called into question by this book is, on the one hand, positivist and empiricist assumptions of historiography, and, on the other hand, the conception of truth as *adaequatio*. *Marbot* tells a story about the impenetrability, about the gap, about the empty space, about the absence that infinitely separates our signs and things in themselves.

The important similarity between Hildesheimer's *Marbot* and Ugričić's *Infinitive* is evident: *Marbot* is a biography of a non-existent person and *Infinitive* is a monograph about a non-existent book. There is a certain empty space at the centre of these works. However, *Infinitive* is a more complex book than *Marbot*. In this chapter, pseudo-Salinger's story "Bringing No Presents, Just Pasts" from *Infinitive* will be used in the interpretation of Hildesheimer's work, but this story will, at the same time, illuminate *Marbot* and open a new set of questions about *Infinitive*. This is the reason why I will leave *Marbot* after this chapter and focus again on the problems of *Infinitive*.

One possible interpretation of *Marbot* and *Infinitive* can be based on Nietzsche's "On Truth and Lies in a Nonmoral Sense" and on the general understanding of postmodernist fiction.

Let us go slowly now. According to Aristotle, we have to differentiate history and poetry:

> It is, moreover, evident from what has been said, that it is not the function of the poet to relate what has happened, but what may happen - what is possible according to the law of probability or necessity. The poet and the historian differ not by writing in verse or in prose. The work of Herodotus might be put into verse, and it would still be a species of history, with meter no less than without it. The true difference is that one relates what has happened, the other what may happen. Poetry, therefore, is a more philosophical and a higher thing than history: for poetry tends to express the universal, history the particular.[95]

This separation of literature and history is subverted in *Marbot: A Biography*. Aristotle's point of view implies that the task of a historian is very simple – he just has to keep the record of reality, nothing more than this. His task is just to chart what happened in the past, and he needs to carefully (and precisely) reconstruct the events from the past with the help of historical documents and other traces. The same can be said about the biographer. This notion of history emphasizes objectivity; the writing of history is a scientific task and historiography is about something actual and real, or about something that was actual once.[96] At the basis of this notion of history lies the understanding of truth as correspondence, and, if we follow Heidegger from "On the Essence of Truth", we can conclude that this correspondence has a double sense:

> 1) the consonance of a matter with what is supposed in advance regarding it;
> 2) the correspondence of what is meant in the statement with the matter, how the statement relates to the world.

This also means that the non-truth can be defined as the non-correspondence of the statement with the matter or as a non-agreement of a being with its essence.

The problem arises with our attempt to explain how this correspondence occurs. In his famous text "On Truth and Lies in a Nonmoral Sense" Friedrich Nietzsche claims that man will never be satisfied with the truth in the form of tautology. But, if this is the case, man will always exchange truth for illusions. He poses a question: what is a word? His reply goes like this: it is a copy in sound of some nerve stimulus. Then he continues:

> But the further inference from the nerve stimulus to a cause outside of us is already the result of a false and unjustifiable application of the principle of sufficient reason. If truth alone had been the deciding factor in the genesis of language, and if the standpoint of certainty had been decisive for designations, then how could we still dare to say "the stone is hard," as if "hard" were something otherwise familiar to us, and not merely a totally subjective stimulation! We separate things according to gender, designating the tree as masculine and the plant as feminine. What arbitrary assignments! How far this

> oversteps the canons of certainty! We speak of a "snake": this designation touches only upon its ability to twist itself and could therefore also fit a worm. (*Schlange*, the German for "snake" is related to the verb *schlingen* "to wind or twist") What arbitrary differentiations! What one-sided preferences, first for this, then for that property of a thing! The various languages placed side by side show that with words it is never a question of truth, never a question of adequate expression; otherwise, there would not be so many languages.[97]

If we want to really seize the truth our designations need to be congruent with things. Pure truth, pure correspondence, is nothing other than the thing itself. This is why the thing in itself, the object of correspondence (the pure truth) is constantly elusive. Nietzsche emphasizes the role of metaphor for human knowing:

> 1) a nerve stimulus is transferred into an image – this is the first metaphor;
> 2) then the image is imitated in a sound – this is the second metaphor.

We believe that the truth is in our possession, but is this belief justified? How can we be so sure if we have nothing else but metaphors for things which do not correspond to the original entities?

We do not have to agree completely with this line of argumentation, but we have to notice that this problem points to the fact that the writing of history is not as straightforward as it seemed at first glance. Since humanity is never satisfied with the truth as tautology this means that the task of a historian is not just to note that something happened – he needs to offer reasons why something happened; he needs to present the sense of the event to his readers. Now we come to the meaning-making function of history. It is a widespread illusion that historians just want to tell the truth about the past - they want to give sense to the past events, and the only way to do this is by narrativization. Hayden White writes:

> Thus, for example, in *The Savage Mind*, Claude Lévi-Strauss has suggested that the formal coherency of any historical narrative consists solely of "a fraudulent outline" imposed by the historian upon a body of materials which could be called "data" only in the most extended sense of the term. Historical accounts are inevitably interpretative, Lévi-Strauss argues, because of "a twofold antinomy in the very notion of an historical fact." A historical fact is "what really took place," he notes; but *where,* he asks, did anything take place? Any historical episode – in a revolution or a war, for example - can be resolved into "a multitude of individual psychic moments." Each of these, in turn, can be translated into a manifestation of some more basic process of "unconscious development, and these resolve into cerebral, hormonal, or nervous phenomena, which themselves have the reference to the physical and chemical order". Thus Lévi-Strauss concludes, historical facts are in no sense "given" to the historian but are, rather, "constituted" by the historian himself "by abstraction and as though under the threat of an infinite regress."[98]

This is the first step – the creation of facts; the second step is the creation of sense. In *Infinitive* we can see that Stewart Greenchurch is very close to Nietzsche when he argues that the sense (or maybe we can even say the truth) of a historical event is constructed tropologically, by the means of *metabasis or narrative castling* (*metabasis of sense*). *Metabasis, narrative castling and metabasis of sense* are all Stewart Greenchurch's names for the tropological creation of sense. In the works of

Hayden White, this creation of sense is called *emplotment*, and, in the work of Nietzsche, it is called chronological inversion (*chronologische Umdrehung*). In *The Will to Power*, Nietzsche writes:

> Chronological inversion, so that the cause enters consciousness later than the effect.- We have learned that pain is projected to a part of the body without being situated there-we have learned that sense impressions naively supposed to be conditioned by the outer world are, on the contrary, conditioned by the inner world; that we are always unconscious of the real activity of the outer world... The fragment of outer world of which we are conscious is born after an effect from outside has impressed itself upon us, and is subsequently projected as its "cause"...
>
> "Inner experience" enters our consciousness only after it has found a language the individual understands - i.e., a translation of a condition into conditions familiar to him-; "to understand" means merely: to be able to express something new in the language of something old and familiar.[99]

Before we come back to Greenchurch, we need to present Paul de Man's interpretation of these passages from Nietzsche's work:

> The argument starts out from a binary polarity of classical banality in the history of metaphysics: the opposition of subject to object based on the spatial model of an "inside" to an "outside" world. As such, there is nothing unusual about the stress on the unreliability, the subjectivity of sense impressions. But the working hypothesis of polarity becomes soon itself the target of the analysis. This occurs, first of all, by showing that the priority status of the two poles can be reversed. The outer, objective event in the world was supposed to determine the inner, conscious

event as cause determines effect. It turns out however that what was assumed to be the objective, external cause is itself the result of an internal effect. What had been considered to be a cause, is, in fact, the effect of an effect, and what had been considered to be an effect can in its turn seem to function as the cause of its own cause.

The main impact of this deconstruction of the classical cause/effect, subject/object scheme becomes clear in the second part of the passage. It is based, as we saw, on an inversion or reversal of attributes which, in this particular case, is said to be temporal in nature. Logical priority is uncritically deduced from a contingent temporal priority: we pair the polarities outside/inside with cause/effect on the basis of a temporal polarity before/after (or early/late) that remains un-reflected.[100]

Stewart Greenchurch's claim that the basic law of narrative is the primacy of purposes (effects) over reasons (causes) shows us that he is an attentive reader of Nietzsche. However, he is an attentive reader of Nietzsche who owes a lot to Paul de Man's interpretation of the quoted passage from *The Will to Power*. Greenchurch claims that the narrative arises with the conversion of causes into reasons, and effects into purposes, and this is achieved by the already described rhetorical operation (primacy of purposes over reasons). This primacy of purposes over reasons (chronological inversion) is actually a linguistic event and it shows us a strange power of language. This strange power can be described as the ability of language to disrupt the linear conception of time. When we narrate about something the basic principle of connecting the events is not causality, but purpose.

In the work of Stewart Greenchurch, the main example of this primacy of purposes over reasons is a museum of natural history. A museum of natural history is a place where everything is conserved; this is the place for brute facts and historical remains. However, all of these facts are presented to us as a narrative - as a narrative about the history of nature. A man is the main reason for the very existence of that museum and the purpose of that place is to tell us (humans) a story about the history of nature. This is the obvious example of narrative castling, because here a man is not the result of the development of the nature, but he is the purpose for telling this story about the development of nature. If we translate this into de Man's terms, it means that a man, in this case, functions as the cause of its own cause.

The narrator of *Infinitive* suggests that we should read J.D. Salinger's unpublished story "Bringing No Presents Just Pasts" as another example of narrative castling. He also claims that Salinger himself sent this story to Stewart Greenchurch, and that we can read it only in the first edition of Greenchurch's *The Axiological Infinitive*. However, we already know that this is not the unpublished story of J.D. Salinger, but a story written by Sreten Ugričić. When we take all this into account, this means that the process of truth-making will be illustrated by the falsely attributed fiction. Before we address the most important problems that this short story poses, we should first read it in its entirety. The main character of this story is Sybil Carpenter, the little friend of Seymour Glass from the real story of J.D. Salinger, "A Perfect Day for Bananafish":

> A long white beach; the sea is very calm, good. Almost all the swimmers have already gone. There is a blue whale at the bottom of the sea. A barefoot girl in the red shorts is squatting at the edge of the water and playing with the pebbles. The little pebbles have acquired their perfect shape slowly, unnoticeably, being washed out and polished by the soft waves.

> She digs into them, throws them from one hand to another, shapes them into a pile, and then destroys and flattens it...She is playing aimlessly, but still as if she's choosing a pebble, her pebble, among all the others.
>
> She is not looking for it, but when she thinks that she has found it, she will name it, place it into her pocket and take it with her to her home, to the city, far away from here. In the shell of her palm, the chosen pebble, with its dim shine, reminds her of a large pearl. Its name is "humbug", the same as her favorite sweet.
>
> Later, much later, in her room – while the stars are shining high above the streets and skyscrapers at night - "humbug", this silent, small, opaque thing, will remind her of these moments before she falls asleep: of the sound of the waves behind her back, of the smells of the last summer, of the horizon that can be reached with your hand, of the big blue whale at the bottom of the sea.
>
> At night, on the night bed table in her room there is "humbug", the pebble of wisdom she once found on the beach. While the good stars – also silent and far enough – twinkle outside. The measureless glittering lace on the blue background is always there. The blue whale is at the bottom of the sea.
>
> The girl is sleeping calmly. Washed and polished by the soft waves, she is slowly acquiring her perfect shape.[101]

"Bringing No Presents Just Pasts" has its place in the seventh chapter of *Infinitive*.[102] It is used to illustrate the basic process of Greenchurch's narratology - the already mentioned metabasis or narrative castling. This is a story about the emergence of value and it shows us how an object with no value is transformed into something valuable and meaningful. At the same time this is also a story about truth. Sybil chooses a pebble and precisely this choice transforms it into a humbug. How is this achieved? A pebble is a pebble, not a humbug. This example shows us how the immediacy of a given is not immediate. When she chooses her pebble Sybil imagines that this pebble is actually in her room. This change of context endows the meaningless object with meaning and it becomes a humbug. However, the already mentioned change of context can happen because Sybil imagines the present as her memory, as something that has already happened. According to Greenchurch, this imagination underlies every creation of sense. The narrator of *Infinitive* interprets Greenchurch and claims that this emphasis on the role of imagination implies that we need to make a clear distinction between the sense and the truth. Greenchurch claims that the sense is older than the truth because we cannot even imagine a non-sensical human experience.

What I just presented is the interpretation of the interpretation of the interpretation. I interpreted the interpretation of Greenchurch's interpretation of pseudo-Sallinger's story. However, we know that "Bringing No Presents Just Pasts" is not Salinger's story and that Stewart Greenchurch and *The Axiological Infinitive* exist only on the pages of Sreten Ugričić's *Infinitive*. This means that the claims about the construction of sense (and about the truth) belong to a non-existent person. Because of that, these claims cannot be interpreted and analyzed as a real theory. If we do that, we will miss something extremely important; we will not take into account the textual nature of *Infinitive*. What should we do in this case? If we continue to claim that the truth is nothing other than correspondence than there is no other way but to discard all these claims. However, another kind of truth may be at work in *Infinitive* and *Marbot*; another kind of truth that is older and more primordial than propositional truth, namely, truth as *aletheia*? And is it possible that these works could enable us to undergo an experience with language? In order to check the validity of these theses, we will have to read the works of Martin Heidegger and to try to connect them with the problems of *Infinitive* and *Marbot.*

In the work of art truth is at work

One question comes before all others: can the reading of Heidegger's texts really be helpful in our examination of *Infinitive* and *Marbot*? For example, Otto Pöggeler claims that in "The Origin of the Work of Art" Heidegger is not interested in art itself. In this text (and in Heidegger's work in general), art is always in the shadow of the *Seinsfrage*. In brief, according to Pöggeler, "The Origin of the Work of Art" does not offer the answer to the question *what is art?* and he states that the main theme of "The Origin of the Work of Art" is not art, but the question of Being.[103] On the other hand, Friedrich von Hermann claims that the main characteristic of Heidegger's thinking is the emphasis on questions and not on answers, and thus he reads "The Origin of the Work of Art" as an incentive for thinking about art.[104] My opinion is that "The Origin of the Work of Art", and other Heidegger's texts, tell us something very important about art. This opinion is based on my readings of Blanchot's and Derrida's works which can be easily perceived as a reworking of Heidegger's poetics. According to Timothy Clark, these two authors rework Heidegger's claims about Hölderlin into notions about literarity in general.[105]

However, this claim leads us to another problem. This is the problem of application. In his two "Prefaces" for *Elucidations of Hölderlin's Poetry* Heidegger claims: "The present *Elucidations* do not claim to be contributions to research in the history of literature or to aesthetics. They spring from a necessity of thought.... These elucidations belong within the dialogue of thinking with a form of poetry whose historical uniqueness can never be proved by the history of literature, but which can be pointed out by the dialogue with thinking."[106] It is fairly obvious that Heidegger's famous essay "The Origin of the Work of Art", and his lectures about George, Rilke, Trakl and Hölderlin, do not function as some kind of universal conceptual map. The main virtue (or the main problem) is that these texts do not offer a universally applicable conceptual framework for the analysis of literary texts. Also, Heidegger's notions (if we can really call them notions?) are not ready-made concepts. They are not portable and they arise from Heidegger's specific way of thinking.

We must bear these difficulties in mind, but, at the same time, short quotations from two "Prefaces" for *Elucidations of Hölderlin's Poetry* can direct us towards possible solution. The keyword is *dialogue,* and, if we really want to follow Heidegger's path of thinking,[107] if we really want to use his texts to elucidate some other works of art, we must try to establish a dialogue between them. Consequently, this means that we need to think dialogically rather than analytically about the works of art in question. In this case, Heidegger's texts open a path of thinking about *Infinitive* and *Marbot*. I will construct this part of my dissertation by moving back and forth from Heidegger's texts to *Infinitive* and *Marbot,* and the other way around. To really think about something means to resist the temptation to reduce it to something familiar. For me, *Marbot* and *Infinitive* are enigmas and need to be recognized as such. In order to accomplish that, I will keep my text as open as possible. My aim is not to construct it as a guide (or as a definitive explanation of these works), but rather to formulate a kind of dialogue, an infinite conversation between Heidegger's texts and the above mentioned literary works.

A good point of departure can be Hildesheimer's biography of Wolfgang Amadeus Mozart. In the "Preface" we encounter the notion of *impenetrable strangeness*. What is that *impenetrable strangeness*? According to Hildesheimer it is the object of his book itself: Mozart.[108] For him, Mozart is obviously an enigma. But, if we approach this problem from the perspective of historiography we will get an answer that can easily sound paradoxical: impenetrably strange is the very sense of a given historical process. How is this possible? The ideal of positivism in historiography was formulated by Leopold von Ranke, and it says that the task of historiographer is to show the past "as it actually was" (*wie es eigentlich gewesen ist*). But Hayden White claims that what we accept as real and true in historiography is only that which wears the mask of sense, of the completeness and fulness which we can only imagine but never experience.[109] Written documents are just traces of the past, not the past itself. They are, at the same time, actual remains of what once was, and, since they are cut from its original context, something that needs constant interpretation and reinterpretation. History is not a mere collection of these traces. Historical discourse is the interpretation of past events by means of narration. First, because the historian can never include all the facts in his historical narrative - he needs to make a selection. Second, because the aim of the historian is to construct the sense of some historical process, he must interpret his material by filling in the gaps in his data. The key moment in this narration of history is the *emplotment* that actually constructs historical facts. The sense is not in the events. It is constructed by the emplotment that makes these events into historical facts. When people try to make sense of the past they must always rely on some kind of emplotment. Emplotment constitutes the basis for deciding what counts as fact. Also, emplotment determines what kind of interpretation is the most suitable for the understanding of constituted facts. The facts are neither given, nor are they found, but they are constructed by the questions of the historian. That is why the governing principle of the historical account can be defined as a "heuristic rule which self-consciously eliminates certain kinds of data from consideration as evidence."[110]

White thus claims that historical discourse is the interpretation of past events by means of narration and the key element of every narration is emplotment. In *Metahistory*, he tries to explain this "deep narrative structure" of historiography. He distinguishes four narrative styles (*viz.* four ways of emplotment) in historiography: romance - Michelet; comedy - Ranke; tragedy - Tocqueville; satire – Burckhardt. By this distinction he points to the common roots of literature and historiography.

Up to some point Stewart Greenchurch follows Hayden White by rephrasing Whites's arguments into his own terminology (as I have already mentioned, Hayden White's *emplotment* becomes *narrative castling* in the work of Stewart Greenchurch). In a manner similar to Hayden White, Greenchurch also argues that the sense of an historical event is constructed tropologically, by the means of emplotment. According to Greenchurch, as we have seen, the basic law of narrative is the primacy of purposes over reasons. This primacy lies at the foundations of every emplotment. Stewart Greenchurch claims that every fact, no matter how insignificant, can be the cause of narrative castling. The basic condition is that this fact must be recognized as a reason that leads to a certain purpose. Some facts can either hinder the plot or not have any influence on it. These facts will be ignored and will have to wait for another narrative, which is based on a different emplotment. Hence, a historian can be wonderstruck while he is watching how *his-story* unfolds and writes itself following the logic of that which he knew nothing about.

So far, everything is clear, but now I will introduce something that can seem a little bit puzzling. It seems that there are no discrepancies between the position of Hayden White and the position of Stewart Greenchurch. Both of them agree that "sense" needs to be divorced from "truth" which is understood as *adaequatio*. But, Greenchurch adds another turn of the screw to this line of argumentation. One thing is clear: emplotment transforms crude facts into the order of sense. These facts are endowed with sense only after the narrative castling. It is obvious that emplotment defines the sense of, for example, some historical event. This also means that emplotment is definitive of narrative, and that sense is infinitive of narrative.[111] Why does Greenchurch claim this? I will try to make this important point a little bit clearer. Before everything else, we need to notice that this is the alteration that Greenchurch adds to Hayden White's theory. According to Greenchurch, sense is the infinitive value because historically defined value is unable to occupy the position of sense. This would be an obvious example of *hybris*. Sense is always infinitive; it can never be definitive. Emplotment can be described as a definition of sense because historical facts are ordered via emplotment. This is the reason why some facts are sensible in one narrative and completely senseless in another. The historiographer chooses his emplotment, and *his-story* becomes definitive of a given historical process (or a definitive of a given historical event).[112] Greenchurch claims that, in most cases, the historiographer is unaware of the sense of his historical narrative. However, this does not mean that the sense is non-existent. This is an interesting addition to Hayden Whites's argumentation. Unfortunately, in our case this leads to the original conundrum, namely, what is infinitive if not the *impenetrable strangeness* itself?

Are we back to the beginning? If we continue to insist that the truth is nothing more than *adaequatio* then the answer is in the affirmative. But, in White's, and especially in Greenchurch's analysis there are several clues that can lead us from this dead end. First, according to Greenchurch, *sense is infinitive of narrative*. This sentence should not be perceived as a revolutionary break from the questioning of truth but as something which lies at the centre of this questioning. It is something that plunges us back into this questioning. From ancient times, philosophy has thought about the connection between truth (sense) and Being (infinitive), and the answer has always been the same: the truth is somehow primordially connected with Being. Second, according to Greenchurch, sense needs to be divorced from truth that is understood as *adaequatio*. This divorce points toward the above mentioned connection between sense and infinitive. It is clear that we are no longer in the realm of propositional truth, which leads to my question: can we treat Greenchurch's sense, not as something completely different from truth, but as another kind of truth? That is, can we treat it as another kind of truth that is older and more primordial than propositional truth, namely, truth as *aletheia*? Or, to put it differently, is the interplay of concealment and unconcealment somehow reenacted in *Infinitive*?

The starting point of my new beginning will be Heidegger's analysis of the traditional concept of truth from *Being and Time* in which he shows the derivativeness of this concept.[113] Heidegger does not provide some new criterion of truth; he is interpreting the essence of truth. What interests him is the sense of truth. For him, truth is something that happens (it is not seen; it is shown). Heidegger investigates what happens in an event in which truth occurs, since he is interested in the sense of this event. The similarity between

Heidegger's and Greenchurch's project is obvious. Greenchurch tells us how the sense of the historical event is created and Heidegger examines the sense of the event of truth.

According to Heidegger, three statements characterize the traditional understanding of truth:

1.) The locus of truth is the proposition (judgement);
2.) The essence of truth lies in the "agreement" of the judgement with its object;
3.) Aristotle, the father of logic, attributed truth to judgement as its primordial locus, he also started the definition of truth as agreement.[114]

After that, Heidegger asks what *agreement* means in general. His response is that agreement is always a relation of something to something. Truth has a relational character, and its basis is, according to the three presented theses, the connection between the ideal content of judgement and the real thing about which the judgement is formed. Heidegger's example is helpful and, at the same time, very illustrative:

> Let someone make the true statement with his back to the wall: "The picture on the wall is hanging crookedly." This statement demonstrates itself when the speaker turns around and perceives the picture hanging crookedly on the wall. What is proved in this demonstration? What is the meaning of confirming this statement? Do we perhaps ascertain an agreement between "knowledge" or "what is known" with the thing on the wall? Yes and no, depending on whether our interpretation of the expression "what is known" is phenomenally adequate. To what is the speaker related when he judges without perceiving the picture, but "only representing it"? Possibly to "representations"? Certainly not, if representation

is supposed to mean here representing as psychical event. Nor is he related to representations in the sense of what is represented, if we mean by that a "picture" of the real thing on the wall. Rather, the statement that is "only representing" is in accordance with its ownmost meaning related to the real picture on the wall. What one has in mind is the real picture, and nothing else. Any interpretation that inserts something else here as what one has in mind in a statement that merely represents falsifies the phenomenal state of affairs about which a statement is made. Making statements is a being toward the existing thing itself. And what is demonstrated by perception? Nothing other than the fact that it is this very being that one has in mind in one's statement. This is further confirmed by the fact that this is pointed out by the being in which the statement is made - which is being toward what is put forward in the statement. What is to be confirmed is that it discovers the being toward which it is. What is demonstrated is the discovering being of the assertion. Here knowing remains related solely to the being itself in the act of demonstration. It is in this being, so to speak, that the confirmation takes place. The being that one has in mind shows itself as it is in itself, that is, it shows that it, in its selfsameness, is just as it is discovered or pointed out in the assertion. Representations are not compared, neither among themselves, nor in relation to the real thing. What is to be demonstrated is solely the being-discovered of the being itself, that being in the how of its being discovered. This is confirmed by the fact that what is stated (that is, the being itself) shows as the very same thing. Confirmation means the being's showing itself in its self-sameness. Confirmation is accomplished on the basis of the being's showing itself. That is possible only in that the knowing asserts and is confirmed is itself a discovering being toward real beings in its ontological meaning.[115]

What this example tells us is quite basic: if the picture did not show itself to me, I would be unable to say anything about it at all. I will clarify this systematically.[116] The aim of the statement *The picture on the wall is hanging crookedly* is to uncover the picture on the wall. Heidegger's example shows us that the propositional truth (truth as correspondence or truth as *adaequatio*) depends on a more primordial truth as *aletheia*. What we have here is not a relation between an inner mental image and some outer object. What we have is a relation between a being as uncovered by the statement and the being itself. Heidegger's point is that the truth of the statement is *Entdeckend-sein* (Being-uncovering). However, there is another important point. The basis of this uncovering is our *In-der-Welt-sein* (Being-in-the-world), the essential disclosedness of Dasein (Dasein's openness of comportment). This means that, in its most basic sense, truth is disclosedness of the world.

Heidegger's important claim is that truth refers not to objects, but to Dasein itself. In *Being and Time,* truth is described as the existential of Dasein. This means that there is no truth without Dasein. More precisely, there can be truth only as long as Dasein is. If we bear in mind pseudo-Salinger's story (and the questions I asked about it) that does not mean we are capable of arbitrarily determining what is truth. Things are present to Dasein because they are meaningful, but they are meaningful only because they have their place in Dasein's world. Richard Polt provides a very useful explanation:

> For example, our geologist is studying a piece of quartz that is undeniably, solidly real. It was real before she studied it, and it will continue to be real once she is done with it. Now, how does this mineral come to have the *meaning* "real" for the geologist? How does it *reveal* itself as a real in her life? How does it make a difference to her that the quartz is real, rather than unreal? According to Heidegger, we cannot answer these questions unless

we investigate how the geologist's existence is rooted in a past, projects toward a future, and falls into present. Thanks to this care structure, she is in a world - a world of many concerns, including her family, religion and profession. Within her world, some things *present* themselves to her in such a way that she can study certain aspects of them with the methods of geology. Reality is the kind of presence that characterizes such aspects of things. Now, neither the quartz nor anything else could present itself to us in the first place without the context in which things can present themselves to us in the first place - and that context is care. Although we are getting ahead of ourselves a little, we can say that care, which is thoroughly temporal provides the context that gives meaning to reality. This is a special case of the general thesis toward which Heidegger is working in *Being and Time*: time provides the context that gives meaning to all modes of Being.[117]

This brings us back to "Bringing No Presents Just Pasts." One possible interpretation of this story is that it is not a story that celebrates relativism. If we bear in mind Polt's example, we come to the conclusion that the pebble (like a piece of quartz) does not depend on Dasein for its location or its existence. However, the reality in which the pebble shows itself, in which it has its place as a humbug, does depend on Dasein's (Sybil) existence. The story speaks about our primary relationship to the world. It shows us how a pebble becomes a meaningful ready-at-hand being. The pebble is what it is in itself, but, at the end of the story, its place has changed. In the world of the little girl, the pebble becomes the humbug; its place in her room endows the pebble with meaning.

The problem of this interpretation is that it is not very illuminative. First, it treats "Bringing No Presents Just Pasts" as a real event and therefore completely ignores the textual nature of this literary work.[118] According to this interpretation, the text is simply a surface behind which real persons and events exist. This explanation fails to deal with the issue of textuality, because it fails to engage with the text as a text. On the one hand, the problem lies in the fact that the story does not describe a real event. On the other hand, this is not an ordinary story. Jerome David Salinger did not write this story, and therefore he did not send it to Stewart Greenchurch. We cannot read it in the first edition of Greenchurch's *The Axiological Infinitive,* because this book does not exist. "Bringing No Presents Just Pasts" and *The Axiological Infinitive* exist only on the pages of Sreten Ugričić's *Infinitive*. The aforementioned interpretation is not very illuminative because it fails to offer any kind of answer to the crucial questions: Are *Infinitive* and *Marbot* just simple hoaxes? If they are, why are they capable of tricking their readers so easily? Maybe a certain problem of presentation is made visible by these works?

In order to highlight this problem, we might return to Dejan Ilić's interpretation of *Infinitive*. First, Ilić makes a recourse to chronology. In order to explain *Infinitive,* he needs a temporal series of events. This is his line of reasoning: the necessary condition of Sreten Ugričić's *Infinitive* is Stewart Greenchurch's *The Axiological Infinitive. The Axiological Infinitive* is something that comes before *Infinitive. Infinitive* is something that comes after *The Axiological Infinitive.* Stewart Greenchurch is the addressor and Sreten Ugričić is the addressee of the message. However, we already know that this is not the case and that *The Axiological Infinitive* exists only on the pages of *Infinitive*. This is not a huge obstacle for Dejan Ilić. When he realises that this is the case, he will proclaim that Stewart Greenchurch is the unnecessary addition to a coherent theoretical position presented in *Infinitive* and he will make recourse to spatiality. In short, he will discard Stewart Greenchurch and his invisible work and claim that the origin of *Infinitive* lies in Sreten Ugričić: *Infinitive* is a straightforward presentation and immediate transcription of Sreten Ugričić's theoretical thought. Yes, it is true, *The Axiological Infinitive* is indeed the origin of *Infinitive*, but this origin is unattainable and unreachable. This is the paradox that Dejan Ilić overlooks and he tries to fix *Infinitive*'s point of origin in the immediacy of the authorial intention.

Jean-François Lyotard, in his analysis of Kant's "Transcendental Analytic", shows us why this operation is problematic and why the supposed immediacy of the given is not actually immediate. Lyotard claims that the philosophy of the subject is characterized by one important trait: it treats a presentation like a situation. This is called metaphysical illusion. Lyotard writes: "The idea of a given (an immediate given) is a way of receiving and censuring the idea of a presentation. A presentation does not present a universe to someone: it is the event of its (inapprehensible) presence. A given is given to a subject, who receives it and deals with it. To deal with it is to situate it, to place it in a phrase universe. We can follow this operation at the beginning of the "Transcendental Aesthetic."[119] After these introductory sentences, Lyotard offers his interpretation of Kant's text:

> The first two pages of the "Transcendental Aesthetic" can thus be broken down into two moments, each of which is structured like a phrase universe. First moment: an unknown addressor speaks matter (as we say, to speak French) to an addressee receptive to this idiom, and who therefore understands it, at least in the sense by which he or she is affected by it. What does the matter-phrase talk about, what is its referent? It does not yet have one, it is a sentimental phrase, the referential function is minor in

it. What is important is its conative function, as Jakobson would have said. The matter-phrase relates only to the addressee, the receptive subject.

Second Moment: this subject passes into the situation of addressing instance and addresses the phrase of space-time, the form phrase, to the unknown addressor of the first phrase, who thereby becomes an addressee . This phrase, as opposed to the matter phrase, is endowed with a referential function. Its referent is called the phenomenon. As Kant writes, sensible impressions are "related to objects" called phenomena. The referential function which then appears results from the capacity the subject has - which is an active capacity-to show the moment and the place of whatever it is that by its matter produces the effect (*Wirkung*) or sensible impression upon the addressee of the first phrase. This is what we call the ostensive capacity: It's over there, It was a little while ago. This second phrase, which applies deictic markers onto the impressions procured by sensation, is called in the Kantian lexicon: intuition.

The "immediacy" of the given, as we see, is not immediate. On the contrary, the constitution of the given requires an exchange of roles between addressor and addressee instances and thus requires two phrases or quasi-phrases: respectively, the one where impression occurs and the one where the putting into (spatio-temporal) form occurs. This permutation involves two partners who alternate between addressor and addressee. Through this dialogical or dialectical linking, a referent is constituted, the phenomenon.[120]

After this passage that sheds more light on some problems of the first chapter of my dissertation,[121] I will resume with the problems of the second chapter. Can we claim that a certain relationship with truth exists in the works of Sreten Ugričić and Wolfgang Hildesheimer? I would not say that we should simply discard the already presented interpretation of pseudo-Salinger's story "Bringing No Presents Just Pasts". This interpretation is a starting point, and the further examination of Heidegger's writings about truth can help us to formulate some kind of answer to the above mentioned crucial questions.

Before proceeding to the analysis of Heidegger's famous text "On the Essence of Truth",[122] we should address one important issue. In *Being and Time* Heidegger states that truth is the existential of Dasein. Disclosedness, in general, is essential to the being of Dasein. Because of that, truth is, in its primordial sense, "the disclosedness of Dasein to which belongs the disclosedness of inworldly beings."[123] However, there is also a catch in all this. On the one hand, things can be unconcealed because Dasein is essentially disclosed (or opened) by care. Care situates Dasein as being-in-the-world, and therefore, Dasein is in truth. On the other hand, falling prey is also a part of Dasein's constitution. This implies that Dasein is usually lost in its world. Heidegger claims: "Because it essentially falls prey to the world, Dasein is in "untruth" in accordance with its constitution of being."[124] Since falling prey is also an essential part of Dasein's constitution, it is implied that the unconcealing of things is always (and at the same time) also, concealing.

I mentioned all this because it can be used to highlight the difference between Heidegger's position in *Being and Time* and his position in later writings. In his later years, Heidegger abandons the project of fundamental ontology and shifts the focus to Being itself. According to William J. Richardson, Heidegger "becomes more and more preoccupied with Being itself, but chiefly in terms of the problem of truth, since the sense of Being is its truth."[125] In this part of the text, I will analyse Heidegger's essay "On the Essence of Truth", and, after that, I will explain the connection between truth and art that is formulated in "The Origin of the Work of Art". This connection (Heidegger's claim that in the work of art the truth is at work) will be the basis of my claim that the truth is at work in the works of Sreten Ugričić and Wolfgang Hildesheimer.

The beginning of the Heidegger's essay "On the Essence of Truth" resembles his analysis in *Being and Time*. He starts with the usual concept of truth and poses his first question: what do we ordinarily understand by truth? The answer is the same as in *Being and Time*: truth is either correspondence or accordance. The next question is concerned with the inner possibility of this accordance. We already know that Dasein's comportment is open to beings. Therefore, correctness is made possible by the openness of comportment. The openness of Dasein's comportment is that which makes accordance and correspondence possible. Consequently, it is clearly stated that truth does not reside in the propositions but in the disclosedness of inwordly beings.

There are no discrepancies with the argumentation that was already formulated in *Being and Time*. However, after Heidegger explains what the basis of our usual concept of truth is, he claims that "the openness of comportment as the inner condition of the possibility of correctness is grounded in freedom. The essence of truth, as the correctness of a statement, is freedom."[126] Does this mean that we again have to go back to the beginning? Is the truth something completely subjective, something that depends upon *human caprice*? *Being and Time* clearly says that the truth is not *human caprice*, and also that truth is Dasein's existential. There is no truth without Dasein. In "On the Essence of Truth", Heidegger goes even further and poses the important question: is freedom really a property of the human being?

What is freedom? Heidegger states that freedom is letting be of beings. What he means by that is the following: "Freedom was essentially determined as freedom for what is opened up in an open region. How is this essence of freedom to be thought? That which is opened up, that to which a presentative statement as correct corresponds, are beings opened up in an open comportment. Freedom for what is opened up in an open region lets beings be the beings they are. Freedom now reveals itself as letting beings be."[127] To let beings be is not something negative. It refers to an engagement with beings, to let beings be as the beings that they are. So, freedom (*letting-be*) is essentially an engagement with the disclosedness of beings. Freedom is exposure to the disclosedness of beings. If this is the case, *human caprice* does not possess freedom. Freedom is not the property of a human being. Quite the contrary, freedom possesses the human being. Heidegger explains: "... freedom, ek-sistent, disclosive Dasein, possesses the human being - so originarily that only it secures for humanity that distinctive relatedness to beings as a whole as such which first founds all history. Only ek-sistent human being is historical... 'Truth' is not a feature of correct propositions that are asserted of an 'object' by a human 'subject' and then 'are valid' somewhere, in what sphere we know not; rather, truth is disclosure of beings through which an openness essentially unfolds [west]."[128] In short, openness of comportment is based on freedom, which is described as a release into openness where Dasein meets other beings.

Since the truth is, at its essence, freedom, and since it is described as letting-be of beings, human beings can also not let beings be as the beings that they are. Beings can either be concealed and covered or unconcealed and uncovered. In this concealing we can notice the non-essence of truth that does not arise from human negligence. Strangely, according to Heidegger, the non-essence of truth arises from the essence of truth, which means that there is an inherent connection between truth and non-truth.

How is this possible? "On the Essence of Truth" tells us that there is an ontic and ontological connection between truth and non-truth. An ontic connection between truth and non-truth can be described with the help of my previous explanation of Heidegger's claim that Dasein is both in truth and in non-truth. One of the most important existentials in *Being and Time* is attunement. Why is attunement so important? The answer: attunement is essentially disclosive and, because of that, it is something that characterizes Dasein ontologically. Heidegger says: "Mood has always already disclosed being-in-the-world as a whole and first makes possible directing oneself toward something... It is a fundamental existential mode of being of the equiprimordial disclosedness of world, being-there-with, and existence because this disclosure itself is essentially being-in-the-world."[129] It is important to bear in mind that not all attunements are equally disclosive. As previously explained, Dasein can also be in non-truth because it can become trapped in an inauthentic attunement, which will show things from a restricted perspective. We are always attuned to the world in some way, and we cannot escape from attunement. Attunement reveals that Dasein is in the world and therefore discloses being-in-the-world as a whole.

The problem arises from the simple fact that in any particular comportment (unconcealing of a particular thing) being-in-the-world becomes obscured. In our particular comportment we always experience the world from a certain perspective (from a certain point-of-view). This brings us to something very important: concealing lies at the heart of unconcealing. First, in unconcealing only one aspect of the unconcealed thing comes to the surface. The other aspects are obscured and retreat into the background. We are limited by our perspective (by our point-of-view) simply because we are thrown into the world and attuned to that world in a particular way. Second, only something that is concealed can be unconcealed, and this means that concealment is ontologically prior to concealment. Letting-be of beings (*unconcealment*) always happens on the background of concealment. That is the reason why William J. Richardson claims:

> Concealment, then is prior to the freedom which comes-to-pass through a particular comportment between There-being (*Dasein*) and individual being. Furthermore, this comportment itself not only leaves concealed the remainder of beings-in their-totality but itself enters into a special relationship with the concealing of what is concealed. This relationship to the concealment of the total ensemble of beings is of such a nature that the concealing *itself* remains concealed. We may speak, then, of a concealing of concealment, sc. what is concealing in There-being's liberating comportment is not only beings-in-their-totality but the fact that the ensemble is concealed and the import of this fact. This concealing of the concealed Heidegger calls "the mystery" (*das Geheimnis*) - the unique and primordial obscurity that enshrouds not individual beings severally but the entire There-being of man.[130]

This concealing remains concealed because we focus on the thing that is unconcealed (being) and not on the process of unconcealing (which always involves concealing). According to

Heidegger, *Being loves to hide*, and that is why letting-beings-be is at the same time concealing. The *Seinsfrage* and the question of truth are intrinsically connected. This structural concealing resembles the forgetfulness of Being (and infinitive). Common reason covers the most important question, and we can easily forget about Being (and infinitive). Both Being and infinitive are somehow always concealed from us, presumably because they cannot be identified (or defined) by being (or fixed by definitive). This is the reason why Heidegger claims in *Being and Time* that "this indefiniteness of the understanding of Being that is always already available is itself a positive phenomenon which needs elucidation."[131] Despite this forgetfulness, the vague and average understanding of Being always lingers in the background. This indefinability of Being (and infinitive) imposes the question of their meaning upon us. In this text, I will argue that the work of art is the place where this question (this enigma) can find its formulation.

In order to explain how truth happens in the work of art, I will start with the question about the piece of equipment, namely with the pair of peasant shoes. This is the place in "The Origin of the Work of Art"[132] where Heidegger tries to explain the equipmentality of the equipment. First, why is he interested in the equipmentality of the equipment? The answer is simply because the usual understanding of artworks is based (and derived) on the previous interpretation of the equipmentality of the equipment. In my work, the prime example of this kind of interpretation is Dejan Ilić's reading of *Infinitive*. In this case, *Infinitive* is understood as equipment with aesthetic quality. Why, then, is the standard definition of the equipmentality of equipment problematic? In order to answer this question we need to go back to *Being and Time*. This recourse will enable us to explain the important distinction between ready-at-hand

and present-at-hand.

In *Being and Time,* Heidegger states that there is no such thing as one piece of equipment or one useful thing because equipment always belongs to the totality of useful things. It is only in this totality that equipment can be what it is. In its essence equipment is *something in order to*. The variations of this *in order to* include *serviceability*, *usability*, *handiness*, etc. The relations named here constitute the above mentioned totality of the equipment. It is important to note that the *something in order to* structure always includes a reference to something. This is why the *something in order to* structure points towards the totality of equipment. Equipment always shows itself as ready-at-hand, and, never in itself, as present-at-hand. Heidegger uses the example of hammering to explain how the totality of equipment always comes before the individual piece of equipment:

> Association geared to useful things which show themselves genuinely only in this association, that is, hammering with the hammer, neither *grasps* these beings thematically as occurring things nor does it even know of using the structure of useful things as such. Hammering does not have a knowledge of the useful character of the hammer; rather, it has appropriated this useful thing in the most adequate way possible. When we take care of things, we are subordinate to the in-order-to constitutive for the actual useful thing in our association with it. The less we just stare at the thing called hammer, the more actively we use it, the more original our relation to it becomes and the more undisguisedly it is encountered as what it is, as a useful thing. The act of hammering itself discovers the specific "handiness" of the hammer. We shall call the useful thing's kind of being in which it reveals itself by itself *handiness*. It is only because useful things have *this* "being-in-themselves", and do not merely

occur, that they are handy in the broadest sense and are at our disposal. No matter how keenly we just *look at* the "outward appearance" of things constituted in one way or another, we cannot discover handiness. But association which makes use of things is not blind, it has its own way of seeing which guides our operations and gives them their specific thingly quality. Our association with useful things is subordinate to the manifold of references of the "in order to". The kind of seeing of this accommodation to things is called *circumspection*.[133]

The equipment is inconspicuous. We use it, and in this usage, it vanishes from our attention. As long as the piece of equipment is serviceable, and as long as it is working properly, we do not pay much attention to it. We simply use it. When we start to think about the specific piece of equipment it changes from ready-at-hand to present-at-hand. Usefulness is not blind, but it always includes a degree of blindness. The problem of the equipmentality of equipment can be easily discerned from the perspective that, in order to determine the equipmentality of equipment, we need to grasp a piece of equipment as ready-at-hand. However, as soon as we focus our attention on a piece of equipment it becomes present-at-hand. When it becomes present-at-hand, this equipmentality of equipment slips through our fingers. When we use the equipment we are too close to it, and this closeness has its blind spot. Therefore, this blind spot prevents us from grasping the equipmentality of equipment. In order to understand the equipmentality of equipment we need some distance from the equipment. Heidegger claims that the work of art can help us with that. The work of art can help us to understand the equipmentality of equipment. This is the reason why Heidegger claims that the work of art is the *Ereignis* of truth.

I will proceed slowly with Heidegger's example from "The Origin of the Work of Art", with the pair of peasant shoes.[134] Heidegger asks the following questions: it is clear that the equipmentality of equipment consists in its utility or serviceability, but how do we understand this utility itself? Also, if we understand this utility, does it mean that we simultaneously understand the equipmentality of equipment? The problem arises from the already described paradox: when we use the equipment we are confronted with its equipmentality, but when we try to grasp this equipmentality, it escapes us. The equipmentality of equipment consists in its usefulness, but this usefulness is based on the reliability of the equipment. The reliability of the equipment can be described as the essential being of equipment. Because of this reliability the peasant woman knows all about her shoes without reflection. According to Heidegger, the usefulness of the equipment is the consequence of this reliability. The essential being of the equipment (equipmentality of the equipment) is reliability. The reliability discloses the equipmentality of equipment, but this reliability is, in turn, disclosed by the work of art (van Gogh's painting). The painting, Heidegger argues, speaks to us about the equipmentality of the equipment; disclosing the essence of equipment, it speaks to us about the truth of beings. In its own way, the work of art opens up the being of beings. This is how Heidegger describes the equipment's reliability: "This equipment belongs to *the earth* and it is protected in *the world* of the peasant woman. From out of this protected belonging the equipment itself rises to its resting-in-self."[135] This place is important because it is a first mention of the relation between the world and the earth.

However, here lurks the trap of oversimplification for the commentators. If we do not take into account this connection between Heidegger's notion of reliability and the world and the earth or if we miss it, we can attempt to oversimplify things. This oversimplification again shows itself as the understanding of truth as correspondence. Although Heidegger explicitly claims that the unconcealment happens in the work of art, we can be tempted to simplify this by turning things around and saying that what is unconcealed is the being in its naked reality - the thing-in-itself (*das Ding an sich*). The second move will be the identification of that naked reality of being with the essence of being. By this procedure, we would come back to the understanding of truth as correspondence. In this line of simplified thinking, unconcealment is not understood as more primordial than correspondence, but rather the other way around. In order to avoid this oversimplification we will need to clarify Heidegger's position. He does not want to suggest that the work of art represents reality, meaning that the truth of the work of art depends on the faithfulness to the represented thing. He rejects Stendhal's ideal from *The Red and the Black* according to which art "is a mirror going along a main road. Sometimes it reflects into your eyes the azure of the sky, sometimes the mud of the quagmires on the road."[136]

To summarize: we first learned what kind of truth is not at work in the work of art. It is not truth as *adaequatio*. Secondly, we learned that it is definitely truth as *aletheia* which is at work in the work of art. Also, we need to notice that in "The Origin of the Work of Art", Heidegger again modifies his understanding of truth. Finally, in this essay, Heidegger also tries to provide the answer to the fundamental question: what is truth if we accept that it can occur ***in*** (or maybe ***as***) art?

In "The Origin of the Work of Art", Heidegger again claims that the truth is the unconcealment of beings. However, there is an important addition:

> And yet: beyond beings - though before rather than apart from them - there is still something other that happens. In the midst of beings as a whole an open place comes to presence. There is a clearing. Thought from out of beings, it is more in being than is the being. This open center is, therefore, not surrounded by beings. Rather, this illuminating center itself encircles all beings - like the nothing that we scarcely know.
>
> The being can only be, as a being, if it stands within, and stands out within, what is illuminated in this clearing. Only this clearing grants us human beings access to those beings that we ourselves are not and admittance to the being that we ourselves are. Thanks to this clearing, beings are unconcealed in certain and changing degrees. But even to be concealed is something the being can only do within the scope of the illuminated. Each being which we encounter and which encounters us maintains this strange opposition of presence in that at the same time it always holds itself back in a concealment.[137]

Heidegger focuses on truth, and he does not mention Dasein anymore. The unconcealment, the opening of the Open, is understood as an interplay of concealment and unconcealment, as togetherness (and strife) of world and earth. Due to the focus of this chapter, it is not relevant to discuss in detail the important terms of *world* and *earth*. Instead, I shall present Heidegger's understanding of truth and connect this understanding with the works of Sreten Ugričić and Wolfgang Hildesheimer. However, some interpretation of *world* and *earth* must be given and Gianni Vattimo's understanding of these terms can be helpful in this case. World and earth are in fact especially pertinent for us because the structural relationship between infinitive and definitive is reenacted in Vattimo's analysis. He says that we can understand the world as *a system beings give rise to within a specifically given horizon or opening of being*. For him, it is important not to identify the earth with nature and world with culture. That would reduce the relationship between these two terms to simple opposition. He claims that in the work of art, the earth can be understood as *a permanent ontological reserve of meaning*[138] that cannot be exhausted by interpretation. Every interpretation defines a world that is founded and opened up by the work of art in question. However, and at the same time, the work of art is a *permanent reserve of new interpretations*. This is the reason why, for Heidegger, the presence of the earth is the important feature of the work of art: a feature of eternal withdrawal. In short, it can be said that the earth is the reservoir of potential meanings that the work in question always holds in reserve.[139]

If we go back to Heidegger, we will see that, for him, earth is something that is essentially self-secluding; world, on the other hand, is always self-disclosing. The strife of world and earth (which becomes that of unconcealment and concealment) happens in the work of art, and this strife is the happening of truth. This strife, this interplay of concealment and unconcealment, as set up in the work, testifies that artistic beauty is one of the ways in which truth happens. When we try to interpret the work of art two things happen simultaneously: unconcealment and concealment. Our interpretation gives rise to a certain horizon or opening of the beings in their being. At the same time, this emergence hides the other possible openings. Every reading is in its essence a misreading. This happening does not arise from our negligence. This is, quite simply, the happening of truth, and truth is, in its essence, the already mentioned interplay between unconcealment and concealment. The strife between concealment and unconcealment is opened up by the work of art, and the truth establishes itself as the strife between these two sides by which the "open center" is won. The truth is described as unconcealment which is, at the same time, concealment. In other words:

> Art shows how a being which presences in unconcealment maintains "the opposition of presence"; to the extent that it is unconcealed, it is also concealed. In the unconcealment the concealment holds sway not only as the non-essence, the self refusal of truth, but also as the counter-essence of the disguise in which one being disguises the other and beings generally disguise Being. Amidst the familiar and common, art wrenches open the space for the uncanny and thus lets every clearing and revealing shatter on the concealment. Truth as it occurs at times as art is unconcealment. Nothing belongs to it as that which holds sway, as concealment and "veil", as the heart and the mystery of unconcealment.[140]

This happening of the truth in the work of art leads to another one of its characteristics: createdness. Heidegger's notion of createdness is important, because it can provide us with the solid basis for the distinction between work and equipment. Both equipment and the work of art have a shared feature in that they are both something that has been brought forth. However, in "The Origin of The Work of Art", Heidegger claims that the work of art and equipment are essentially different because equipment can never be the happening of truth. This is because the main characteristic of equipment is its serviceability, its usefulness, and, as long as it is working perfectly, a piece of equipment vanishes in its serviceability. The production of equipment is finished when this equipment is ready for use. This means that the material used for the production of equipment is used up. On the other hand, the createdness of the work of art is different from every other bringing forth. What makes this createdness different is that it is created into the created work. That is to say, in the work of art createdness is created into the work of art in a way that causes it to stand out from the work of art itself. Createdness of the work of art makes us aware that the work is. This awareness remains hidden if we treat the artwork in the same way as we treat the equipment. If we treat the artwork as equipment endowed by aesthetic quality, createdness remains concealed. The work of art makes us aware that the unconcealedness of being has happened. It makes us aware that the work is something rather than nothing. The usefulness (or serviceability) is one of the main characteristics of equipment, but the work of art does not disappear in this usefulness. Rather, it draws attention to itself and to the simple fact that it is something rather than nothing. According to Christopher Fynsk:

> The work somehow brings forth the fact that it is *figure of...* something - the event of truth. But truth is no thing that is, and is nowhere other than in the work; so we might say no more than that it is the figure of... nothing, other than itself. This is to say, if we follow out the logic of this argument, that the work shows figurality itself.[141]

We can clearly discern the parallels with *Infinitive* and *Marbot* and this notion of createdness. Both works make their createdness explicitly visible. They make it visible because *Infinitive* is a monograph, but a monograph of a non-existent book; whereas, *Marbot* is a biography of a non-existent man. Their basis is pure nothingness (non-existent man and non-existent book), but *Infinitive* and *Marbot* are something rather than nothing. The fact that they arise from nothing is something that makes their createdness visible. We can clearly see their createdness, but we still do not know what their relationship is with truth. In other words, how is the truth at work in these works? In order to make the connection, we will have to examine Heidegger's claim that language is essentially poetry.

The power of naming

The work of art is not exhausted in its createdness. According to Heidegger, the work of art is the event of truth, namely, a becoming and happening of truth. This means that the essence of art is the establishment of truth in the work. Truth establishes itself in the work as the opposition between clearing and concealing. To which Heidegger than adds something very important: "Truth, as clearing and concealing of that which is, happens through being poeticized. All art, as the letting happen of the advent of the truth of beings, is, in essence, poetry."[142] It is obvious that Heidegger claims that poetry has a privileged position among arts, but this is not the end. Something much more important is at stake here and Heidegger adds:

> Language, by naming beings for the first time, first brings beings to word and to appearance. This naming nominates beings *to* their being and *from* out of that being. Such saying is a projection of the clearing in which announcement is made as to what beings will come into the open as. Projecting [*Enwerfen*] is the releasing of a throw [*Wurf*] as which unconcealment sends itself into beings as such. This projective announcement immediately becomes a renunciation of all dim confusion within which beings veil and withdraw themselves.
>
> Projective saying is poetry: the saying of world and earth, the saying of the arena of their strife and, thereby, of all nearness and distance of the gods. Poetry is the saying of the unconcealment of beings. The prevailing language is the happening of that saying in which its world rises up historically for a people and the earth is preserved as that which remains closed. Projective saying is that in which the preparation of the sayable at the same time brings the unsayable as such to the world. In such saying, the

concepts of its essence - its belonging to world-history, in other words - are formed, in advance, for a historical people.

Poetry is here thought in such a broad sense, and at the same time in such an intimate and essential unity with language and the word, that it must remain open whether art, in all its modes from architecture to poesy, exhausts the nature of poetry.[143]

How can we clarify these claims? We need to go slowly and our starting point could be Heidegger's sentence: "When we go to the well, when we go through the woods, we are always already going through the word "well," through the word "woods," even if we do not speak the words and do not think of anything relating to language."[144] Our common understanding says that language is a simple tool for communication and for the exchange of information. Because this is the main purpose of language it needs to be as transparent as possible. This also implies the understanding that the language of everyday communication is the norm and that poetic language is derivative. We already know that, for Heidegger, things are not that simple. The already stated primacy of poetry certainly depends on the importance and primacy of language.[145] I will go back to the previous example *The picture on the wall is hanging crookedly.* This sentence is true if I see that the picture is really hanging crookedly. But, what do I see? I see picture as a picture and a wall as a wall because I am in some language in which concepts "picture" and "wall" possess some meaning. Our concepts are always tied to some linguistic expression and therefore language is part of our revelation of the world. Things are always revealed to us within a linguistic context. According to Karsten Harries: "Our conceptual space is inseparably intertwined with some language. To be in a world is to inhabit some language."[146]

In his later writings, Heidegger goes even further than this. For him, to be a human being means to dwell in language and because of that language will be described as *the house of Being*. Only by virtue of language man is exposed to beings: language makes beings manifest and language preserves them as such. At the first glance, language is the property of a man - it is his tool for communication. But, if language provides *the possibility of standing in the midst of the openness of beings* then it cannot be just a simple tool. Language is not just our tool for communication; language *brings beings as such for the first time into the Open*. Oversimplifying, we can say that language is the background on which the things become apparent.[147]

What about poetry?[148] Poetry is important because we need to understand the essence of language from the essence of poetry and not the other way around. We can see that in "The Origin of the Work of Art" Heidegger understands art as a possibility for an open place, namely, for the taking place of the openness in which being is able to appear. Poetry has an important role in this essay because it enables the openness to show itself. We have to bear in mind the connection between the essence of poetry and the establishment of truth: the establishment of truth is the clearing in which Being comes to pass. In his essay "Hölderlin and the Essence of Poetry",[149] Heidegger states that poetry happens in language and that its material is language. Because it happens in language, poetry can be understood only if we provide the answer to the question: what is the essence of language? The essence of language is *the founding of Being through words* - naming.[150] Language names, it gives names to beings. According to Heidegger, "poetry is a founding by the word and in the word."[151] Poetry has the ability to name beings and this naming does not merely provide a name for some entity that is already known in some way.

Poetry is the founding of Being in the word. Without naming there is no openness. In the poetic word the being is named as what it is and in poetry beings become known as beings. Poetry re-enacts the original naming which is the origin of our everyday language. What is established in poetry is the Open and in this essay the Open is interchangeable with Being. The word brings into the Open and maintains the thing in that Open.

A good illustration of what Heidegger is trying to say can be found in "The Nature of Language"; namely, in the last verse of Stefan George's poem "The Word": "Where word breaks off no thing may be."[152] This verse tells us something very important about the relation between word and thing. Heidegger states that we can understand the verse in the following way: there can be no thing where the word is missing or, more precisely, there can be no thing where that which names the being is missing. It is important to note that naming is not understood as a mere sign for something that already exists. To emphasize this Heidegger again paraphrases George's verse: "No thing is where the word, that is, the name is lacking. The word alone gives being to the thing."[153] It is important to note that the word is not just able to name a being that is already there. The word grants the being presence and this is why the word is not just a mere reference or a tool for communication. In short, poetry, the original naming allows being to arise. But, how is this possible? Is a mere word really capable of bringing a thing into being?

First, an interesting analogy can be established between Heidegger and J.L. Austin. However, it is important to note that, in this work, I do not claim that Heidegger's *naming* and Austin's *performative* are identical. Heidegger's understanding of naming is very complex and Austin's performative can help us to illuminate it. Like Heidegger, Austin is interested in the strange power of language (its active function) and, at the very beginning of *How to Do Things with Words* he says that the truth as correspondence will not be his guiding principle: "It was too long the assumption of philosophers that the business of a 'statement' can only be to 'describe' some state of affairs or to 'state some fact' which it must do either truly or falsely."[154] According to Austin, truth/falsehood criterion can only be applied to the utterances that are called constatives. Constatives are sentences that report a certain state of affairs. For example, if my friend says "it is raining outside", I will look through the window and see if his statement is true or false.

However, there is another kind of utterance because language has the ability to perform actions and not just to report on them. These utterances are called performatives and they act through process of their enunciation:

> 1.) they do not "describe" or "report" or constate anything at all, are not "true or false"; and
>
> 2.) the uttering of the sentence is, or is a part of, the doing of an action, which again would not normally be described as saying something.[155]

We might say that Austin seeks in his notion of performative something that Heidegger assigns to the act of naming - the essence of language, its active function. However, we need to be careful; we must not equate naming and performative. Performative and naming are not one and the same. When we come back to Heidegger's naming the limitations of Austin's conception of performative will become visible. But, before that, we can use Austin's conception of performative to come as near as possible to the understanding of naming.

According to Austin, naming (in its narrow sense) is a typical performative. For example, "I name this ship Titanic". Other examples of performative utterances are promises ("I promise to pay my debt") or bets ("I bet you 5 pounds that it will rain tomorrow"). It is obvious from these examples that performative utterances do something and that they are neither true nor false. In the case of performatives, uttering is doing - to say something means to do something. This implies that performative utterances have the ability to change the world because they can bring into being the thing they name. If performatives cannot be true or false then what criterion is applied to them? According to Austin, it is the criterion of felicity or infelicity; performatives can be successful or unsuccessful. The condition of their success is their conformity to the established rules. In Heidegger's notion of naming, the rules themselves are being established.

After he made a distinction between performative and constative utterances, Austin tries to formulate a linguistic criterion that will enable us to recognize performatives. But, in this process he encounters a serious problem - the existence of implicit performatives. Shoshana Felman explains this problem in the following way:

> For although linguistic criteria that might formalize the distinction [between constatives and performatives] do exist, they prove to be neither exhaustive nor at all absolute. The principal grammatical criterion is the asymmetry that occurs, in certain verbs (henceforth recognized as "performative verbs"), between the first person of the

> present indicative, active voice, and the other persons and tenses of the verb: whereas the first person, by uttering the verb in the present tense, effectively carries out the designated act ("I *promise*," I *swear*,", "I *guarantee*," "I *name* this ship the *Liberty*," "I *call* the meeting *to order*" - said by presiding officer), all other forms of the word are descriptions, not acts; they only state or report the event ("I promised," "he swears," "he names the ship...," "she called the meeting to order," and so on). But this criterion is insufficient, for we find other expressions that do not include an explicit performative verb and yet still belong to the category of the performative because they too accomplish an action and lie outside the reach of the truth/falsity criterion. The imperative, for example, "Go away!", may be seen as an ellipsis of the performative "I *order* you to leave." Or the sign "Beware of the dog" can be translated by the performative "I warn you that this dog bites." Thus we have to distinguish between explicit and implicit performatives. But as soon as we acknowledge the existence of implicit performatives, it is difficult to find any sentence that would not fall into this category. For even constative utterances might imply the ellipsis of "I note," "I affirm," "I declare" : these expressions too, in the last analysis, do no more than carry out linguistic *acts* which are neither true nor false but which on the other hand may be successful or unsuccessful, felicitous or infelicitous.[156]

This means that constative utterances can also perform actions. Every constative utterance can imply a simple "I state," "I affirm," etc. and thus can become performative. Like performatives, constative utterances are also actions of stating, affirming, etc. With the notion of implicit performatives the original distinction is not just loosened, things are much more serious. Now, constative utterances become just a particular type of performatives.

Let us analyze the following statement: "Language is essentially performative." This statement can easily lead us into aporia. It is clear that this statement emphasizes the active function of language, namely - performative function of language. However, the only way to claim that language is active, that it functions performatively is through the constative utterance "Language is essentially performative." Jonathan Culler states:

> The propositions that perform the illocutionary act of stating necessarily claim to do nothing but merely display things as they are; yet if you want to show the contrary—that claims to represent things as they are in fact impose their categories on the world— you have no way to do this except through claims about what is or is not the case. So when Nietzsche claims that truth is but a moving army of metaphors and metonymies whose metaphoricity has been forgotten, he can only do this in statements that seem to claim to be true. More generally, the claim that declarations are acts of language that suppose and impose the categories rather than refer to what exists independently of language cannot avoid recourse to a language of declaration. "The deconstruction," writes de Man, "states the fallacy of reference in a necessarily referential mode". The argument that the language of philosophical constatation is in fact performative takes the form of constative statements.[157]

Are we closer to the truth of *Infinitive* and *Marbot*? If the role of performatives is so important, can we say that this power of language is shown in *Infinitive* and *Marbot*? To be more precise, can we say that the truth which is at work in these two works is the truth of language? Or, that these two works of art enable us to undergo an experience with language? *No thing is where the word is lacking and the word alone has the capability of giving being to things.* Can we say that *the word can be where the thing is lacking because it has the power to give being to things*? Is this the "message" of *Infinitive* and *Marbot*? Maybe we can read these works as the testimonies to the power of language that creates Andrew Marbot, Stewart Greenchurch and *The Axiological Infinitive* out of nothing?

We already know that Hildesheimer's work is not just a successful parody of the classical historical biography. This work is much more complicated because it draws our attention to the "impenetrable strangeness" of every historical subject. *Marbot: A Biography* shows us that narrativization plays a crucial role in every attempt to give sense to past events: the sense of every event is constructed tropologically. The construction of sense is one of the main themes of *Infinitive* and it is clearly visible in pseudo-Salinger's story "Bringing No Presents, Just Pasts." However, this pseudo-Salinger' story is just the first step - *Infinitive* as a whole offers much more than a simple explanation of this process. For example, in the case of this work, a story about a theoretical position comes-to-pass in the shape of this theoretical position. Dejan Ilić's reading of this story about a certain theory becomes a reading of that theory; *Infinitive*, for him, is not a literary, but a theoretical work. In the hands of Dejan Ilić, a narrative about a certain theory becomes that theory itself. This is the best illustration of the performative aspect of *Infinitive.* Maybe we can say that in the works of Sreten Ugričić and Wolfgang Hildesheimer language is understood as the power or as the activity capable of bringing things into being. Valéry's words from his "Preface" to Gustave Cohen's *Essai d'explication du "Cimetière marin"* can be really instructive in this case: "If I am questioned, if anyone wonders.... what I 'wanted to say' in a certain poem, I reply that I did not want to say but wanted to make, and that it was the intention of making which wanted what I said."[158]

However, at this moment, we need to be extremely careful and to note that Heidegger's notion of naming is much more complex than Austin's understanding of performative. First, the power of language is not at man's (or the poet's) disposal. As I already stated, Heidegger claims that language is not a tool used by a man; man is the one used by language. According to Heidegger, *man is a man only insofar as he is devoted to the call of language; insofar he is used for language, to speak it.* ("But man is capable of speaking only insofar as he, belonging to Saying, listens to Saying, so that in resaying it he may be able to say a word.")[159] Heidegger states that the essence of language lies in the Saying (*Sage*). He says that Saying means to show or to let appear, but this appearance will be at the same time unconcealing and concealing. If we explain Heidegger's naming by a rash reference to Austin's performative this will be an obvious simplification. The importance and meaning of naming are not that simple. What is called into being in naming does not become present in the sense of the things that are present-at-hand. This is why Heidegger's naming is not identical with Austin's performative. Something shows itself in an appearing which is at the same time withdrawing and concealing. For example, in the case of *Infinitive*, Stewart Greenchurch and *The Axiological Infinitive* appear, but never as present-at-hand (or even as ready-at hand) objects. *The Axiological Infinitive* and its author become present as an appearance which simultaneously unconceals and conceals. Their presence is given as the infinite withdrawal.[160]

We have to come back to "Where the word breaks off no thing may be" and try another explanation. In "The Nature of Language" we can find another perspective on this problem. If the word *is* then it must be some sort of a thing simply because a thing is. In Heidegger's words: "If the word is to endow the thing with being, it too must be before any thing is - thus it must inescapably be itself a thing."[161] Are we faced with a paradox? Does this mean that one thing (word) gives being to another thing? We have to bear in mind that, according to Heidegger, something *is* only where the appropriate word exists for the being. The appropriate word names thing as a being. Does this mean that the role of poetry (and poetic word) is to grasp it and to express it by making it beautiful?

This is not the case and everything is much more complicated. The word is no-thing and *is* is not a thing. We can never find *is* as a thing connected to a thing. However, a similarity exists between *is* and the word. Heidegger states that we can never say that the word *is*, but only that *it gives*. Gives what? The word gives Being. Heidegger also claims:

> We are familiar with the expression "there is, there are" on many usages, such as "There are strawberries on the sunny slope", *il y a, es gibt*, there are strawberries; we can find them as something that is there on the slope. In our present reflection, the expression is used differently. We do not mean "There is the word" - we mean "by virtue of the gift of the word there is, the word gives..." The whole spook about the "giveness" of things, which many people justly fear, is blown away. But what is memorable remains, indeed it only now comes to radiant light. This simple, ungraspable situation which we call up with the phrase "it, the word gives," reveals itself as what is properly worth of thought, but for whose definition standards are still lacking in every way.[162]

Heidegger's reading of Georg Trakl's poem "Winter Evening"[163] can help us to understand this giving. This poem is perfectly understandable and there are no unfamiliar or unclear words. The topic of the poem is a winter evening or, to put it a little bit differently, the poem describes a winter evening. But this poem is not a simple description:

> The poem's title is "A Winter Evening." We expect from it the description of a winter evening as it actually is. But the poem does not picture a winter evening occurring somewhere, sometimes. It neither merely describes a winter evening that is already there, nor does it attempt to produce the semblance, leave the impression, of a winter evening's presence where there is no such winter evening. Naturally not, it will be replied. Everyone knows that a poem is an invention. It is imaginative even where it seems to be descriptive.... The poem, as composed, images what is thus fashioned for our own act of imaging. In the poem's speaking the poetic imagination gives itself utterance.[164]

The poem and its winter evening, however, are not the expressions of the writer's imagination. The poem names the snow that strikes the window, it names the vesper bell and the winter evening time in general. But, we must remember that Heidegger claims that the nature of language is not exhausted in signification. This brings us back to Heidegger's understanding of naming and he explains:

> What is this naming? Does it merely deck out the imaginable familiar objects and events - snow, bell, window, falling, ringing - with words of a language? No. This naming does not hand out titles, it does not apply terms, but it calls into the word. The naming calls. Calling brings closer what it calls. However this bringing closer does not fetch what is called only in order to set it down in closest proximity to what is present, to find a place for it there. The call does indeed call. Thus it brings the presence of what was previously uncalled into a nearness. But the call, in calling it here, has already called out to what it calls.

> Where to? Into the distance in which what is called remains, still absent... The calling calls into itself and therefore always here and there - here into presence, there into absence.[165]

The things that are called are present in the call. What is the call?[166] The explanation of the call will again show us why naming is not identical with the performative. In order to explain what the call is, we need to go back to *Being and Time* once more (especially to section 56). Heidegger describes conscience as the kind of calling and the call is understood as a kind of discourse. But what is called in a call is not formulated in words. Dasein is calling and Dasein is also called in this calling. It is Dasein that is called about and Dasein is called to its own and unique existence. Dasein that calls is in *Angst* and the call is uncanny. The call of Dasein is an appeal to Dasein to be authentic. But, what is spoken in this discourse that is described as calling? Strictly speaking nothing is described in the call of conscience, because the call is not an utterance. The call does not give information and "'nothing' is called to the self which is summoned, but the self is summoned to itself, to its ownmost potentiality of being."[167]

Things in the poem, things that are called are not present in the same way as, for example, present-at-hand things. The poem brings things into presence, but that presence is always turned toward something that is infinitely absent. The poem calls things, but they are not called among the things present. In our case, *The Axiological Infinitive* is not present in the same way as, for example, the table and the chairs in my kitchen or the computer on my desk. What we have here is "presence sheltered in absence." Heidegger writes: "The place of arrival which is also called in the calling is a presence sheltered in absence. The naming call bids things to come into such an arrival."[168] The call of *Infinitive* brings forth Stewart Greenchurch's *Axiological Infinitive* in the same way and this work is present as absent.

Can we say that the truth of *Infinitive* lies in this presence as absence, in this unconcealing as concealing? We can, because *Infinitive* is not a work that blindly celebrates the power of words - it is a work that provides an experience with language. This experience happens in *Infinitive* when we glimpse at the abyss behind the supposed fullness. I will try to explain how the abyss shows itself in *Infinitive*.

In order to show this abyss behind the supposed fulness, I will use two texts of Maurice Blanchot: "Literature and the Right to Death" and "The Language of Fiction". The relationship between Maurice Blanchot and Martin Heidegger is very complex and multi-layered, but my perspective on it will be mainly influenced by Levinas's text "The Poet's Vision". We already know that Heidegger claims that the unconcealment happens on the background of concealment and that in the poem we do not have a simple presence, but *a presence sheltered in absence*. A certain change of emphasis happens in the work of Maurice Blanchot; he follows Heidegger, but he will emphasize things in a different way. This change of emphasis will lead to an important difference between Blanchot and Heidegger.

In his text about *The Space of Literature*, Emmanuel Levinas mentions this important difference between Blanchot and Heidegger that is based on the aforementioned change of emphasis: "Already in Heidegger, art, beyond all aesthetic meaning, made 'the truth of being' shine forth, but it shared that ability with other forms of existence. Blanchot sees art's vocation as exclusive. But above all, writing does not lead to the truth of being. One might say that it leads to the errancy of being - to being as a place of going astray, to the uninhabitable. Thus one would be equally justified in saying that literature does not lead there, since it is impossible to reach a destination. The errancy of being - more external than truth. In Heidegger, an alternance of nothingness and being also occurs in the truth of being; but Blanchot, contrary to Heidegger, does not call it truth, but non-truth. He insists on this veil of the "no", this inessential character of the ultimate essence of the work.... In Blanchot, *the work uncovers, in an uncovering that is not truth*, a darkness."[169]

Blanchot agrees with Heidegger that literature is bound to language. The literary work of art is a work of language. In "Literature and the Right to Death", he connects the power of naming with Hegelian negativity. Again, this enables him to form an agreement with Heidegger - no thing can be where its name is missing.[170] However, for Blanchot, the basis for this presence sheltered in absence are annihilation and death. Also, the presence sheltered in absence can be noticed not only in poetry, but also in the language of everyday:

> The word gives me the being, but it gives it to me deprived of being. The word is the absence of that being, its nothingness, what is left of it when it has lost being - the very fact that it does not exist. Considered in this light, speaking is a curious right. In a text dating from before *The Phenomenology*, Hegel, here the friend and kindred spirit of Hölderlin, writes: "Adam's first act, which made him the master of the animals, was to give them names, that is, he annihilated them in their existence (as existing creatures)." Hegel means that from that moment on, the cat ceased to be a uniquely real and became an idea as well. The meaning of speech, then, requires that before

any word is spoken, there must be a sort of immense hecatomb, a preliminary flood plunging all of creation into a total sea. God had created living things, but man had to annihilate them. Not until then did they take on meaning for him, and he in turn created them out of the death into which they disappeared; only instead of beings (*êtres*) and, as we say, existants (*existants*), there remained only being (*l'être*), and man was condemned not to be able to approach anything or experience anything except through the meaning he had to create.[171]

In order to create meaning, the language of everyday annihilates the existence of the very being it designates. However, according to Blanchot, it still refers to it through the being's disappearance. Precisely this absence becomes the essence of being. So far, Blanchot follows Heidegger.

Blanchot argues that the situation is a little bit different in the language of literature. The already mentioned difference in emphasis between him and Heidegger becomes visible on this background. Blanchot claims that literary language is actually governed by an important contradiction. The language of literature is not interested in the presence sheltered in absence, but in this absence itself. This is how Blanchot describes this interest:

> In speech what dies is what gives life to speech; speech is the life of that death, it is "the life that endures death and maintains itself in it." What wonderful power. But something was there and is no longer there. Something has disappeared. How can I recover it, how can I turn around and look at what exists *before*, if all my power consists of making it into what exists *after*? The language of literature is a search for this moment which precedes literature. Literature usually calls it existence; it wants the cat as it exists, the pebble *taking the side of things*, not

man but the pebble, and in this pebble what man rejects by saying it, what is the foundation of speech and what speech excludes in speaking, the, Lazarus in the tomb and not Lazarus brought back into the daylight, the one who already smells bad, who is Evil, Lazarus lost and not Lazarus saved and brought back to life.[172]

Blanchot makes an important transition in this passage. He first stays within the boundaries of Mallarméan poetics. He first speaks about the materiality of words and how words in literature become like things. However, at the very ending of this passage, he makes an important move and this move will become crucial in his interpretation of the myth of Orpheus. Literature turns its attention not to things, but toward absence itself. Orpheus desires to see the invisible Eurydice in the same way as literature desires Lazarus who is in the tomb and not Lazarus brought back into the daylight.

The similar problem is presented in Blanchot's essay "The Language of Fiction."[173] This essay will enable us to illuminate further the change of emphasis that happens in the work of Blanchot and to connect it with the problems of *Infinitive* and *Marbot*. Again, we can notice that in "The Language of Fiction" Blanchot is influenced by Heidegger's depiction of presence that is sheltered in absence. He states that the words in the literary work do not play the same role as words in everyday language. His example is the simple sentence that can be the part of our everyday existence, but at the same time we can find it in Kafka's *The Castle*: "The head clerk called." In both cases, the words are exactly the same and we pass over them quickly. However, one important difference arises. For example, as an ordinary clerk I very well know who is the head clerk and all other things that relate me to him; this knowledge of mine is in a certain way limitless because the context is boundless. In the other case, as the reader of Kafka's novel, I am in a completely opposite position - I am infinitely ignorant about the world that is evoked in a book and my ignorance is also an important part of the nature of the evoked world. This ignorance, this destitution, and non-knowledge is always implied by fiction. According to Timothy Clark, this ignorance has two important consequences: our senses of the words in the literary work suffer from a certain lack; and, simultaneously, they have the power to originate what they seem to simply represent.[174]

Let us now presume that *Infinitive* is a real monograph about the equally real philosopher and his most important work. If this is the case then *The Axiological Infinitive* will have the power to influence our perception of *Infinitive*, it will be our point of reference. Something in the real world will have the function of guarantee - it will be able to tell us how successful *Infinitive* is. The simple comparison will give us the answer whether or not Stewart Greenchurch's work is represented faithfully. In order to decide if Ugričić's work is successful and true we will first have to read the work of Stewart Greenchurch and then make a decision. This is how truth as correspondence functions. But, as we know, we cannot turn to *The Axiological Infinitive* because this work is unconcealed (and in a strange way present) only on the pages of *Infinitive*. The author of *Infinitive* is in the same position as the readers of his book - they both share the same ignorance about *The Axiological Infinitive*.

After this initial distinction between the language of everyday and the language of fiction, we should examine one important similarity. This similarity, this feature that everyday language shares with the language of fiction is negativity. This negativity is already mentioned in "Literature and the Right to Death." In the language of fiction, the negativity is just more visible than in the language of everyday. Our everyday language does not give us the fullness of things, but is cut off from them. Things are negated because we are in a language of signs. The basis of the language of signs is replacement: things are replaced with signs. This is why Blanchot claims that our everyday words need to be as close as possible to nothing: "Invisible, not letting anything be seen, always beyond themselves, always on this side of things, a pure awareness crosses them, so discreetly that it itself can sometimes be lacking. Everything then is nullity. And yet, understanding does not stop occurring; it even seems that it attains its point of perfection. What could be richer than this extreme destitution?"[175]

We should not forget the sentence that we already mentioned: "The head clerk called." The words are the same in the language of everyday and in the language of fiction (it is the same sentence), but the attitude of recipient/reader is different. This attitude can divulge the important difference: in the language of fiction we do not depart from a reality that surrounds us (from our everyday context), but from a reality that is evoked in the book. The words in the work of art suffer from a primordial lack and we cannot understand them with the help of a simple connection with concrete references. This is also Heidegger's point in the analysis of "A Winter Evening": the poem does not describe a winter evening that occurs in some place and in some time. Sreten Ugričić's work does not describe a book that precedes *Infinitive*. The head clerk is named and he comes into existence in the pages of *The Castle* and he continues to exist only as a verbal entity, not as a real person. Blanchot summarizes these similarities and differences between the language of everyday and the language of fiction in the following passage:

> The sentence in the story and the sentence in daily life both have the role of a paradox. To speak without words, to make oneself understood without saying anything, to reduce the heaviness of things to the agility of signs, the materiality of signs to the movement of their signification - it is this ideal of a pure communication that is at the heart of universal talk, of this way of speaking that is so prodigious, in which, while people speak without knowing what they say and understand what they do not listen to, words in their anonymous usage are no more than ghosts, absences of words, and by that itself, in the midst of the most deafening noise, empower a silence that is probably the only one in which man can rest, as long as he lives. The language of real existence wants to unite these two opposing characteristics: for as long as it is given us, a real thing among things, which we arrange like an experience and which we do not need to make ours in order to use, it is also an act tending to go into thin air before it is accomplished, supported only by the emptiness of a possible intention, as near as one can imagine to non-existence. A sign of the superabundance of beings, to be itself as a trace and sediment of the world, of society, and of culture, it is pure only if it is nothing. On the other hand, the sentence in the story puts us in contact with the unreality that is the essence of fiction and, as such, it aspires to become more real, to be made up of a language that is physically and formally valid, not to become the *sign* of beings and objects already absent (since imagined), but rather to *present* them to us, to make us feel them and live them through the consistency of words, the luminous opacity of things.[176]

If absence is so important then it is wrong to say that literature is about something - literature is that something itself.[177] If we say that *Infinitive* is about something then what is that "something"? Obviously *The Axiological Infinitive*. But, that "something" is essentially nothing - a non-existent book. This non-existent book is produced on the pages of *Infinitive* and this book is evoked as a work that is infinitely absent. Does *Infinitive* embody Flaubert's ideal? Is *Infinitive* "a book about nothing, a book dependent on nothing external, which is held only by the strength of its style, just as the earth suspended in the void depends on nothing external for its support? Is this a work with no subject or the book in which the subject is invisible or infinitely absent?"[178] *Infinitive* can produce an uncanny feeling because in this work a certain "object" is called into presence (*The Axiological Infinitive*), but only in order to be returned to its original absence. The essential word of *Infinitive* is *The Axiological Infinitive*, but this essential word is nothing else than the appearance of something that has always and already disappeared.

Blanchot's essay "Encountering the Imaginary"[179] can help us to shed more light on *Infinitive*. *Infinitive* is a tale of one event and on its surface it looks like a simple narrative - it is a narration about the encounter with Stewart Greenchurch's *The Axiological Infinitive*. But, this encounter is in fact an extraordinary event that eludes the forms of everyday time and also the world of ordinary truth. In his essay, Blanchot quotes Plato from *Gorgias*: "'Listen to a beautiful tale. Now you will think it is fable, but I believe it is a tale. I will tell you what I am going to tell you as a true thing.'"[180] *Infinitive* begins and ends in the completely opposite way because the narrator tells us: "It is possible to read this monograph as a novel" and "It is possible (least wrong) to read this monograph as a novel..."The criterion of common truth clearly states that "novel" is not truth, but the product of imagination and therefore - a beautiful lie.

Because of that, maybe the beginning and ending of *Infinitive* are closer to the old Epimenides paradox?[181]

This self-referentiality of *Infinitive* points to the fact that this tale is not a narration of the event, but the event itself. However, this event is peculiar: at the same time *The Axiological Infinitive* precedes *Infinitive*, but also Greenchurch's book is brought into presence only when we finish the last page of *Infinitive*. Blanchot writes:

> Narrative is the movement towards a point, a point - one that is not only unknown, ignored, and foreign, but such that it seems, even before and outside of this movement, to have no kind of reality; yet one that is so imperious that it is from that point alone that the narrative draws its attraction, in such a way that it cannot even "begin" before having reached it; but it is only the narrative and the unforeseeable movement of the narrative that provide the space where the point becomes real, powerful and alluring.[182]

Infinitive is reflexive and self-referential, but not only that. In the basis of *Infinitive* lies the relation with *The Axiological Infinitive*, and *The Axiological Infinitive* is nothing in itself - infinite absence. This means that *Infinitive* is not (and it can never be) a simple repetition of *The Axiological Infinitive*. *Infinitive* and *The Axiological Infinitive* are not one, although they depend on each other. Without *The Axiological Infinitive* there can be no *Infinitive*, but also without *Infinitive* Greenchurch's work cannot come into existence. Timothy Clark gives expression to this paradox in the following way:

> Topologically, the movement between this *récit* and its event is that of a spiral whose spiraling inwards is ceaseless, asymptotic... The movement of relation 'includes the point or level where the reality which the

récit describes, can ceaselessly merge with its reality as *récit*. To ceaselessly merge is a process inherently unfinished in which the *récit* and its event never fully merge.[183]

However, there is one place where the works of Blanchot and Ugričić merge - the myth of Orpheus. In the tale about Orpheus and Eurydice we can notice the similarities between the works of Maurice Blanchot and Sreten Ugričić.[184] Eurydice is not present, but she means everything to Orpheus. She is, above all other things – beautiful. He descends into Hades for her and goes to the other side of the night, into the other night. There she is, alone and without him, although she cannot be without him. Once found by Orpheus, Eurydice again stays behind: the infinitive which always escapes its definition. Life in her presence is uncertain, she is so impermanent, but she has the greatest importance for Orpheus. Of course, he cannot resist, he must turn his gaze back and look at her. But, at that very moment, Eurydice disappears and Orpheus comes back to history: infinitive cannot be defined because it defines everything else.

Eurydice is the extremity that art is capable of reaching and Orpheus wants to bring this extremity into the daylight, he wants to define her and to make her real. Orpheus can do almost everything, he just cannot look into the face of Eurydice - because, at that moment, her importance turns into nothingness, into unimportance. But, not to turn back, not to look at her would be an even bigger mistake: Orpheus desires to see that invisible Eurydice; he wants to have the completeness of her death living in her. This is what Orpheus searches in the Underworld, what drives him forward: he wants to see what the night hides - the other night and the concealment which becomes visible.

Orpheus is forced to turn back because he never stopped looking at Eurydice. Only in his song, he saw her invisible and touched her untouched. His destiny is to sing about Eurydice, but he is Orpheus only in the song that helps him to form a relationship with his beloved: he can be himself only in the presence of her eternal absence. Only the song gives him the power over Eurydice, the song in which she is already lost and Orpheus himself infinitely dead.[185]

In his text "'Affirmation Without Precedent': Maurice Blanchot and the Criticism Today",[186] Leslie Hill explains the dual logic of this story. On the one hand, this is a story that celebrates the power of art. This power is indirect, and the art can save from death because it is able to transfigure the object of mourning. This object is substituted by an image that has the essential features of the absent object. On the other hand, Orpheus does not descend into the Underworld in order to produce the work of art. His aim is to bring Eurydice back - he wants Eurydice herself. To be more precise, he wants something that cannot be brought into daylight. He produces the work, but the work is not enough. Like the song of Orpheus, *Infinitive* "relies for its existence on something it cannot therefore embody. The work resists elucidation. It alludes to a secret which cannot be divulged by the work, but which nevertheless lies within the work at an intangible distance from the work, as a kind of secret without secret, simultaneously veiled and yet unveiled, and in itself irreducible to any disclosure or disclosing of truth, visible or invisible."[187]

In one of his previous works Sreten Ugričić asks: "How is it possible that the disappearance of some beings only affirms their true presence?"[188]

The answer is given in *The Axiological Infinitive*.

CHAPTER THREE:
THE IMAGINARY AND ITS VICISSITUDES

We will only ask: just as the statue glorifies the marble, and insofar as all art means to draw into the light of day the elemental deep which the world, in order to affirm itself, negates and resists, doesn't the language of the poem, of literature, compare to ordinary language as the image compares to the thing? One likes to think that poetry is a language which, more than others, favors images. This is probably an allusion to a much more essential transformation - the poem is not a poem because it contains a certain number of figures, metaphors, comparisons; on the contrary, the poem's particular character is that nothing in it functions as an image. So we must express what we are seeking differently: in literature, doesn't language itself become altogether image? We do not mean a language containing images or one that casts reality in figures, but one which is its own image, an image of language (and not a figurative language), or yet again, an imaginary language, one which no one speaks; a language, that is, which issues from its own absence, the way the image emerges upon the absence of the thing; a language addressing itself to the shadow of events as well, not to their reality, and this because of the fact that the words which express them are, not signs, but images, images of words, and words where things turn into images.

Maurice Blanchot, *The Space of Literature*

The impossibility of beginning

The central point of the work is the work as origin, the point which cannot be reached, yet the only one which is worth reaching.

Maurice Blanchot, *The Space of Literature*

In previous chapters, it seemed possible to begin with a story. However, in the case of this chapter, the only possible beginning is from the impossibility of beginning. Therefore, the fundamental *Stimmung* of this chapter is completely different. This *Stimmung* (and also a dilemma) is best described by the words of the old Egyptian scribe who is called Khakheperresnb: "Would I had phrases that are not known, utterances that are strange, in new language that has not been used, free from repetition, not an utterance that has grown stale, which men of old have spoken?"[189] The answer to this dilemma is a straightforward "never" and therefore, in my answer, I would like to follow Blanchot and to add: "A story? No. No stories ever again."[190] However, this is not the end and the situation is even more difficult. In short, this chapter stems from the Beckettian feeling of exhaustion, from the feeling "that there is nothing to express, nothing with which to express, nothing from which to express, no power to express, no desire to express, together with the obligation to express."[191] In this situation, the only solution that seems viable is copying and imitation. Therefore, I have decided to follow the advice that was formulated by the (imaginary) friend of Miguel de Cervantes Saavedra: "All that has to be done is to make the best use of imitation in what one writes; and the more perfect the imitation the better the writing."[192] In short, the advice is this: the better you copy, the better will be your writing.[193]

My decision is to start by copying myself and I will again restate the basic problem of this work. This study revolves around *Infinitive* which can be described as a monograph; namely, a book about another book. However, the problem lies in the fact that this other book and its author, Stewart W. Greenchurch, do not exist – or, to be more precise, they exist only on the pages of Sreten Ugričić's *Infinitive*. What we have here is a certain bending of a text toward itself, but the question is immediately posed: how can we understand this strange self-referencing that is happening in *Infinitive*. In my previous chapter, the notion of *createdness* helped me to explain the already mentioned peculiar characteristic of *Infinitive*. Let me recall that both *Infinitive* and Hildesheimer's *Marbot* make their createdness explicitly visible. They make it visible because *Infinitive* is a monograph, but a monograph on a non-existent book; *Marbot*, on the other hand, is a biography of a non-existent man. Their basis is pure nothingness (a non-existent book and a non-existent man), but *Infinitive* and *Marbot* are something rather than nothing. The fact that they arise from nothingness is something that makes their createdness visible.

Or, to repeat the words of Christopher Fynsk:

> The work somehow brings forth the fact that it is *figure of...* something - the event of truth. But truth is no thing that is, and is nowhere other than in the work; so we might say no more than that it is the figure of... nothing, other than itself. This is to say, if we follow out the logic of this argument, that the work shows figurality itself.[194]

However, this notion of createdness does not offer a final solution to the paradox of *Infinitive* and *Marbot*. Even after this explanation, the paradox is very much alive. It is alive, because the notion of createdness answers only to the one demand of the work while, at the same time, obscures the other. If we follow the interpretation of Blanchot's writings offered by Leslie Hill,[196] we will discern that these two demands are:

1) the demand for the work (createdness)
2) the demand of worklessness

Both of these demands show themselves in the myth of Orpheus. In this story, the gaze of Orpheus is at the same time inevitable and necessary; it is a clear response to the demand of worklessness which claims that the most important thing is not the work, but the nothingness from which the work arises.

Blanchot claims:

> That the work must be the unique clarity of that which grows dim and through which everything is extinguished -- that it can exist only where the ultimate affirmation is verified by the ultimate negation -- this requirement we can still comprehend, despite its going counter to our need for peace, simplicity, and sleep. Indeed, we understand it intimately, as the intimacy of the decision which is ourselves and which gives us being only when, at our risk and peril, we reject -- with fire and iron and with silent refusal -- being's permanence and protection. Yes, we can understand that the work is thus pure beginning, the first and last moment when being presents itself by way of the jeopardized freedom which makes us exclude it imperiously, without, however, again including it in the appearance of beings. But this exigency, which makes the work declare being in the unique moment of rupture -- "those very words: it is, "the point which the work brilliantly illuminates even while receiving its consuming burst of light -- we must also comprehend and feel that this point renders the work impossible, because it never permits arrival at the work. It is a region anterior to the beginning where nothing is made of being, and in which nothing is accomplished. It is the depth of being's inertia [*désoeuvrement*].

> Thus it seems that the point to which the work leads us is not only the one where the work is achieved in the apotheosis of its disappearance -- where it announces the beginning, declaring being in the freedom that excludes it -- but also the point to which the work can never lead us, because this point is always already the one starting from which there never is any work.[196]

I turn, then, to the notion of worklessness by exploring the following question: does this bending of a text toward itself somehow testify about the impossibility of beginning and about worklessness? In order to provide an answer to this question, I will return to works cited in my previous chapters, starting with Cervantes's *Don Quixote* and the question of the relationship between the Part II and the Part I of *Don Quixote*. I will seek to connect these works with Blanchot's interpretation of the myth of Orpheus, thereby making visible the problem of the imaginary. First, a certain perspective on the imaginary (inspired by Blanchot's writings) will be presented. I will, then, offer a critique of the imaginary that will be based on the text of Emmanuel Levinas, "The Reality and Its Shadow." The imaginary (the basic feature of art) is problematic, because, according to Levinas, it enables the evasion of responsibility.

As Roberto González Echevarría points out, *Don Quixote* is now widely considered as a single book, but it actually has two parts. The first part was published in 1605, and the second in 1615. Between them lies also Avellaneda's apocryphal sequel to the Part I that was published in 1614. One of the most important characteristics of the Part II (which is written by Cervantes) is that in this book Don Quixote and Sancho Panza are recognized by other characters because they read the Part I of *Don Quixote*. Not just that, Sanson Carasco is this time capable of defeating Don Quixote only because he has read Part I of the novel. Roberto González Echevarría explains that "the world is a stage in Part II with roles and plots sacrificed for the protagonists by other characters. There is no solid ground outside fiction; everything is caught in an infinitely receding sequence of fictions."[197] In a more poetical way, this situation presented in Part II is described by Calderon in his famous drama *Life is a Dream*:

> What is this life? A frenzy an illusion,
> A shadow, a delirium, a fiction.
> The greatest good's but little, and this life
> Is but a dream, and dreams are only dreams.[198]

However, we must not forget that, in the case of *Don Quixote*, what we have is not just a simple recognition between the characters, but, more importantly, the novel capable of critical thinking about itself.

Imitation is the key for the understanding of *Don Quixote*. For example, Alonso Quijano pretends that he is Don Quixote, who in turn imitates Amadis of Gaul. It is clear from the very beginning that Don Quixote tries to imitate the adventures of errant knights that are described in literary works. Therefore, his main goal is to turn life into art and he can be considered as the precursor of Flaubert's Emma Bovary (similar misfortunes will happen to her in Flaubert's masterpiece).[199] In his text "Don Quixote and the Invention of the Novel", Antonio J. Cascardi emphasizes the role of imitation: "Imitation is at once a guiding thread in Don Quixote's mock-heroic project to emulate the virtuous heroes of the books of chivalry, but it was also the literary means by which Cervantes sought to re-cast the language and conventions associated with the pre-novelistic discourses available to him. These two models converge insofar as Don Quixote's imitation of examples proceeds by the imitation of literary text."[200]

The nature of this project that is based on imitation is best described in Foucault's text about *Don Quixote*.[201] Foucault points out that the basis of Don Quixote's imitation is the attempt to prove that what books are telling is true: "Don Quixote reads the world in order to prove his books and the only proofs he gives himself are the glittering reflections of resemblances."[202] However, his story is much more than a simple testament about the discrepancy between fiction and reality. In this book we can see how the resemblances between signs and reality are vanishing into thin air. At the same time, however, this book is not just a catalogue of Don Quixote's defeats. First, as Foucault explains in another book, a certain form of madness which does not offer a way back to truth and reason is presented in Cervantes' work.[203] This madness is so strong that not even death is capable of bringing peace to the errant-knight and his erring becomes infinite:

> The death of Don Quixote takes place in an atmosphere of calm, where links with reason and truth have at last been renewed. The Don's madness has become aware of itself at a stroke, and falls away as stupidity before his very eyes. But the onlookers are unconvinced: 'they were certain that he was in the grip of some new madness.' This indefinitely reversible ambiguity can only be decided by death. Madness dissipated blends seamlessly into the imminence of the end: 'one of the signs that he was really dying was the ease with which he had turned from a madman into a sane man.' But death brings no peace, and madness will triumph again, a truth derisory in its eternity, beyond the end of a life delivered from madness only by its own ending. The senselessness of his life pursues him, and ironically he

is immortalized only by his madness, which becomes his imperishable life in death.[204]

Don Quixote's madness, his adventures and failures are presented in the novel of Miguel de Cervantes, therefore, in writing and within a book. This points to the fact that the real topic of this novel is not an impotence of writing, but its strange power. The writing became so powerful that it was capable of presenting (by its own means) even the possibility of its own failure. This very turning back of a presentation upon itself, under the guise of a failure, will become a new power. Foucault explains it in the following way:

> Yet language has not become entirely impotent. It now possesses new powers, and powers peculiar to it alone. In the second part of the novel, Don Quixote meets characters who have read the first part of his story and recognize him, the real man, as the hero of the book. Cervantes's text turns back upon itself, thrusts itself back into its own density, and becomes the object of its own narrative. The first part of the hero's adventures plays in the second part the role originally assumed by the chivalric romances. Don Quixote must remain faithful to the book that he has now become in reality; he must protect it from errors, from counterfeits, from apocryphal sequels; he must fill in the details that have been left out; he must preserve its truth. But Don Quixote himself has not read this book and does not have to read it, since he is the book in flesh and blood.... Between the first and second parts of the novel, in the narrow gap between those two volumes, and by their power alone, Don Quixote has achieved his reality - a reality he owes to language alone, and which resides entirely inside the words. Don Quixote's truth is not in the relation of the words to the world but in that slender and constant relation woven between themselves by verbal signs. The hollow fiction of epic exploits has

become the representative power of language. Words
have swallowed up their own nature as signs.[205]

Similar traits of *Don Quixote* are also perceived by Borges and on their basis he formulates something that can be called "an ontological argument." He claims that one of the greatest enjoyments of Miguel de Cervantes is the game with shifting mirrors that produces a confusion between two worlds: the world of the reader and the world of the book. For example, one of the books present in Don Quixote's library is Cervantes's *Galatea*. However, this is not the end, and we also have a scene in which one of the characters in the novel (the barber) gives his judgement on Miguel de Cervantes. So, the invention, or even the form of a dream of Cervantes, criticizes its own maker. Also, as I already mentioned in one of my previous chapters, we learn that Cervantes is not the real author of *Don Quixote,* only its stepfather: his novel is a translation of Cide Hamete Benengeli's writings. There are many more ambiguities like this in *Don Quixote* and, as we already know, they culminate in the Part II when the main characters of *Don Quixote* are, at the same time, the readers of Cervantes's novel. What is the main consequence of these ambiguities? Borges gives us the following answer to this question:

> Why does it disturb us that Don Quixote be a reader of the Quixote and Hamlet a spectator of Hamlet? I believe I have found the reason: these inversions suggest that if the characters of a fictional work can be readers or spectators, we, its readers or spectators, can be fictitious. In 1833, Carlyle observed that the history of the universe is an infinite sacred book that all men write and read and try to understand, and in which they are also written.[206]

This game with shifting mirrors can be used for blurring the boundaries between reality and fiction and a lot of interpretations of *Don Quixote* and Borges are written about this line of argumentation. However, this is not the line of argumentation that I would like to pursue and my intention is different. I accept that the above mentioned arguments point toward an ontological problem, but I argue that this problem is actually concerned with the ontology of literature.

According to Paul de Man, in the works of Jorge Luis Borges *infamy* functions as an aesthetic principle and the fiction has infamy at its heart.[207] The examples of infamy (and duplicity) are: imitation, plagiarism, madness, impersonation, etc. Infamy is also connected with the strange and dangerous power that mirrors possess. In "Tlön, Uqbar, Orbis Tertius", Borges mentions the following quotation from the article on Uqbar: "For one of those gnostics, the visible universe was an illusion or (more precisely) a sophism. Mirrors and fatherhood are abominable because they multiply and disseminate that universe."[208] As we already know, the article on Uqbar does not exist, but *one of those gnostics* exists in a strange way. This is another example of the text bending toward itself and Borges quotes the words that he attributed to one of his characters in his previous story "The Masked Dyer, Hakim of Merv": "The world we live in is a mistake, a clumsy parody. Mirrors and fatherhood, because they multiply the parody are abominations."[209] The game with shifting mirrors again happens before our eyes and it leads de Man to the following conclusion:

> Poetic invention begins in duplicity, but it does not stop there. For the writer's particular duplicity (the dyer's image in "Hakim") stems from the fact that he presents the invented form as if it possessed the

attributes of reality, thus allowing it to be mimetically reproduced, in its turn, in another mirror-image that takes the preceding pseudo-reality for its starting-point. He is prompted "by the blasphemous intention of attributing the divine category of being to some mere [entities]". Consequently, the duplication grows into a proliferation of successive mirror-images.... This mirror-like proliferation constitutes, for Borges, an indication of poetic success. The works of literature he most admires contain this element; he is fascinated by such mirror-effects in literature as the Elizabethan play within the play, the character Don Quixote reading *Don Quixote*, Scheherazade beginning one night to retell verbatim the story of *The Thousand and One Nights*. For each mirrored image is stylistically superior to the preceding one, as the dyed cloth is more beautiful than the plain, the distorted translation richer than the original, Menard's Quixote aesthetically more complex than Cervantes's.[210]

This *regressus ad infinitum*, in the same way as the story "Pierre Menard, Author of the *Quixote*", points to the very interesting characteristic of literature, namely to its (im)possibility. In this short story, the (im)possibility shows itself as the paradox of originality. In order to understand this (im)possibility, we need to be attentive to this main paradox of Borges's story. Menard's project was not to compose another *Don Quixote*, but to produce a couple of pages which would be completely identical with the ones of Miguel de Cervantes. Borges's story "Pierre Menard, Author of the *Quixote*" is the original work, but its originality rests upon the unoriginal project of its main character. However, this project is not just "unoriginal" (it will not produce something completely new, but reproduce Cervantes's text *word by word*), but also impossible. In Borges's story, the narrator presents us one part of Pierre Menard's letter: "'My undertaking is not difficult, essentially... I should only have to be immortal to carry it out.'"[211] However, the result of this impossible project will be Menard's *Invisible Work* which is, according to the narrator of "Pierre Menard, Author of the *Quixote*", verbally identical with Cervantes's text, but also infinitely richer. In his influential essay "The Literature of Exhaustion", John Barth addresses this problem of "the unoriginal originality": "But the important thing to observe is that Borges *doesn't* attribute the *Quixote* to himself, much less recompose it like Pierre Menard; instead he writes a remarkable and original work of literature, the implicit theme of which is the difficulty, perhaps the unnecessity, of writing original works of literature. His artistic victory, if you like, is that he confronts an intellectual dead end and employs it against itself to accomplish new human work."[212]

Don Quixote and "Pierre Menard, Author of the *Quixote*" are both referring to some point of beginning outside of themselves and both of these works are trying to attain and to appropriate that *arche* which proves to be, not just unattainable, but impossible. Are we back to the beginning of this text and to the words of Khakheperresnb: "Would I had phrases that are not known, utterances that are strange, in new language that has not been used, free from repetition, not an utterance that has grown stale, which men of old have spoken?"[213] This circle has a paradoxical nature and we have to explore it. After that, with a little help from Ugričić's *Infinitive*, we might come to realize that we never had a circle in front of ourselves, but something completely different - a spiral that goes into infinite depths.

Foucault speaks about the very important narrow gap between Part I and Part II of *Don Quixote* and I am interested in exploring what happens in the gap between *Infinitive* and *The Axiological Infinitive*. Precisely in the gap between

Infinitive and *The Axiological Infinitive* lies the encounter between these two works. This encounter is the necessary pre-condition of *Infinitive*, and *The Axiological Infinitive* is the origin of this work. However, a strange reversal happens before our eyes in the form of a realization that Stewart Greenchurch and his masterpiece exist only on the pages of Sreten Ugričić's *Infinitive*. How is this possible? It is possible because *Infinitive* is not a narration of an event, but an event itself or, to paraphrase the words of Hölderlin, what appears in *Infinitive* is not a change of representation, but the representation itself.[214] The necessary consequence of this appearance is the short circuit in the flow of time. Time ceases to exist and we are faced with the time of time's absence:

> It is the time when nothing begins, when initiative is not possible, when, before the affirmation, there is already a return of the affirmation....The time of time's absence has no present, no presence. This "no present" does not, however, refer back to a past.... The irremediable character of what has no present, of what is not even there as having once been there, says: it never happened, never for a first time, and yet it starts over, again, again, infinitely. It is without end, without beginning. It is without a future. What appears is the being deep within being's absence, which is when there is nothing and which, as soon as there is something, is no longer. For it is as if there were no beings except through the loss of being, when being lacks. The reversal which, in time's absence, points us constantly back to the presence of absence -- but to this presence as absence, to absence as its own affirmation (an affirmation in which nothing is affirmed, in which nothing never ceases to affirm itself with the exhausting insistence of the indefinite)...[215]

The already described proliferation of images (in *Don Quixote* and in the works of Jorge Luis Borges) reflects this time paradox and opens the realm of fascination. As John Blegen points out in his essay on Blanchot: "the fascinated person is not in charge of his attention; his attention is in charge of him."[216] Endless repetition and proliferation of images is in fact the movement toward absence that is the origin of the work. Or, to quote Maurice Blanchot: "The central point of the work is the work as origin; the point which cannot be reached, yet the only one which is worth reaching."[217]

This brings us back to the myth of Orpheus. Why is this story so important for Blanchot? The most important moment in this story is the gaze of Orpheus and this gaze conveys the (non)essence and (non)truth of literature. It also unveils its (im)possibility. This gaze is the response of Orpheus to the second demand, to the demand of worklessness. John Gregg offers a valuable insight:

> Creative activity, therefore, seems to begin at a stage in which artists feel confident in their ability to have control over the raw materials of their craft. This initial confidence tends to waver, however, as they make further advances, and it is eventually replaced by impersonality, passivity, and fascination. In order to write—to have the ultimate Orphic encounter of experiencing the presence of absence—it is necessary to write already as a prelude to this moment, as if writing were the exercise of a power.
>
> This situation plays a major role in determining the importance that the myth has for Blanchot insofar as temporality is concerned. The adverb "déjà" in the statement "pour écrire, il faut déjà écrire" as well as the sequence of events recounted by the myth in which Orpheus first plays his music in order to enter Hades and at some later moment interrupts it when he turns to look at Eurydice is potentially misleading. It is really too simple to say (as we just did) that an initial stage of

confidence is subsequently overwhelmed by fascination and loss of power. These two forms of singing (and writing) are not related to each other in the same way that two events in linear, chronological succession would be, for the writing of passivity and the writing of power are in a relationship of mutual contamination from the start. To say that worklessness follows an earlier exercise of power is only half right. There is no such sens unique in Blanchot's exigency that he describes as "circular," which is to say that it is a reversible situation: passive writing not only "follows" active writing but "precedes" it as well (as if one could assign precise points on a circle that is in perpetual motion). It is more appropriate to think of temporality in the nocturnal world of artistic activity in terms of repetition and synchronicity than in terms of the unicity and chronological sequence of events. If we do so, we realize that Orpheus's decision to look at Eurydice never takes place a first time; it has always already happened.... Blanchot cherishes the myth of Orpheus, "le mythe inépuisable" that he never tires of alluding to, because it tells the story of an event that always already has had to have taken place in order to occur.[218]

This temporal paradox that is described in the myth of Orpheus and its relation to the image (and imaginary) will provide the basis for the next part of this book. In the following part, I will try to explore this relation with the help of Alain-Fournier's great novel *The Lost Estate* (*Le Grand Meaulnes*).[219] However, before I do that, I will have to explain why I chose this work. At the first glance, *The Lost Estate* has no similarities with *Infinitive* and *Marbot*. These two works are about a non-existent book and about a non-existent person, while *The Lost Estate* is based on the event that actually happened to its author. Stewart Greenchurch's *The Axiological Infinitive* and Hildesheimer's Andrew Marbot are an imaginary book and an imaginary person. On the other hand, the central event in *The Lost Estate* is something real, something that actually happened. However, what happens when an event like this becomes a part of some literary work? I will try to show that this event is a peculiar one and I will also try to underline its connections with the myth of Orpheus.

Encountering the imaginary: The case of Alain-Fournier

In an indescribable way our looks tangled together. I seemed to be looking at my own reflexion. Suddenly I was entangled in utmost confusion, not sure which of us was which. We were like halves of one being, joined in some mysterious symbiosis. I fought to retain my identity, but all my efforts failed to keep us apart. I continually found I was not myself, but him. At one moment I actually seemed to be wearing his clothes. I fled from the room in utter confusion: afterwards did not know what had happened, or if anything had.

Anna Kavan, *Ice*

I looked up at that dark window and thought of how it was said that acute insomniacs often experience a kind of queasy blurring of the lines between dreams and wakefulness, their waking lives taking on some of the surprising tedium of a nightmare. Maybe the midnight disease was like that, too. After a while you lost the ability to distinguish between your fictional and actual worlds; you confused yourself with your characters, and the random happenings of your life with the machinations of a plot.

Michael Chambon, *Wonder Boys*

È uno strano dolore.
Piano.
Morire di nostalgia per qualcosa che non vivrai mai.

Alessandro Baricco, *Seta*

What do I want to achieve with this text? Another question that is closely associated with this first one is: what will this text be? I will offer the answer immediately: it will be a piece of literary criticism. Another, more elaborate answer is: it will be a search for the meaning of a certain literary work (Alain-Fournier's *The Lost Estate*). In my text, this meaning will be understood as the origin of a literary work; as a cause of *The Lost Estate*.[220] Therefore, the role of my text will be a mediating one (mediation between the reader and the work) and the explanation that I will offer will follow the laws of causality. Because of all this, it will be best to describe my text as *the extrinsic approach to the study of literature*.[221] I will search for an essential event that will explain *The Lost Estate*; for an event that does not belong to literature because:

> Whoever asserts literature in itself asserts nothing. Whoever looks for it looks for only what is concealed; whoever finds it finds only what is on this side of literature or, what is worse, beyond it. That is why, finally, it is non-literature that each book pursues as the essence of what it loves and wants passionately to discover.[222]

Therefore, let us pretend that this text will revolve around non-literature, about a certain event that makes *The Lost Estate* possible. How are we going to talk about it? Simply, via the self-effacement of criticism. This piece of literary criticism will efface itself in two ways. First, as Blanchot explains in "What is the Purpose of Criticism?", every criticism is characterized by a perpetual movement toward self-effacement.[223] Apparently, the task of criticism is simple and obvious: criticism has to make the work more understandable and to introduce this work back into the world. However, in this process, criticism cannot add anything to the work and, in the end, it is the work that seems to speak for itself.[224] Second, my text will be a narrative about encounter; a narrative that will sometimes use a technique of false attribution (and tweaked quotations) that is also used in *Infinitive*. It will aspire to look like criticism, but it will ultimately efface itself as criticism .

The story that I want to tell is very simple: this is a story of boy meets girl. However, one must be careful: although this is a story of boy meets girl, this is not a love story. Let us presume that this story begins on June 1, 1905, on Ascension Thursday, when Henri-Alban Fournier decided to go to Paris to visit one art exhibition (Fifteenth Salon de la Société Nationale des Beaux-Arts). Maybe we can use Chris Marker's masterpiece as the springboard for our own narrative? In this movie, we hear: "On this particular Thursday, the boy whose story we are telling was bound to remember the warm sun, the stairways going down to the Seine, and a girl's face. Nothing sorts out memories from ordinary moments. Later on they do claim remembrance when they show their scars. That face will become the image that will stay with him for the rest of his life. Had he really seen it? Or had he invented that tender moment to alleviate all the pain that was about to come?"[225]

Young Henri-Alban was instantly enchanted and he discreetly followed the girl until she entered into a big house in the Saint-Germain boulevard. He correctly presumed that this is the place where the girl of his dreams was living and, overwhelmed by the desire to see her again, he started to come in front of this house every day. Finally, after three days, he saw her again and this is how he described this second encounter:

> A second's hesitation - a detour - she disappears behind a group, a bus, some conductors, then suddenly there she is on my pavement, on the pavement where I'm walking, fairly slowly, straight towards her as now she quickens

her step. Three, four people pass by us - and then I'm in the cloud of the lace of her boa, of her boa, of her dress, and I say as she passes, very close, in a voice I can't recapture, so close she hears, so quickly she's gone by, without reflecting, 'You are beautiful'. She's gone past - I think she's at her door, is going in, has disappeared, and without fully knowing what I'm doing, I move across to the left hand pavement where the flower-seller is, where I turn slowly round, where I wait for the window - now I shall know this is the minute... the window doesn't open - and then suddenly there She is, coming out again, *there* in front of me, walking quickly, looking straight in front of her (I say to myself half-aloud: My destiny, my whole destiny, my whole destiny - you exaggerate when you speak aloud to yourself) goes into the bus office - where is she going? This Sunday morning filled with the cries of flower-sellers, of sunshine, light colored costumes coming from Mass, light colored costumes going to Mass, light colored costumes going to lunch somewhere. Is she going to lunch somewhere? I wait back on my pavement because on her account I'm afraid of the window.

The tram car. She gets on. Me too. Going up the three steps, our glances meet, her eyes turn away, stare elsewhere, slightly amused but very dignified terribly dignified. Now I'm on the platform. I don't think of anything in particular. I'd like to catch sight of her skirt. When is she going to get off? I think I glimpse her hand. Can't think of anything any more - long, long - where will she get off? - question...

Now she gets off - so gently, and the brown train of her dress is in front of my eyes, the whole long brown train - I've got to be very careful not to step on it. Ten steps along the pavement and I'm up with her by her right side and not too moved at first, without knowing what I'm doing, without knowing, I say to her: 'Say you forgive me for saying you were beautiful - for having followed you for so long.‘

Oh! With such finality! In a little voice so firm and disdainful, which leaves me shattered and crestfallen, classes her as one of those lovely young ladies who can go out walking by themselves, and puts me in my place in the gutter, shattered and crestfallen.

She goes on her way... crosses the square.[226]

But Henri-Alban did not give up easily. He followed her into the church of Saint-Germain-des-Prés. At one point he lost her in the crowd, but he managed to find her again in The Church of the Sacred Heart. Again he tried to speak to her, again she moved away from him; again he followed her. At the tram station, she finally spoke and the description of this conversation can be found in Henri-Alban's letters, but this is also the most important scene in *The Lost Estate*. Henri-Alban talked to her and, at first, he simply repeated his words: "You are beautiful." They talked and he found out that her name is Yvonne. He replied: "The name I had given you was prettier." "What's the use? What's the use?", she replied softly whenever he suggested anything. Their essentially one-sided conversation ended when she declared pensively: "We're two children. We've been foolish... Farewell, don't follow me."[227] These words marked the end of their talk. She left him and after three years Henri-Alban remembers her departure:

I leaned against the pilaster of the bridge and watched her depart. For the first time since I'd known her, she turned around and looked back at me. I took a few steps forward to the next pilaster, dying to rejoin her. Then, when she was much further away, she turned right round a second time, stood perfectly still, and looked back at me, before she disappeared forever. Was this because, silently, from the distance, she wanted to reinforce her order that I shouldn't follow her? Or was it to let me see her face to face for one more time? I've never discovered the answer.[228]

The similarities between the events from Alain-Fournier's life and the events described in the novel are obvious. The description of Yvonne in *The Lost Estate* is exactly the same as her portrait in Alain-Fournier's notes and letters of 1905. Their dialogue is also identical. As Martin Turnell correctly noticed, the meeting with Yvonne is both the central event in the novel and in Alain-Fournier's life.[229] This offers an interesting possibility for the interpretation of *The Lost Estate* - we can try to read it as an autobiographical novel. The most important characters in the novel can be identified as the real persons from Alain-Fournier's life. However, Robert Gibson goes even further and claims that three main characters (Augustin Meaulnes, François Seurel, Frantz de Galais) are just reflections of different aspects of Alain-Fournier's personality.[230] Does this means that Fournier managed to construct a world whose residents are just the images of himself? Is this the case even with the female characters in the novel? The model for Valentine was Alain-Fournier's perception of his lover Jeanne and therefore Valentine can be perceived as the projection of Jeanne, but what about Yvonne? Is Yvonne real or just a reflection of, and occasion for, movements within him? In *Repetition*, Kierkegaard formulates this possibility: "The girl has, again, no actuality, but is simply a reflection of, and occasion for, movements within him. The girl has enormous significance for him. He will never be able to forget her. But that through which she has significance is not herself, but her relation to him."[231] Alain-Fournier and Kierkegaard are interested in different things, but this possibility that *the girl is simply an echo of something that precedes her* links them together. In Kierkegaard's work, we also have an interesting game with shifting mirrors. Kierkegaard's pseudonym in this book is Constantin Constantius (a person interested in the philosophical problem of repetition). However, he becomes a confidant of a young man who was, like Kierkegaard, engaged to a young girl and then he changed his mind. This means that a young man is another reflection of Kierkegaard's personality because his situation mirrors the one from Kierkegaard's life: his broken engagement with Regine Olsen. This possibility that the girl "is simply a reflection of, and occasion for, movements within him" is important for me because it opens the possibility that the other can appear from the inside not just from the outside. I will leave this question open for now and first focus on the male characters in the novel.

The main character in the novel, Augustin Meaulnes, can be perceived as the embodiment of all Alain-Fournier's ideals. Augustin Meaulnes is the person who Alain-Fournier wanted to be. François Seurel, narrator of the events described in *The Lost Estate,* is, according to some interpretations, another double of Alain-Fournier. While Meaulnes was his ideal, Alain-Fournier lived most of his childhood as Seurel (or he believed that this was the case). In his book, Martin Turnell claims that both Seurel and Meaulnes are indeed Fournier's doubles. Alain-Fournier's father was the teacher at Epineuille-Fleuriel and Meaulnes was the name of the neighbouring village.[232] Frantz de Galais is the inverted image of Meaulnes, but also the embodiment of certain aspects of Alain-Fournier's personality that he did not like in himself. These characteristics are selfishness and a melodramatic way of looking at life. This is why Robert Champigny claims that Frantz is the false Meaulnes. He also states that in his love experiences Alain-Fournier behaved more like Frantz and less like Meaulnes. Alain-Fournier's childhood memories and his way of behaviour are ascribed to Seurel, but, in the description of his sister, some important details also belong to Frantz.[234]

These examples suggest that Alain-Fournier really tried to write something that can be called an autobiographical novel. Another question is: did he manage to achieve this? Did he manage to achieve immortality by leaving several imprints of himself in *The Lost Estate*? In order to answer this question, let us turn to an example from Maurice Blanchot's *The Book to Come*. In "The Secret of the Golem", Blanchot examines Adolf Bioy Casares's science fiction novel *Morel's Invention* and writes:

> In Bioy Casares's narrative, *Morel's Invention* - which Borges has assigned a place among the great successes - we are told the story of a man who, fleeing political persecution, finds refuge on an island where he is safe because a kind of plague has left it deserted. A few years before, a rich man with some friends, had built a hotel there, a chapel and a "Museum", but the epidemic seems to have chased them away. Thus the exiled man lives there for some time in the anguish of extreme solitude. One day he sees a young woman, and then some other people, who reoccupy the hotel and lead, in this wilderness, leading an incomprehensible life of amusement. So he must again flee, he must hide himself, but the attraction of this young woman whom he hears called Faustine, the enchanted indifference she shows him, this world of celebration and happiness seize him. He approaches her, he speaks to her, he touches her, he appeals to her - all in vain. He must come to a decision: he does not exist for her, he is as if dead in her eyes, and might not he be dead, in fact? Let us advance to the climax: the organizer of this little company is the scholar who has succeeded in winning from persons and things an absolute image, one that strikes all the senses as an identical and incorruptible double of reality. The scholar, without their knowing it, has "filmed" his friends, in each instant of their lives, for a week that will be eternal and that begins again each time the tides set in motion the mechanism that runs

the projectors. Until now, the narrative is only ingenious. But a second denouement is reserved for us, in which the ingenuity becomes moving. The fugitive lives, then, close to the images, he lives close to the fascinating young woman to whom little by little he feels attached, but not attached enough; he would like to enter into the circle of her indifference, enter into her past, modify the past in accord with his desire. A plan comes to him: to adapt his gestures and words to the gestures and words of Faustine, so that they can respond to each other like an allusion to what a spectator would think was their happy intimacy. Thus he lives for an entire week during which putting an image-taking machinery into movement, he causes himself to be reproduced, becoming in his turn an image and living wonderfully in this imaginary intimacy. Naturally, he hastens to destroy the version of the week in which he does not exist. From now on he is happy, in a sort of heaven - happiness and eternity for which he must pay (for this is the price) with his death, for the beams are mortal.

Happiness, unhappiness of the image. In this situation, might the writer not be tempted to recognize, rigorously described, many of his dreams, his illusions, and his torments, up to the naïve, insinuating thought that, if he dies of them, he will pass on a little of his life into the figures eternally animated by his death?[235]

Blanchot's analysis puts us on the right track and we need to examine the characters in Alain-Fournier's novel a little bit closer. The most important characters in the novel (Augustin Meaulnes, François Seurel, Frantz de Galais) become permanently changed by something. From a certain moment they can never be what they were and, in the cases of Meaulnes and Seurel, they can never be who they truly are. This displacement is presented in its most simplest form in the case of Frantz de Galais. At the beginning he is presented as a rich and spoiled kid, but after his love failure he becomes a vagrant.[236]

However, the cases of Meaulnes and Seurel are much more complicated. The most obvious assumption is that Meaulnes is changed by his experience in *le pays sans nom*. But, how can we describe that experience? It is a dreamlike experience and Meaulnes is aware of that.[237] He recognizes this dreamlike quality, but he still (and always in vain) *tries to depart for the land that he belongs to; tries to leave for the land that does not exist*. The entrance into *le domaine mystérieux* is like the entrance into a dreamworld and it corresponds to our entrance into a world of fiction. However, as Martin Turnell points out, Meaulnes's entrance into a dream is prepared by another dream.[238] He suddenly remembered that dream during the first night away from Sainthe-Agathe, in the abandoned cattle shed or sheepfold. It was cold and he had lost his blanket on the road:

> So he tried to think of other things. Chilled to the bone as he was, he remembered a dream, or rather a vision that he had as a small child - something he had never mentioned to anyone. One morning, instead of waking up in his room where his trousers and his coats where hanging, he found himself in a long green room with tapestries like forest greenery. The light flowing into this place was so sweet that you felt you could taste it. Beside the nearest window, a girl was sewing, with her back turned to him, as though waiting for him to wake up. He had not had the strength to slip out of bed and walk through this enchanted mansion. He had gone back to sleep. But the next time, he swore that he would get up - tomorrow morning, perhaps![239]

The real-life experience of Alain-Fournier (meeting with Yvonne) resembles Meaulnes's experience at the lost estate. However, this is the experience that Meaulnes recounts to Seurel and, after that, Seurel (narrator of the novel) presents it to us. It is an experience and not a dream, but this experience possesses the power that makes it similar to dreams.

Why did Meaulnes tell about his dream experience in *le pays sans nom* to Seurel? In order to share an intimate moment with his friend? Not likely. It looked more like Meaulnes's attempt to establish himself as the character in this fantastic story. Meaulnes is clearly confused by his dreamlike experience and his retelling is basically an attempt of appropriation. He is a stranger, the uninvited guest at the strange fête in *le pays sans nom* - he has a constant feeling of not belonging. He does not belong because he was not himself there, he only resembled, not even himself, but a strange Someone in his place. Non-identical with himself, he was like a character in the book. For Meaulnes, *le domaine mystérieux* is the place of pure similitude. We can use Blanchot's explanation and claim that "he feels like a stranger because he is not truly there to grasp his dreamlike experience. He is a stranger because the I of the dreamer does not have the meaning of the real I. One could even say that there is no one in the dream and therefore, in some sense no one to dream it; whence the suspicion that when we are dreaming, it is just as easily someone else who is dreaming and who dreams us, someone who in turn, in dreaming us, is being dreamed by someone else, a premonition of the dream without dreamer, which would be the dream of the night itself."[240] Meaulnes's insecurity about his experience is the reason for sharing it with Seurel. Thus the game of shifting mirrors becomes visible and it tells us something about dreaming and writing. In his text

Dreaming, Writing, Blanchot provides a useful explanation of what is happening here:

> The one who dreams turns away from the one who sleeps; the dreamer is not the sleeper: sometimes dreaming that he is not dreaming and therefore that he is not sleeping; at other times dreaming that he is dreaming and thus, through this flight into a more inner dream, persuading himself that the first dream is not a dream, or else knowing that he is dreaming and then awakening into a very similar dream that is nothing other than an endless flight outside the dream, a flight that is an eternal fall in a similar dream (and so it is through other twists and turns). This perversion (whose disturbing consequences for the state of wakefulness Roger Caillois has described in a precious book) seems to me tied to a question that surfaces naively, perfidiously in each of our nights: In the dream, who is dreaming? Who is the "I" of the dream? Who is the person to whom one attributes this "I" of the dream admitting that there is one? Between the one who sleeps and the one who is the subject of the dream's plot, there is a fissure, the hint of an interval and a difference structure; of course it is not truly another, another person, but what is it? And if, upon awakening, we hastily and greedily take possession of the night's adventures, as if they belonged to us, is it not with certain feeling of usurpation (of gratitude as well)? Do we not preserve the memory of an irreducible distance, a distance of the peculiar sort, the distance between me and myself, but also the distance between each of the characters and the identities - even certain - that we lend them, a distance without distance, illuminating and fascinating, which is like the proximity of the remote or contact with the faraway? An intrigue and a questioning that refer us to an experience of the writer when, in a narrative, poetic, or dramatic work, he writes "I" not knowing who says it or what relation he maintains with himself.

> In this sense, the dream is perhaps close to literature, at least to its enigmas, its glamour, and its illusions.[241]

In *The Lost Estate,* it is evident that after his visit to *le pays sans nom* Meaulnes is not who he was.[242] He is aware that something important happened to him, something that turned him into a different person. However, was he ever who he really is? Maybe this fissure, this feeling of alienation is not provoked just by the already mentioned dreamlike experience; maybe this feeling was always already present? In order to answer this question, we will need to examine the relationship between Meaulnes and Seurel and to come back to the meeting with Yvonne.

At the very beginning of the novel Seurel describes the intrusion of Meaulnes into his world:

> But someone came and swept me away from all these tranquil, childish joys - someone who snuffed out the candle that had cast its light on my mother's gentle face as she prepared our evening meal; someone who turned off the light around which we gathered as a happy family on those evenings, after my father had closed the wooden shutters across the French windows.[243]

However, it is important not to take Seurel's representation of Meaulnes for granted: Seurel is a perfect example of an unreliable narrator. The word that is constantly repeated in *The Lost Estate* is "the adventure." Seurel's aim is to tell us "the adventure story" and the role of its hero is reserved for Augustin Meaulnes. Like Alonso Quijano, François Seurel found a consolation in books, but he did not decide to become a hero from the novel, he did not decide to become Don Quixote. He decided to create a hero out of Meaulnes. This is the place where the problems arise. In short, Meaulnes cannot be what Seurel wants him to be and Seurel's wishes are the source of constant displacement and estrangement for both of them.

Meaulnes wants to follow Seurel's wishes and this desire alienates him from himself - he becomes like a character in a book, a stranger to himself. In turn, this estrangement effects even Seurel. He idealizes Meaulnes and he finds Yvonne for him. He organizes their meeting, but he is really in love with Yvonne, not Meaulnes. Therefore, he is the one who was supposed to marry her, not Meaulnes. However, all this is impossible for Seurel because he is not the hero of his story - he is just the narrator. But, Meaulnes is also not a hero. This is not a love story and this is not an adventure story. Nevertheless, even at the very end when Meaulnes finally comes back home to his daughter, Seurel cannot stop his romanticizing and this impulse produces another displacement for him:

> I had stepped back a bit to see them better. Filled with wonder, and a sense of slight disappointment, even so, I realized that the girl had at last found the companion for whom she had unconsciously been waiting. I felt that The Great Meaulnes had come back to deprive me of the only joy that had left me. And already I imagined him, one evening, wrapping his daughter in a cloak and setting off with her for some new adventure.[244]

These various displacements that are presented in the novel are interesting because they bring us closer to the one important problem. If it is true that Seurel, Meaulnes and Frantz are images of Alain-Fournier's personality, how is this effect of estrangement in them and between them possible? Maybe it is true that Alain-Fournier has no other personality other than the one that can be seen in *The Lost Estate*. Maybe it is true that this work is a fateful reflection of his personality.

However, in the words of Blanchot this truth will sound like this: "'I no longer have any personality other than the one which suits this work.' But what suits the work is perhaps that 'I' have no personality. Clemens Brentano, in his novel *Godwi*, speaks eloquently of 'the nullification of oneself' which is effected in the work. And perhaps it is a question of a still more radical change which does not consist in a new disposition of the soul and mind, which is not limited to removing me from myself, 'nullifying' me, and which is not linked to the particular content of a given book either, but rather to the fundamental demand of the work."[245]

What we also need to notice is that there is an infinite distance between Seurel and Meaulnes, infinite distance that cannot be bridged by any means. As I already mentioned, although he loves Yvonne, Seurel cannot marry her because he is the narrator and not the hero of the novel.[246] This distance and difference between Meaulnes and Seurel also offers a possibility for answering the question as to why Meaulnes is unable to recognize Frantz when he comes to his school. Meaulnes simply cannot recognize his (inverted?) reflection in the mirror.

According to the usual understanding, the image is something that comes after the object. Something was present and then it was caught as an image. In our case, different aspects of Alain-Fournier's personality are represented as the main characters in *The Lost Estate*. However, it is also the case that, when something becomes an image, this something automatically becomes ungraspable, unreal and impossible. It seems that *The Lost Estate* offers an intimate comment on Alain-Fournier's personality, but the images of Seurel, Meaulnes and Frantz at the same time open a realm where all possibility of intimacy is practically destroyed. As in the image, something seems to be present on the pages of this novel, an encounter of some sorts, but at the same time nothing seems to be really present. Where is it? It is not here, but also it is not somewhere else. Maybe nowhere? However, if it is nowhere then it means that nowhere is here.[247] In short, what we have is the constant play of displacement and estrangement and this will lead us to the reexamination of the fateful meeting with Yvonne.

What did the aftermath of this meeting look like? Exactly one year after Alain-Fournier first saw Yvonne he went to the place of their meeting. After that, he wrote to his sister:

> Last Thursday, on Ascension Day, I went to the Société Nationale des Beaux Arts. I was as beautiful as an angel in my dark suit, with my long hair and my black hat. But, I didn't really expect anything, anything at all, and the result was that nothing happened, that nothing could have happened.[248]

To his best friend (and his sister's future husband), Jacques Rivière he said:

> She didn't come.
>
> For a long time I'd told myself simply this: one Thursday, on Ascension Day, we lived that beautiful episode which I've described to you. we have no acceptable way of re-establishing contact, and all that we had in common between us, as the saying goes, is that we knew the day and the time and the place of our extraordinary adventure. So I kept telling myself: she *might* come.
>
> But for a long time now, I've known that she *couldn't* possibly come, and now, more than at any other time, I know how right I was.

> In any case, even if she had come, she would not have been the same.
>
> And if she ever does come, she will not be the same...[249]

These two passages tell us something crucial: like Eurydice, Yvonne was always already lost. She was never really present and her importance for Alain-Fournier lies in her fleeting presence that is actually absence. She was never a real being, but always already the image of herself. The hopelessness of Alain-Fournier and the hopelessness of Meaulnes were not provoked by the actual events - this loss and this absence were there from the very beginning. It is easy to find the real Yvonne and *le pays sans nom,* but both Alain-Fournier and Meaulnes are unable to find the objects of their desire. Seurel and Jasmin Delouche will need to do that for Meaulnes. Is it because Meaulnes never really wanted to find *le pays sans nom*? Both Meaulnes and Alain-Fournier are aware that the objects of their desires are unreal and impossible. Their shared experience (the meeting with Yvonnne) is perceived as a dream also because of the artificiality of these experiences. Meaulnes's experience happens within Frantz's wedding party and the whole atmosphere of this event is invented and directed by Frantz. Maybe this allows us to say that the Meaulnes's meeting with Yvonne happens in a dream that was dreamt by Frantz? Yvonne, whom both Alain-Fournier and Meaulnes met, is not a real being, but a model that already existed in dreams. Their love toward her is remembrance, but remembrance of something that never happened. Meaulnes will never really love Yvonne and he will never really be her husband. Therefore, *The Lost Estate* cannot be perceived as a compensation for the loss that Alain-Fournier suffered in the real life. In this case, real life and literature are inextricably connected and the novel is not a simple repetition of something that happened in reality.

From the very beginning Yvonne is an echo, an echo of something that precedes her. What precedes Yvonne? Nothing else but her double, the image of Yvonne. As David Arkell describes, Henri-Alban met Yvonne 1 in October 1903, during the train journeys between Bourg-la-Reine and Paris. She was accompanied by her friend and Henri-Alban followed them. David Arkell describes Alain-Fournier's adroitness: "As they approached the Panthéon, which is situated on the island of its own, he doubled back round the other side and, just as they were noting his, advanced toward them head-on. Emerging thus from behind the monument almost magically, he swept off his hat and greeted them as old friends. The pick-up was impeccable."[250] Their relationship lasted for eighteen months and after that it ran out of steam. Robert Gibson correctly notices the reason for the end of the affair: "Whatever her physical or intellectual or emotional qualities, Yvonne 1 possessed one attribute which prevented Fournier for loving her on his own highly imaginative terms: she was readily accessible."[251]

However, it is not only the case that Yvonne 2 is the echo of Yvonne 1, but Meaulnes is also an echo of Seurel and Alain-Fournier is an echo of Henri-Alban. Henri-Alban needed the meeting with Yvonne in order to become Alain-Fournier. Robert Champigny notices that Alain-Fournier's desire for repetition lies at the basis of *The Lost Estate*. But, as I already said, this novel is not a simple example of the author's desire for return. The situation is a little bit more complicated by mediation: Alain-Fournier remembers what happened to Henri-Alban and Seurel presents Meaulnes's adventure to us. Meaulnes and Alain-Fournier do not search for Yvonne, but themselves outside themselves. They want to meet themselves before they became who they are, they want to meet the ones who met Yvonne. They want to erase the lack that constituted them. The best proof is offered by Alain-Fournier himself: "Dans cette journée que je me suis donnée pour errer au travers de moi-même à la recherche de ce désir, j'ai eu comme jamais je ne l'avais eue, la sensation violente et par instants presque hallucinatoire qu'en effet je voyageais au travers de moi-même."[252] Although Yvonne is created by their dreams, they cannot control the effects of their creation and this creation changes them and makes them perpetually absent from themselves. This fateful meeting with Yvonne is the limit that they cannot cross; both the impossibility and the possibility; in short, it is a meeting with literature.

How is this possible? The origin of *The Lost Estate* is the event that happened in the real world. However, literature is the very thing that enabled this event to take place. Robert Champigny writes: "The soul which Fournier lends to Yvonne is a prefabricated house which was magically assembled when the girl appeared."[253] Until the end of his life, Yvonne remained the unattainable image for Alain-Fournier, he did not try to meet her again. Instead she became his inspiration and an ever-present obsession. David Arkell tells us what influenced Alain-Fournier: "Early reading of Fromentin's 'Dominique' may have had something to do with it. In that novel the hero meets the love of his life while still a schoolboy. She marries another but he is content to yearn. They both yearn for the rest of their lives. It is one of the many forerunners of 'Brief Encounter'. Also involved was Maeterlinck's 'Pelléas et Mélisande', and inevitably Debussy's music, which in those days had swept most young men in Paris off their feet. His first words to her ('Vous êtes belle') come from Act 1, Scene 1 - as does the line 'Je ne suis pas d'ici', which Fournier was later to use more than once about himself. Yvonne's 'Nous sommes deux enfants' is adapted from an idea in Act III. The incident in which her dress gets caught and torn is to be found Act IV, Scene 3 ('Ma robe s'est accrochée aux clous de la porte. Voyez, elle est déchirée.') To cap it all, he later told his sister that he'd hoped that Yvonne, when asked her name would answer 'Mélisande.'[254] This is the very reason why neither Alain-Fournier nor Meaulnes never really tried to find Yvonne - both of them recognized the aesthetic nature of their love. In short, both of them were in love with the image of Yvonne. This is why the only thing left for Meaulnes is to leave Yvonne to die because he does not want her in flesh and blood but he wants her as an image. Like Orpheus, in Blanchot's interpretation of the myth, Alain-Fournier does not want Yvonne "in her daytime truth and her everyday appeal, but wants her in her distance. He is not interested in the intimacy of a familiar life, but in the foreignness that excludes all intimacy, and wants, not to make her live, but to have living in her the plenitude of her death."[255]

This encounter with the imaginary is important because it shatters the linear conception of time. This is not a simple case of intertextuality, but a situation where literature in a strange way precedes itself. This is what enables Michel Guiomar to claim that:

> Alain-Fournier's inspiration as a novelist did not come from the woman he called Yvonne de Galais. On the contrary, it was a novel, still deeply hidden and still unknown to him but planned in advance in every detail which provoked the Encounter in the Cours-la-Reine, ensuring that the first exchange of glances would be already pre-determined by profound tendencies within Alain-Fournier himself.[256]

If we follow Blanchot's remarks from his essay "Encountering the Imaginary" we can say that *The Lost Estate* is the narrative of one extraordinary event, the narrative of an Encounter. This Encounter really happened, Henri-Alban lived it through and he needed to become Alain-Fournier (who in turn needed to become both François Seurel and Augustin Meaulnes) in order to tell us about it. However, this narrative is a movement toward Yvonne, toward a point that can never be attained, but this point is, at the same time, something that makes this very narrative possible. "All the ambiguity stems from the ambiguity of time, which enters into play here, and which allows us to say and feel that the fascinating image of the experience is, at a certain moment present, while this presence does not belong to any present, and even destroys the present into which it seems to introduce itself. It is true, Henri-Alban actually walked the streets of Paris and, one day, on a certain date, he encountered Yvonne. He can thus say: now, this is happening now. But what has happened now? The presence of a person in its infinite distance. And what has he touched in the present? Not the event of the encounter become present, but the opening of this infinite movement that is the encounter itself, an encounter that is always apart from the place and the moment in which it is spoken, for it is this very apartness, this imaginary distance, in which absence is realized and only at the end of which the event begins to take place, a point where the real truth of the encounter occurs, from which, in any case, the language that utters it wants to take birth. Always still to come, always already past, always present in a beginning so abrupt that it cuts off your breath, and still unfurling as the return and the eternal new beginning."[257]

In Blanchot's interpretation of the myth, Orpheus's fate was to sing a song about Eurydice, a song in which she is already lost and Orpheus himself infinitely dead. It seemed so appropriate for Alain-Fournier to disappear like Augustin Meaulnes, the hero of his story. What happened that day (September 22, 1914) in the Forest of Saint Rémy? We can only guess. Maybe a scene like the one described in *The Writing of the Disaster*: Lieutenant Fournier enters the forest and while his company is slowly moving he looks through the branches and "looks up towards the ordinary sky, with clouds, grey light—pallid daylight without depth. What happens then: the sky, the same sky, suddenly open, absolutely black and absolutely empty, revealing (as though the pane had broken) such an absence that all has since always and forever been lost therein—so lost that therein is affirmed the vertiginous knowledge that nothing is what there is, and first of all nothing beyond."[258] He hears the gunfire and the bullets start to fly. A sudden pain in his chest brings him to the ground and he is unable to move. While he is slowly fading away he thinks: "When the end draws near, there no longer remain any remembered images; only words remain. It is not strange that time will confuse the words that once represented me with those that were symbols of the fate of them who accompanied me for so many years. I have been Alain-Fournier; shortly, I shall be No One, like Seurel, like Meaulnes; shortly, I shall be all men; I shall be dead."[259]

Levinas on literature: "Reality and Its Shadow"

Art is the pre-eminent exhibition [ostension] in which the said is reduced to a pure theme, to absolute exposition, even to shamelessness capable of holding all looks for which it is exclusively destined. The said is reduced to the Beautiful, which supports Western ontology.

Emmanuel Levinas, *Otherwise than Being or Beyond Essence*

In the first chapter, I tried to show that it is misguided to think that language is just a simple tool for communication and that the author's intention can function as a stable guarantor for the meaning of some text. In the second chapter, I wrote about the relationship between literature and (non) truth and I emphasized the role of absence in literature. In my third chapter, I offered an illustration of Blanchot's thesis that in literature language becomes its own image. If we assume that what I wrote so far is at least plausible, will it be possible to pose the question about the relationship between art and ethics? Is this a valid question or a superfluous one (maybe art is something that is beyond ethics)?

Emmanuel Levinas claims that this is an important question and his essay "Reality and Its Shadow" offers a direct answer to it.[260] However, before I proceed to the analysis of this essay, it must be noticed that Levinas's views on artwork are complex and problematic. He does not offer a coherent and unambiguous aesthetic theory, but the already mentioned relationship between ethics and aesthetics is something that interests him very much. One thing is clear, he shows hostility toward art in "Reality and Its Shadow" and his view on the imaginary is a negative one. Robert Eaglestone claims that Levinas's antipathy toward art is based on two reasons:

First, Levinas wishes to reject ontological claims for art as something which can give us knowledge of the absolute (for example, Hegel's claim that 'art has vocation of revealing the truth') or which claim for art a transcendent role beyond ethics and truth (Nietzsche's claims for art, for example). Perhaps more significantly, he also rejects Heideggerian claims for art which argue that art as poetry is 'founding' or an 'origin'... Levinas assigns art a secondary status, at the same level as straightforward materiality.

Second, Levinas's work is troubled by the problem of representation. In Levinas's work, up to and including *Totality and Infinity*, ethics stem from the face-to-face relationship, guaranteed by the assumption of presence. To suggest that presence is only re-presented in material forms, to confuse the issue of presence with the issue of how presence is represented, is to challenge the actual face-to-face relationship with the other, one of Levinas's most central ideas. It is because of this that Levinas is suspicious of the idea of representation, in art or otherwise, and either ignores representation or attempts to circumvent it...

Levinas in his early work insists that all art is mimetic.... Readers of Auerbach's *Mimesis* will realize that, combined with Levinas's two suspicions or problems, this means that art comes under a double exclusion. First, ontologically, an art work has for Levinas, only an illusory being. Second, as representation or mimesis, the artwork is excluded because of Levinas's distrust of the act of representation itself.[261]

Therefore, following Eaglestone, I will undertake the reading of Levinas in two steps. I will first present Levinas's views on art from the already mentioned essay "Reality and Its Shadow", and, at the beginning of my next and final chapter, I will try to put these views into a broader context of Levinas's philosophy.

Levinas begins "Reality and Its Shadow" by seemingly accepting something that he calls the usual understanding of art. This usual (and general) understanding gives art a privileged position in our lives. According to it, art is an expression and this expression is based on cognition. Immediately after these claims are pronounced, "Reality and Its Shadow" takes one unusual turn: "An artist - even a painter, even a musician - tells. He tells of the ineffable."[262] Why is this an unusual turn? It is strange because, according to Levinas, this general understanding of art is can also be found in the work of Martin Heidegger. It is not a reference to "The Origin of the Work of Art" because this essay was published in 1950, and "Reality and Its Shadow" in 1948. However, there is a curious parallelism between Levinas's statement and Heidegger's famous claim about van Gogh's painting:

> The equipmental being of equipment was discovered. But how? Not through the description and explanation of a pair of shoes actually present. Not through a report on the process of shoemaking. And not through the observation of the actual use of shoes as it occurs here and there. Rather, the equipmental being of equipment was only discovered by bringing ourselves before the van Gogh painting. It is this that spoke.[263]

So, at the very beginning it seems that Heidegger and Levinas agree about the work of art. Art is more real than reality because it can tell us the truth about reality - it possesses the power of unveiling; it is capable of unveiling the essence of beings. However, immediately after the ending of the first paragraph, this apparent agreement between Levinas and Heidegger begins to be questioned. If it is really the case that art has the power of unveiling, how can we explain the existence of criticism? Criticism accepts the already mentioned general and common understanding of art, but its very existence poses some important questions. According to Levinas, the reason why criticism exists is because the public is not satisfied with the simple aesthetic enjoyment; the public wants to speak and the critic is "defined as the one that still has something to say when everything has been said, that can say about the work something else than that work."[264]

This is an important moment because it marks the exact place where Levinas moves away from Heidegger. He claims that art is *neither language nor knowledge* and goes on a quest to rehabilitate criticism; to prove that criticism does not lead a parasitic existence. According to Levinas, the very existence of criticism testifies that something is wrong with art:

> If art originally were neither language nor knowledge, if it were therefore situated outside of 'being in the world' which is coextensive with truth, criticism would be rehabilitated. It would represent the intervention of the understanding necessary for integrating the inhumanity and inversion of art into human life and into the mind.[265]

This passage clearly shows that Levinas does not accept Heidegger's understanding of art. Robert Eaglestone (and also Seán Hand[266]) claim that "Reality and Its Shadow" is a text with clear overtones from Plato; namely, a text where Levinas criticizes Heidegger with the help from Plato. This is true, but there is also another dimension of this essay. The reference to Plato offers a rather simplified view on Levinas's position in this important text. To demonstrate this, I will go back to Plato's dialogue *Ion*.[267] The return to *Ion* will first disclose a line of argumentation similar to the one in "Reality and Its Shadow", but it will also show one important difference between Levinas and Plato.

In *Ion*, the victim of Socrates's cross-examination is a rhapsode and, at the very beginning, Socrates wants to know something about the nature of his art. However, before we continue, we need to have one important thing in mind: the rhapsode and the poet are not the same. The rhapsode is a performer of epic poetry, but also the interpreter of poetry.

The problems arise very soon, namely when Socrates asks: "Does Ion's techne apply to all poets?" Ion's answer is: "No, it only applies to Homer, because he is the greatest of all poets." However, in order to claim that Homer is the greatest poet, Ion's knowledge needs to possess some comparative basis. In the course of the dialogue, it will become evident that Ion does not know anything about other poets. When this fact comes to the surface it will enable Socrates to claim that Ion does not have any knowledge because he does not possess *techne;* the possession of *techne* would enable him to be knowledgeable about all poets and their works. Moreover, since Ion does not have any *techne*, he does not know what he is talking about when he talks about charioteering in Homer. Only a charioteer can judge Homer's remarks on charioteering and not Ion. Why is this remark important? It is important because it will allow Socrates to claim that Ion's power is not based on knowledge, but on inspiration. Therefore, this dialogue is a veiled attack on poetry itself, because it also implies that poetry is never based on knowledge.

So far, so good, because this is exactly the same line of argumentation that can also be found in "Reality and Its Shadow." However, the fact that Ion is not a poet complicates things. Ion is not only a performer of poetry, but at the same time its interpreter. To put it more precisely, he is *the interpreter of the interpreter*. The poet is inspired by the Muse and the rhapsode is inspired by the work of a poet. This is why Ion is *the interpreter of the interpreter* or, a critic. Levinas claims that literary criticism is important because it challenges *artistic idolatry* and because it is capable of functioning as a bridge between art and the intelligible world. However, according to Plato, both poetry and criticism are not *techne*, but something irrational. It is true, Levinas does not agree with Heidegger and he criticizes his understanding of art, but his point of reference is not only Plato. In order to illuminate Levinas's position better I will proceed with the analysis of "Reality and Its Shadow."

Levinas claims that art is essentially disengaged: "a work would not belong to art if it did not have this formal structure of completion, if at least in this way it were not disengaged."[268] The work of art is self-sufficient and complete in itself and it is disengaged from the world. What is the meaning of this disengagement?, asks Levinas. Because it is complete in itself, art refuses any kind of dialogue, and also it is not the place where *aletheia* happens. At the very end of the section titled "Art and Criticism", Levinas says:

> Art does not know a particular type of reality; it contrasts with knowledge. It is the very event of obscuring, a descent of the night, an invasion of shadow. To put it in theological terms, which will enable us to delimit however roughly our ideas by comparison with contemporary notions: art does not belong to the order of revelation. Nor does it belong to that of creation, which moves in just the opposite direction.[269]

This is an important moment in the text because it helps us to perceive that we can read "Reality and Its Shadow" with the help of Blanchot's works. A brief return to the second chapter will enable us to understand why is this the case.

Heidegger, as we have seen, connects art and *aletheia,* but he also says that in the work of art unconcealment happens simultaneously with concealment. The strife between concealment and unconcealment is opened up by the work of art, and the truth establishes itself as the strife between these two sides by which the "open center" is won. The truth is described as unconcealment which is, at the same time, concealment. Otto Pöggeler provides a useful explanation:

> Art shows how a being which presences in unconcealment maintains "the opposition of presence"; to the extent that it is unconcealed, it is also concealed. In the unconcealment the concealment holds sway not only as the non-essence, the self refusal of truth, but also as the counter-essence of the disguise in which one being disguises the other and beings generally disguise Being. Amidst the familiar and common, art wrenches open the space for the uncanny and thus lets every clearing and revealing shatter on the concealment. Truth as it occurs at times as art is unconcealment. Nothing belongs to it as that which holds sway, as concealment and "veil", as the heart and the mystery of unconcealment.[270]

Blanchot will take this interplay between concealment and unconcealment from Heidegger, but he will accentuate it differently. In "The Language of Fiction", the most important thing will become the very obscurity itself (together with non-knowledge) that art brings with itself. In this text the art will be described as the very event of obscurity. The sentence in fiction will enable us to experience this obscurity or "the luminous opacity of things."[271] This will be precisely Levinas's point in "Reality and Its Shadow." Levinas claims that the image is connected with the non-truth of being. This non-truth of being is not a strange residue of being, but, as Heidegger already explained, something that happens simultaneously with disclosing - an interplay of concealment and unconcealment. Levinas writes:

> A being is that which is, that which reveals itself in its truth, and, at the same time, it resembles itself, is its own image. The original gives itself as though it were at a distance from itself, as though it were withdrawing itself, as though something in a being delayed behind being... The whole of reality bears on its face its own allegory, outside of its revelation and, its truth. In utilizing images art not only reflects, but brings about this allegory. In art, allegory is introduced into the world, as truth is accomplished in cognition . These are two contemporary possibilities of being... The discussion over the primacy of art or of nature - does art imitate nature or does natural beauty imitate art? - fails to recognize the simultaneity of truth and image. The notion of shadow thus enables us to situate the economy of resemblance within the general economy of being. Resemblance is not a participation of a being in an idea (the old argument of the third man shows the futility of that); it is the very structure of the sensible as such. The sensible is being insofar as it resembles 'itself, insofar as, outside of its triumphal work of being, it casts a shadow, emits that obscure and elusive essence, that phantom essence which cannot be identified with the essence revealed in truth. There is not first an image - a neutralized vision of the object - which then differs from a sign or symbol because of its resemblance with the original; the neutralization of position in an image is precisely this resemblance.[272]

In order to explain what Levinas means by all this, we first need to focus on the section "The Imaginary, the Sensible, the Musical" where Blanchot's writing can provide a useful explanation. In this section of "Reality and Its Shadow", Levinas claims that the basic procedure of art "consists in substituting for the object its image."[273] It is important to note that in art the object is substituted by its image, not by its concept. The image neutralizes our relationship with the real object and this substitution is also the birthplace of aesthetic disengagement and disinterestedness. According to Levinas, the best description of this artistic disinterestedness is blindness to concepts.

Images possess a strange power - they are able to fascinate us, to enchant us. Levinas also says that, since it marks a hold over us, the image is essentially musical. According to Levinas, "images impose themselves on us without our assuming them"[274] and he uses the notion of rhythm to describe this passivity that is visible in poetry and music. He claims that "rhythm represents a unique situation where we cannot speak of consent, assumption, initiative or freedom, because the subject is caught up and carried away by it." This means that Levinas understands rhythm as the transition from oneself to anonymity; in rhythm, the subject loses the connection with itself; it ceases to experience himself as himself. Josh Cohen recognizes the influence of Nietzsche in this reference to the artwork's essential musicality:

> It is hard to avoid hearing the resonance of the early Nietzsche in this description of aesthetic experience, and more particularly of *The Birth of Tragedy*'s thesis of the essential musicality of the artwork. For Nietzsche, music symbolizes a sphere which is earlier than appearance and beyond it. The Dionysian musician is the dissolution of every determinate form, exposing us to the horror of individual existence; himself imageless, he is nothing but original pain and reverberation of the image. Levinas's account of the artwork points up the same reversion to nothingness, the withdrawal of objects from the world which would confer determinate meaning on them, yielding to that imageless music through which a quality

can divest itself of objectivity — and consequently of all subjectivity.... The avowed hostility of 'Reality and Its Shadow' to art is thrown into relief by this Nietzschean reverberation, for, as will be seen, Levinas's ethics is heavily staked in the sober renunciation of ecstatic Dionysiac intoxication.[276]

However, although the echoes of Nietzsche are present in "Reality and Its Shadow", the subject's loss of connection with himself can be illuminated with the help from Blanchot. In "The Essential Solitude", Blanchot claims that to write means to surrender to the fascination of time's absence.[277] He claims that the time's absence is not a negation of time, rather "it is a time when nothing begins, when initiative is not possible... It is a time without negation, without decision, when here is nowhere as well, and each thing withdraws into its image while the 'I' that we are recognizes itself by sinking into the neutrality of a featureless third person."[278] In writing, fascination casts its spell over language and there is a profound link between fascination and the loss of personality. Fascination is essentially linked to the neutral. In writing, the writer loses the power to say "I" and writing breaks the connection between writer's word and himself. Blanchot claims that what speaks in the writer who lost the power to say "I" is" the fact that, in one way or another, he is no longer himself; he isn't anyone any more. The third person substituting for the 'I': such is the solitude that comes to the writer on account of the work... The third person is myself become no one, my interlocutor turned alien; it is my no longer being able, where I am, to address myself and the inability of whoever addresses me to say 'I'; it is his not being himself."[279] An artist is the person who is fascinated by the image and, as happens to Alain-Fournier, he experiences the events in his life in the third person. The events in his life are like images. For the artist, even his own life looks like some adventure from a book - even before he can be called an artist, he is always already in the imaginary where he feels himself as other and where he cannot speak in the first person. Again, we encounter the paradox of Orpheus. In order to become an artist he needs to create images, but he can do that only because he is always already no one and infinitely dead - because he belongs to the realm of imaginary. The destiny of Orpheus was to sing about Eurydice, but he is Orpheus only in the song in which he sings about her.

In the section titled "Image and Resemblance", Levinas will continue to analyze the already mentioned relationship between the object and its image. The imaginary world of art is clearly unreal, but what can we say about its unreality? In order to say something about this unreality of art, Levinas draws a distinction between image and concept. He claims that in the concept the object is grasped and precisely this grasping enables us to maintain a relationship with the real object. On the other hand, the role of image consists in neutralizing this relationship.

His main point is that resemblance is not a mere result of a comparison between the object and its image. Resemblance is the ground on which the image exists. The thing is, simultaneously, what it is and its own image. Or, to put it differently, being is, at the same time, something that is disclosed in truth, but also something that resembles itself - its own image. Levinas uses the following example to explicate his position:

> Being is not - only itself, it escapes itself. Here is a person who is what he is; but he does not make us forget, does not absorb, cover over entirely the objects he holds and the way he holds them, his gestures, limbs, gaze,

thought, skin, which escape from under the identity of his substance, which like a torn sack is unable to contain them. Thus a person bears on his face, alongside of its being with which he coincides, its own caricature, its picturesqueness. The picturesque is always to some extent a caricature. Here is a familiar everyday thing, perfectly adapted to the hand which is accustomed to it, but its qualities, color, form, and position at the same time remain as it were behind its being, like the 'old garments' of a soul which had withdrawn from that thing, like a 'still life.' And yet all this is the person and is the thing. There is then a duality in this person, this thing, a duality in its being. It is what it is and it is a stranger to itself, and there is a relationship between these two moments. We will say the thing is itself and is its image. And that this relationship between the thing and its image is resemblance.[280]

According to Levinas, in the work of art the object is substituted by its image. When we are looking at the image, we are well aware that we are not looking at the object - we are not deceived. We are well aware that the object is absent and that essential absence is constitutive for the work of art. However, the image is not a simple absence - in the image we have presence that is sheltered in absence. In order to clarify all this we need to take another recourse to Blanchot, namely to his essay "The Two Versions of the Imaginary."[281]

Blanchot claims that an essential connection between the image and absence exists. The image needs absence and neutrality and Blanchot claims that the strangeness of the cadaver is also the strangeness of the image. The cadaver is not the living person, it is not the same as the person that once lived, but it is not the other person. Therefore, the corpse is something that is incapable of establishing a convincing presence and it shows us a relation between here and nowhere.

When this relation shows itself, the corpse begins to resemble himself and this resemblance unveils the absolute neutrality of death. Blanchot writes:

> Himself: is this not an ill-chosen expression? Shouldn't we say: the deceased resembles the person he was when he was alive? "Resembles himself" is, however, correct. "Himself" designates the impersonal being, distant and inaccessible, which resemblance, that it might be someone's, draws toward the day. Yes, it is he, the dear living person, but all the same it is more than he. He is more beautiful, more imposing; he is already monumental and so absolutely himself that it is as if he were doubled by himself, joined to his solemn impersonality by resemblance and by the image… Let us look again at this splendid being from which beauty streams: he is, I see this, perfectly like himself: he resembles himself. The cadaver is its own image. It no longer entertains any relation with this world, where it still appears, except that of an image, an obscure possibility, a shadow ever present behind the living form which now, far from separating itself from this form, transforms it entirely into shadow. The corpse is a reflection becoming master of the life it reflects -- absorbing it, identifying substantively with it by moving it from its use value and from its truth value to something incredible -- something neutral which there is no getting used to. And if the cadaver is so similar, it is because it is, at a certain moment, similarity par excellence: altogether similarity, and also nothing more. It is the likeness, like to an absolute degree, overwhelming and marvelous. But what is it like? Nothing.[282]

If we come back to "Reality and Its Shadow", we will see that this is exactly Levinas's position in regard to the image. However, an important question needs to be posed after this: what are the consequences? What happens when the image is not the image of something? In his text on Levinas, Thomas

Carl Wall provides the answer to this question. He also connects "Reality and Its Shadow" with Blanchot's writings and claims that art opens the impersonal and "the imaginary space left empty of all substance and inhabited by no one - the space that being spills out into, beside itself."[283] This is the very space in which the incessant rustling of the *il y a* can be heard.

After this relationship between art and image is described, Levinas starts a new section that is entitled "The Meanwhile." In this section, we find the claim that every artwork is essentially a statue. The already mentioned withdrawal of art from the real world reveals its fundamental plasticity. Every artwork is a statue because it freezes time:

> Within the life, or rather the death, of a statue, an instant endures infinitely: eternally Laocoon will be caught up in the grip of serpents; the Mona Lisa will smile eternally. Eternally, the future announced in the strained muscles of Laocoon will be unable to become present. Eternally, the smile of the Mona Lisa about to broaden will not broaden. An eternally suspended future floats around the congealed position of a statue like a future forever to come. The imminence of the future lasts before an instant stripped of the essential characteristic of the present, its evanescence. It will never have completed its task as a present, as though reality withdrew from its own reality and left it powerless. In this situation the present can assume nothing, can take on nothing, and thus is an impersonal and anonymous instant.[284]

This also means that the artist is incapable of giving a real life to his images. He can only give them a caricature of life. Radical passivity is the ruling principle of art and the stoppage of time is precisely what makes this radical passivity visible. Art revels in a present that is immune to the future. The adequate name for this eternal present is, according to

Levinas, fate. The novel has its own and unique time and this is a time of a nightmare. Levinas writes: "In the instant of a statue, in its eternally suspended future the tragic simultaneity of necessity and liberty can come to pass: the power of freedom congeals into impotence. And here too we should compare art with dreams: the instant of a statue is a nightmare. It is not that an artwork reproduces a time that has stopped: in the general economy of being, art is the falling movement on the hither side of time, into fate."[285] Because it stops the flow of time art is something inhuman.[286] It is disengaged from the world, it is foreign to any kind of initiative and therefore it is fundamentally irresponsible. In the eternal present we can never be free and we cannot assume responsibility. In short, the time of the artwork is not our time and the artwork lies outside of time. This will lead Levinas to claim that: "There is something wicked and egoist and cowardly in artistic enjoyment . There are times when one can be ashamed of it, as of feasting during a plague."[287]

In the last section of the essay ("For Philosophical Criticism") the solution to this problem of irresponsibility is given. Criticism shows itself as something extremely important because it is capable of bringing the artwork back to the world. Criticism becomes the practice capable of saving the art from itself. Levinas insists that even "the most lucid writer finds himself in the world bewitched by its images. He speaks in enigmas, by allusions, by suggestion, in equivocations, as though he moved in a world of shadows, as though he lacked the force to arouse realities, as though he could not go to them without wavering, as though, bloodless and awkward, he always committed himself further than he had decided to do, as though he spills half the water he is bringing us. The most forewarned, the most lucid writer none the less plays the fool.

The interpretation of criticism speaks in full self-possession, frankly, through concepts, which are like the muscles of the mind."[288]

However, there is a huge problem with this emphasis on the role of criticism because one thing is taken for granted; this thing is the differentiation between art and criticism. Maurice Blanchot writes about this distinction in "What is the Purpose of Criticism?" At the very beginning, it appears that he agrees with Levinas that the role of criticism is a moderating one. Its role is to connect art and real world. However, if this is the case, then criticism lacks any substance of its own; it derives its substance entirely from art. Blanchot writes:

> When Heidegger comments on Hölderlin's poems, he says (I paraphrase): Whatever commentary might be, it will always, in regard to the poem, remain superfluous, and the last, most difficult step of interpretation is the one that leads it to become transparent before the pure affirmation of the poem. Heidegger also makes use of this figure: in the noisy tumult of non poetic language, a poem is like a bell suspended in midair, on which light snow falling would be enough to make it chime, an imperceptible crashing nevertheless capable of harmoniously upsetting it to the point of discord. Perhaps commentary is just a little snowflake making the bell toll.[289]

This leads Blanchot to a paradoxical conclusion that criticism is a perpetual movement toward self-effacement. The more criticism establishes itself the more it points to the work of art about which it comments. The task of criticism is to make the work more understandable, to introduce this work back into the world, but, in doing that, it cannot add anything to the work and, in the end, it is the work that seems to speak for itself. Blanchot says: "Critical discourse, having neither lasting effect nor reality, would like to dissolve within creative affirmation: it is never criticism that speaks, when it speaks; it is nothing... Criticism is nothing, but this nothingness is precisely that in which the literary work, silent and invisible, allows itself to be what it is... Critical discourse is this space of resonance within which the unspoken, indefinite reality of the work is momentarily transformed and circumscribed into words."[290]

However, this disappearance and self-effacement of criticism before the work does not mean that criticism is a simple vulgarization of the work. Precisely this feature makes criticism inseparable from the inner workings of a literary text. As we previously saw with the example of *Infinitive,* one of the most important features of this work is its inability to coincide with itself. Its basic condition is something that is necessarily prior to it (Greenchurch's *The Axiological Infinitive*), but crucially this book is something that has no existence outside *Infinitive.* Therefore, to use the words of Timothy Clark, *Infinitive* is like "a spiral whose spiraling inwards is ceaseless and asymptotic."[291] *The Axiological Infinitive* is the eternally absent basis of *Infinitive* that perpetually divorces this work from itself. This fundamental feature of literature enables Leslie Hill to formulate the following claims about the relationship between literature and criticism:

> For a while on the one hand literature's non-coincidence with itself is what makes literary criticism possible, since without it the critic would simply have nothing to say, so on the other, for the exact same reason, no criticism, by the power of its discourse, can ever overcome the incompletion of the work it seeks to make its own. The artwork cannot endorse or validate the words of the critic, and literary criticism is quickly brought to the

uncomfortable realization not only that it is entirely parasitical on the artwork, but also that its own discourse is necessarily superfluous to the existence of the work. Ironically, however, if this were not the case, criticism again would have little alternative but to fall silent. Paradoxically, then, it is the inability of literary criticism to guarantee the truth of what it says about the artwork that is the best, nay only, hope of its longevity. Its survival, in other words, is not a result of the discursive authority or rigor it prides itself on possessing, but a function of its founding, inescapable impotence.[292]

This problematizes Levinas's endorsing of criticism, but it does not address the fundamental problem of art's apparent irresponsibility. In order to address this problem we will have to examine the role of art in the broader context of Levinas's philosophy.

CHAPTER FOUR:
THE POSSIBILITY OF ETHICS

The cuckoo calls from the well of my mind,
more echo than thought, as it fades through the wind
and flickers away to the silence beyond
like the voice, in myself, of another.

John Burnside, *Insomnia in Southern Illinois*

When I am alone, I am not alone, but, in this present, I am already returning to myself in the form of Someone. Someone is there, where I am alone. The fact of being alone is my belonging to this dead time which is not my time, or yours, or the time we share in common, but Someone's time. Someone is what is still present when there is no one. Where I am alone, I am not there; no one is there, but the impersonal is: the outside, as that which prevents, precedes, and dissolves the possibility of any personal relation.... When I am alone, the light of day is only the loss of a dwelling place. It is intimacy with the outside which has no location and affords no rest. Coming here makes the one who comes belong to dispersal, to the fissure where the exterior is the intrusion that stifles, but is also nakedness, the chill of the enclosure that leaves one utterly exposed. Here the only space is its vertiginous separation. Here fascination reigns.

Maurice Blanchot, *The Space of Literature*

Levinas's (im)possibility

In "Reality and Its Shadow", Levinas directly addresses the possibility of a relationship between art and ethics. The question is: is art capable of being ethical? Or, in Levinas's terms, can we encounter the other in art? As we have already seen, in "Reality and Its Shadow", Levinas's answer is a resounding "no." However, his other works contain numerous references to the famous literary works of European literature. He often cites Shakespeare and Dostoyevsky; *Totality and Infinity* begins with a quotation from Rimbaud and Levinas is fascinated by Vasily Grossman's realist novel *Life and Fate*. What is the function of these references? Do they contradict Levinas's previous claims about art and literature? In most cases, the references to literary works are used to exemplify certain philosophical ideas. However, in some cases, literary references lose their ornamental status and become much more important. I will start with *Existence and Existents* in order to further illuminate Levinas's claim from "Reality and Its Shadow" that art is essentially disengaged. After that, the position of art in *Totality and Infinity* will be presented. At the end of the first section, I will offer reading of "The Poet's Vision" and "The Other in Proust" that can open a possibility for a relationship between literature and ethics.

Chapter 4 ("Existence Without a World") of Levinas's *Existence and Existents* is devoted to the exoticism of art, and presents a perspective that is similar to the one we have already considered in "Reality and Its Shadow." Levinas even begins in a similar way by stating that the work of art is essentially disinterested and disengaged from the world. This is why it is perceived as exotic. The basic procedure of art (the substitution of the object by its image) produces disinterestedness and disengagement. However, Levinas also claims:

> What is called the disinterestedness of art does not only refer to the neutralization of the possibilities of action. Exoticism modifies the contemplation itself. The "objects" are outside, but this outside does not relate to an "interior"; they are not already naturally "possessed." A painting, a statue, a book are objects of *our* world, but through them the things represented are extracted from our world.
>
> Even the most realistic art gives this character of *alterity* to the objects represented which are nonetheless part of our world. It presents them to us in their nakedness, that real nakedness which is not absence of clothing, but we might say the absence of forms, that is, the non-transmutation of our exteriority into inwardness, which forms realize. The forms and colors of a painting do not cover over but uncover the things in themselves, precisely because they preserve the exteriority of those things.[293]

In these two paragraphs, Levinas mentions several salient things. First, he insists that the relationship between literature and real world is not straightforward. The works of art can claim to represent reality, but precisely the notion of representation is problematic for Levinas. Representation extracts the represented objects from *our* world. Second, he also claims that this extraction from *our* world gives the represented things a character of alterity. Therefore, they are, at the same time, something completely other, but also something that belongs to *our* world. Most importantly, Levinas writes that, in art, objects are presented to us *in their nakedness* that is understood as *the absence of forms*. Although this can be used as a starting point for a positive perspective, Levinas will continue to criticize "the exoticism of art" and its supposed "disinterestedness." In *Totality and Infinity*, *nakedness* and *the absence of form* will be associated with Levinas's understanding of the face. In short, he will claim that the face expresses itself *kath auto* (according to itself), but his views on art will remain negative.

Levinas also says that in our everyday language exists an essential connection between words and their meaning. However, a certain detachment of words from their meaning happens in poetry. According to Levinas, in poetry, a word "detaches itself from its objective meaning and reverts to the element of the sensible..."[294] In poetry, a word acquires the power of ambiguity and the multiplicity of meanings. The loss of connection between word and its objective meaning is the basis for the exoticism of art. It is now clear that by exoticism Levinas refers to this essential disengagement of art. This is simply the elaboration of the same argument from "Reality and Its Shadow." However, this elaboration is produced by the covert reference to Mallarméan aesthetics. Levinas claims that a certain materialization of words is always happening in literature.

This materialization is one of the important topics of Blanchot's "Literature and the Right to Death." In this essay, the act of naming is also described as the negation of the real. However, Levinas takes for granted that negation is stabilized in the language of everyday. Or, maybe he does not take into account this negativity at all? Maybe he assumes that some kind of presence exists in the language of everyday, but also in the philosophical discourse? I will come back to this problem of presence in my analysis of the most important part of *Totality and Infinity* (Part B of section 3 that is entitled "Face and Ethics").

This brings us back to the already mentioned problem of naming. Blanchot's interpretation of the myth of Orpheus shows that literature is interested in negativity (absence) itself. Blanchot describes this interest in the following way:

> In speech what dies is what gives life to speech; speech is the life of that death, it is "the life that endures death and maintains itself in it." What wonderful power. But something was there and is no longer there. Something has disappeared. How can I recover it, how can I turn around and look at what exists *before*, if all my power consists of making it into what exists after? The language of literature is a search for this moment which precedes literature. Literature usually calls it existence; it wants the cat as it exists, the pebble *taking the side of things*, not man but the pebble, and in this pebble what man rejects by saying it, what is the foundation of speech and what speech excludes in speaking, the, Lazarus in the tomb and not Lazarus brought back into the daylight, the one who already smells bad, who is Evil, Lazarus lost and not Lazarus saved and brought back to life.[295]

As I already mentioned in the second chapter, the materiality of language is the important feature of Mallarméan poetics, but, in Blanchot's interpretation, this materiality leads us toward absence itself. Let us proceed slowly and carefully in following Blanchot's exposition. In literature, Blanchot claims, words start to show themselves as opaque things.

> A name ceases to be the ephemeral passing of nonexistence [a concept] and becomes a concrete ball, a solid mass of existence; language, abandoning the sense, the meaning which is all it wanted to be, tries to become senseless. Everything physical takes precedence: rhythm, weight, mass, shape, and then the paper on which one writes, the trail of ink, the book. Yes, happily language is a thing…[296]

However, although the language of literature suspends the relationship between the word and a thing, although the word becomes an opaque thing, something strange happens. Precisely the meaninglessness of literary language becomes something meaningful. Rodolphe Gasché describes this paradox in the following way: "In its quest for what language excludes, literature discovers signification in general, but not as a transcendental in the strict sense of language's capacity to make something appear, but as an inescapable degree zero of meaning to which even the meaningless must bend. Literature thus experiences the condemnation of language to signify, its inability to disappear, and stop making sense."[297] This paradox will discern a certain agreement between Blanchot and Levinas:

> When literature refuses to name anything, when it turns a name into something obscure and meaningless, witness to the primordial obscurity, what has disappeared in this case—the meaning of the name—is really destroyed, but signification in general has appeared in its place, the meaning of the meaninglessness embedded in the word as expression of the obscurity of existence, so that although the precise meaning of the term has faded, what asserts itself now is the very possibility of signifying, the empty power of bestowing meaning—a strange impersonal light.[298]

Blanchot and Levinas agree that this detachment of words from their meaning and their consequent materiality sheds "a strange impersonal light" and points toward "something which is not in its turn an object or a name, which is unnameable and can only appear in poetry."[299] According to both of them, the materiality of words enables us to notice the very fact of the *il y a*.

The description of the *il y a* is an extremely important moment in *Existence and Existents*. It starts as a thought-experiment: "Let us imagine..." Art and imagination, condition any approach to the *il y a*. First, the materiality of words leads us toward the *il y a*. Second, Levinas turns to fictionalization (in the form of "Let us imagine...") so that he can describe the experience of the *il y a*. Third, statements of literary characters (Hamlet, Macbeth and Phaedra), the works of Huysmans, Zola, Maupassant and Blanchot (*Thomas l'obscure*), together with "the hallucinatory reality" of Rimbaud are evoked to provide a further illustration of the *il y a*.[300] It all points to the fact that literature and the *il y a* are inextricably linked. Moreover, the experience of literature is the experience of the *il y a*.

This is how Levinas describes the *il y a*:

> Let us imagine all beings, things and persons, reverting to nothingness. One cannot put this return to nothingness outside of all events. But what of this nothingness itself? Something would happen, if only night and the silence of nothingness. The indeterminateness of this "something is happening" is not the indeterminateness of a subject and does not refer to a substantive. Like the third person pronoun in the impersonal form of a verb, it designates not the uncertainly known author of the action, but the characteristic of this action itself which somehow has no author. This impersonal, anonymous, yet inextinguishable "consummation" of being, which murmurs in the depths of nothingness itself we shall designate by the term *there is*. The *there is*, inasmuch as it resists a personal form, is "being in general." [...]
>
> When the forms of things are dissolved in the night, darkness of the night, which is neither an object nor

the quality of an object, invades like a presence. In the night, where we are riven to it, we are not dealing with anything. But this nothing is not that of pure nothingness. There is no longer *this* or *that*; there is not "something." But this universal absence is in its turn presence, an absolutely unavoidable presence. It is not the dialectical counterpart of absence, and we do not grasp it through thought. It is immediately there. There is no discourse. Nothing responds to us, but this silence; the voice of this silence understood and frightens like the silence of those infinite spaces Pascal speaks of. *There is*, in general, without it mattering there is, without our being able to fix a substantive to this term. *There is* is an impersonal form, like in it rains, or it is warm. Its anonymity is essential. The mind does not find itself faced with an apprehended exterior. The exterior — if one insists on the term — remains uncorrelated with an interior. It is no longer given. It is no longer a world. What we call the I is itself submerged by the night, invaded, depersonalized, stifled by it. The disappearance of all things and of the I leaves what cannot disappear, the sheer fact of being in which one *participates* whether one wants to or not, without having taken the initiative, anonymously. Being remains, like a field of forces, like a heavy atmosphere belonging to no one, universal, returning in the midst of the negation which put it aside, and in all the powers to which that negation may be multiplied.[301]

This passage offers the answer to the question: what is the ontological significance of the materiality of words? According to Levinas, it enables us the experience of the *il y a*. The *il y a* is described as the presence of absence. Even when all beings have disappeared, something remains. This something is the presence of absence, the pure exteriority and the possibility of an existence without existents. The *il y a* is the experience of the presence of absence. The experience of art is the experience of the *il y a* and what happens in that experience is the dispossession of the self. Subjectivity is dissolved in this pure exteriority. As I already mentioned in the previous chapters of this dissertation, Blanchot claims that the fundamental movement of writing is the passage from *je* to the impersonal *il*. This also shows that art and the *il y a* are essentially linked.

It is also impossible to hide in the *il y a* (in this experience of the world without beings and without subject). The *il y a* destroys every possibility of a shelter. This means that the experience of the *il y a* is also the experience of the ultimate exposure. Levinas writes: "Before this obscure invasion it is impossible to take shelter in oneself, to withdraw into one's shell. One is exposed. The whole is open upon us. Instead of serving as our means of access to being, nocturnal space delivers us over to being."[301]

According to Levinas, the fundamental *Stimmung* of the *il y a* is horror. In order to explain why this is the case, Levinas will first connect the *il y a* with *participation* and, after that, with *the impossibility of death*. The notion of participation has an important place in "Reality and Its Shadow." In this essay, participation is connected with rhythm, but also with the impersonality and the subject's foreignness to itself. Participation and rhythm are the essential features of the work of art and they enable the passage "from oneself to anonymity", or, in Blanchot's language, the passage from *je* to *il*. In "Reality and Its Shadow", Levinas claims that these two terms block any possibility of ethics. In participation, the subject loses the connection with itself and slips into impersonal existence. This impersonal existence is characterized by the loss of agency which is the main condition for the appearance of ethics.

Since the experience of art is the experience of the *il y a*, this means that art is incapable of surmounting this impersonality. Art traps us in the existence without a world and therefore it cannot be ethical. The *Stimmung* of horror characterizes participation precisely because of this threat of impersonality (or the loss of personality). Levinas writes:

> To be conscious is to be torn away from the *there is,* since the existence of a consciousness constitutes a subjectivity, a subject of existence, that is, to some extent a master of being, already a name in the anonymity of the night. Horror is somehow a movement which will strip consciousness of its very "subjectivity." Not in lulling it into unconsciousness, but in throwing it into an *impersonal vigilance,* a *participation,* in the sense that Lévy-Bruhl gives to the term.[303]

Horror, as he describes it, can be also an anxiety about death. Horror has the ability to depersonalize the subject and thus leads it toward the *il y a*. Horror discloses "the impossibility of death, the universality of existence even in its annihilation."[304] Levinas offers a couple of literary examples to illustrate this impossibility of death. The most important ones come from Shakespeare - the ghost of Hamlet's father and the ghost of Banquo. For Levinas, these ghosts offer "a decisive experience of the 'no exit' from existence."[305] The role of these ghosts is to disclose the impossibility of death.

We will attempt to elaborate further the impossibility of death with the help of Maurice Blanchot's work. According to Blanchot, there is an essential connection between language and death. In "Literature and the Right to Death", this connection is established through negation. Our analysis of naming already showed us that negation enables mastery over things. Blanchot describes this power in the following way:

> I say, "This woman." Hölderlin, Mallarmé, and all poets whose theme is the essence of poetry have felt that the act of naming is disquieting and marvelous. A word may give me its meaning, but first it suppresses it. For me to be able to say, "This woman," I must somehow take her flesh-and-blood reality away from her, cause her to be absent, annihilate her. The word gives me the being, but it gives it to me deprived of being. The word is the absence of that being, its nothingness, what is left of it when it has lost being - the very fact that it does not exist. Considered in this light, speaking is a curious right. In a text dating from before *The Phenomenology*, Hegel, here the friend and kindred spirit of Hölderlin, writes: "Adam's first act, which made him master of the animals, was to give them names, that is, he annihilated them in their existence (as existing creatures)." Hegel means that from that moment on, the cat ceased to be a uniquely real cat and became an idea as well. The meaning of speech, then requires that before any word is spoken, there must be a sort of immense hecatomb, a preliminary flood plunging all of creation into a total sea. God had created living things, but man had to annihilate them. Not until then did they take on meaning for him, and he in turn created them out of the death into which they had disappeared; only instead of beings (*êtres*) and, as we say, existants (*existants*), there remained only being (*l'être*), and man was condemned not to be able to approach anything or experience anything except through the meaning he had to create.[306]

This is a way to perceive death as possibility. Moreover, in this interpretation, death shows itself as the crucial possibility. Basically, the possibility of language is based on death and in death lies the possibility of speaking. However, the language of literature, unlike everyday language, goes toward this negativity in itself; it seeks a moment that precedes literature. Precisely this search (which is described in the myth of Orpheus) enables the experience of the impossibility of death.

In *The Space of Literature*, Blanchot turns to Kafka. He claims that Kafka understands art as the ultimate power and mastery. However, he is aware that this understanding is essentially paradoxical. Kafka claims that death is the primary motivation for writing and its justification. The writer withdraws from the world and he writes in order to die peacefully. However, he is capable of writing only if he can die peacefully. This is a temporal paradox that we already met in the analysis of the myth of Orpheus and this time it is associated with writing. Again, as John Gregg explains, Blanchot refers to something "that always already has had to have taken place in order to occur."[307] In "Death as Possibility", this paradox is described in the following way:

> The writer, then, is one who writes in order to be able to die, and he is one whose power to write comes from an anticipated relation with death. The contradiction subsists, but is seen in a different light. Just as the poet only exists once the poem faces him, only after the poem, as it were -- although it is necessary that first there be a poet in order for there to be a poem -- so one senses that if Kafka goes toward the power of dying through the work which he writes, the work itself is by implication an experience of death which he apparently has to have been through already in order to reach the work and, through the work, death. But one can also sense that the movement which, in the work, is the approach to death, death's space and its use, is not exactly the same

> movement which would lead the writer to the possibility of dying. One can even suppose that the particularly strange relations between artist and work, which make the work depend on him who is only possible within the work -- one can even suppose that such an anomaly stems from the experience which overpowers the form of time, but stems more profoundly still from the ambiguity of that experience, from its double aspect which Kafka expresses with too much simplicity in the sentences we ascribe to him: *Write to be able to die -- Die to be able to write.*[308]

Blanchot also poses the following questions: can death be mastered? Can I make it my own? Is suicide one possible way of mastering death? Blanchot uses the example of Arria to show that this is not possible and this example refers to the impossibility of death. The example of Arria is the example of heroic death. When she saw the hesitation of her husband, she took his dagger, stabbed herself, drew this dagger back out and offered it to her husband with the following words: "It is not painful." However, "Arria's impassivity is no longer the sign of the preservation of her mastery, but the sign of an absence, of a hidden disappearance, the shadow of someone impersonal and neutral."[309]

This shadow brings us back to Levinas's point about the impossibility of death from *Existence and Existents*. What Levinas describes in this work is actually a moment of *dédoublement* that testifies to the impossibility of death in a manner that is linked to the doubling described by Blanchot in the example of Arria. Arria is at the same time herself and her double; the pervasive passivity and neutrality of death turns her into her own image. This is the reason why *I* cannot die - there is no *je* in death, only an impersonal *il*. This is how the idea of authentic death becomes transformed into an endless passivity of dying. In *my* death, there is no *I* anymore. Therefore, this death can never be mine. I am plunged into an infinite abyss of the *il y a* where consciousness becomes dissolved into unbearable anonymity. Art is essentially linked with death and it discloses the impersonality and anonymity that remove me from myself and divest me of the power to say *I*. Levinas and Blanchot agree that art is capable of all this and this is the important reason why Levinas is so critical toward art.[310]

Is it possible to perceive this passage from *je* to *il* as a sign of alterity that does not come from the outside, but from the inside? Levinas claims that this is not possible and he describes the passage from *je* to *il* as a spurious or finite alterity. At the beginning of *Totality and Infinity,* he writes:

> The I is identical in its very alterations in yet another sense. The I that thinks hearkens to itself thinking or takes fright before its depths and is to itself an other. It thus discovers the famous naïveté of its thought, which thinks "straight on" as one's "follows ones's nose" [*...qui pense "devant elle", comme on marche "devant soi"*]. It hearkens to itself thinking and surprises itself being dogmatic, foreign to itself. But faced with this alterity the I is the same, merges with itself, is incapable of apostasy with regard to this surprising "self." Hegelian phenomenology, where self-consciousness is the distinguishing of what is not distinct, expresses the universality of the same identifying itself in the alterity of objects thought and despite the opposition of self to self. "I distinguish myself from myself; and therein I am immediately aware that this factor distinguished from me is not distinguished. I, the selfsame being, thrust myself away from myself; but this which is distinguished, which is set up unlike me, is immediately on its being distinguished not distinction for me." The Difference is not a difference; the I, as other,

is not an "other."....The alterity of the I that takes itself for
another may strike the imagination of the poet precisely
because it is but the play of the same: the negation of the
I by the self is precisely one of the modes of identification
of the I.[311]

We arrive then, at *Totality and Infinity*. "Reality and Its Shadow" is a text that is completely devoted to the problem of art, and *Existence and Existents,* as we have seen, contains a chapter that deals with the same problem. This is not the case with *Totality and Infinity*, where we find only scattered remarks about art and where it is always mentioned in a negative and disparaging way. There are, however, two main lines of argumentation pertinent to our analysis that are also interwoven in the volume. The first line of argumentation has already been indicated; it is the one that stems from "Reality and Its Shadow." The second line of argumentation has clear Platonic influences and is connected with Levinas's understanding of the face. Therefore, I will first focus on the most important part of *Totality and Infinity* (Part B of section 3 that is entitled "Face and Ethics) and after that I will show how the argumentation of this part of the book is linked with the one from "Reality and Its Shadow" and *Existence and Existents.*

Before everything else, we have to make an important distinction between "the nakedness of the face" and "the disclosure of the thing illuminated by its form."[312] This distinction is vital because it refers us back to "Reality and Its Shadow" and to the notion of resemblance.[313] According to Levinas, being is doubled by its form in a manner that is exploited by art. Form prevents alterity from manifesting itself and this is the crucial reason why art cannot be ethical.

The possibility of a relation between the Same and the Other is the main problem of Levinas's ethics. In order for this relation to be ethical, it needs to be a face-to-face relation. Levinas claims that the face-to-face relation founds language because language is primordially enacted as conversation. Therefore, Levinasian ethics grants a special privilege to language and considers language as a nontotalizing relation with the other. Since language is essentially conversation and since the essence of language is a relation with the other, this also means that a face is actually faced in language.[314] Levinas writes:

> "Language is a relation between separated terms. To the one the other can indeed present himself as a theme, but this presence is not reabsorbed in his status as a theme... The fact that the face maintains a relation with me by discourse does not range him in the same; he remains absolute within the relation."[315]

In Part B of section 1, Levinas claims that language enables "the revelation of the other" by instituting a relation that cannot be reduced to the subject-object relation. This revelation is constitutive for language as such. It is constitutive because the basic presupposition of language is the presupposition of interlocution and plurality. Levinas says: "Discourse is thus the experience of something absolutely foreign, a *pure* "knowledge" or "experience, *a traumatism of astonishment.*"[316]

If we accept this, then we need to pose another important question: how can the face appear in language without the loss of its fundamental alterity? How can the other remain transcendent and infinitely foreign? In order for this to happen an autosignification of the face is necessary. The face expresses itself *kath auto* (according to itself) and Levinas claims:

> In expression a being presents itself; the being that manifests itself attends its manifestation and consequently appeals to me. This attendance is not the *neutrality [le neutre]* of an image, but a solicitation that concerns me by its destitution and its Height. To speak to me is at each moment to surmount what is necessarily plastic in manifestation. To manifest oneself as a face is to *impose oneself* above and beyond the manifested and purely phenomenal form, to present oneself in a mode irreducible to manifestation, the very straightforwardness of the face to face, without the intermediary of any image, in one's nudity, that is, in one's destitution and hunger...
>
> Expression does not radiate as splendour that spreads unbeknown to the radiating being - which is perhaps the definition of beauty.[317]

The manifestation of the face is not a manifestation because the face has the ability to represent itself without representation. This is possible because, according to Levinas, the face is fully present. In Levinas's work, ethics is based on the face-to-face relation and this relation is guaranteed by the assumption of presence.[318] As the quoted passage suggests, in *Totality and Infinity,* Levinas understands art in Platonic terms (as representation or *mimesis*) and therefore it cannot be ethical.[319] As we have seen in "Reality and Its Shadow", in the work of art the object is substituted by its image and this means that the artwork is unethical because it freezes the face and turns it into a mask.

Although the relation with the other happens in language, in "Rhetoric and Injustice", Levinas openly claims: "Not every discourse is a relation with exteriority."[320] In this place, Levinas's position is Platonic and he understands rhetoric in a narrow sense. For him, rhetoric is simply persuasion. Therefore, he states that, in rhetoric, the other is not approached to be faced, but from an angle and in order to be persuaded into something. Since rhetoric is described as persuasion, it means that some hidden agenda is always present in rhetoric. This is why rhetoric (together with art) is essentially violent and unjust.

If we stop here, Levinas's view on art will remain unproblematic, coherent, and unambiguously negative. However, there are two texts that significantly complicate his position: "The Poet's Vision" and "The Other in Proust."

Levinas's essay "The Poet's Vision" is dedicated to the analysis of Blanchot's *The Space of Literature*. Levinas presents Blanchot's main arguments and also focuses on the difference between Blanchot's and Heidegger's theoretical positions. Also, in relation to Blanchot's writings on literature, he poses an essential question:

> How can the Other (which Jankélévitch calls the *absolutely other* and Blanchot "eternal streaming of the outside") appear, that is, be for someone, without already losing its alterity and exteriority by that way of offering itself to view? How can there be appearing without power?[321]

In light of the statements from Levinas we have considered thus far, we should assume that his answer will be that the absolutely other cannot appear in literature. According to him, art and literature are essentially unethical. However, in "The Poet's Vision" his answer is completely different:

> The mode of revelation of what remains *other*, despite its revelation, is not the thought, but the language, of the poem. Its privilege, in Blanchot's analyses, does not consist in leading us further than knowledge. It is not telepathic: the outside is not distant. It is what appears - but in singular fashion - when all the real has been denied: realization of that unreality. Its way of being, its nature, consists in being present without being given, in not delivering itself up to the powers, since negation has been the ultimate human power, in being the domain of the impossible, on which power can get no purchase, in being a perpetual dismissal of the one who discloses it.[322]

In "The Poet's Vision", Levinas associates literature with the negation of the world and with the *il y a*. But, in this essay, literature is not dismissed as, for example, in "Reality and Its Shadow" or in *Existence and Existents*. The important point of this essay is the possibility that the *absolutely other* can somehow appear in literature.

If we now take into consideration Levinas's essay "The Other in Proust", the situation becomes even more complicated. The essay begins in a way that follows "Reality and Its Shadow." Levinas again situates the artist in the realm of imaginary. However, in "The Other in Proust", Levinas formulates two important theses that subvert the argumentation from the earlier essay.

The first thesis can be related to the story we considered in Chapter 3 concerning Alain-Fournier and Yvonne. In this case, however, the main protagonists are the narrator of *Remembrance of Things Past* and Albertine. According to Levinas, the mystery that lies at the heart of Proust's work is the mystery of the other:

The story of Albertine... is the narrative of the inner life's sudden intensification brought about by an insatiable curiosity about the alterity of the other, at once empty and inexhaustible. The reality of Albertine is her evanescence in her very captivity - a reality made up of nothingness. She is a prisoner, though she has already disappeared, and she has disappeared though a prisoner - since despite the strictest surveillance she retains a dimension of secrecy. The objective facts Proust is able to gather about her after her death do not dispel the doubt that surrounded her when her lies disguised her fugues. When she is no longer there to defend her absence, when evidence abounds, leaving no room for doubt, the doubt remains intact. Albertine's nothingness uncovers her total alterity.[323]

Just as Alain-Fournier is infatuated by Yvonne's infinite absence, Marcel is drawn toward Albertine:

Marcel did not love Albertine, if love is a fusion with the other, the ecstasy of one being before the perfections of the other, or the peace of possesion. Tomorrow he will break with the young woman, who bores him. He will take that trip he has been planning for a long time. The story of Marcel's love is laced with confessions apparently designed to put in question the very consistency of that love. But that non-love is in fact love; that struggle with the ungraspable, possession; that absence of Albertine, her presence.[324]

Another, more important thesis can then be found in the middle of this essay. Let us recall that in Chapter 3, we addressed the question: Is Yvonne real or is she just a reflection of Alain-Fournier and the occasion for movements within him? If the answer to this question is "yes", then the possibility that the other can appear from the inside (and not just from the outside) is opened. Namely, the affirmative answer opens the possibility that a "spurious alterity" (Levinas's characterization of the passage from *je* to *il* in *Totality and Infinity*) is in fact the *absolutely other*.

This is precisely what happens in "The Other in Proust." Levinas begins this essay with the presentation of Proust's many faces. He poses the following questions: how is this possible? What enables so many different interpretations of *Remembrance of Things Past*? The answer lies in the essential ambiguity (or indeterminacy) of Proust's work: "It is obvious that this ambiguity is the very light that bathes Proust's poetry. The contours of the events, persons and things, despite the accuracy of delineation, the sculpting of personality traits and characters, remain in total indeterminacy."[325]

This essential ambiguity is produced because in the work of art the object is substituted by its image. However, this doubling that happens in the work is not perceived as something negative in "The Other in Proust." In this essay, doubling is described as auto-referentiality because, in the work of Marcel Proust, "the true emotion is always the emotion of the emotion... Proustian reflection, dominated by a separation between the *I* and its state, imparts its own accent to the inner life by a kind of refraction. It is as if *I* were constantly accompanied by another self, in unparalleled friendship, but also in a cold strangeness that life attempts to overcome. The mystery in Proust is the mystery of the other."[326]

This is crucial for our analysis because Levinas does not write here about the simple division within *I*, but about the possibility that *I* can become "the other within the self." In *Totality and Infinity*, this possibility is dismissed, but in "The Other in Proust" it is described as the necessary condition for the encounter with the absolutely other. This doubling of the very encounter with the other, this "I becoming other" is something that needs to happen so that the ethical encounter can become possible.[327] Again, we are faced with the temporal paradox from the myth of Orpheus; with an encounter "that always already has had to have taken place in order to occur."[328]

Jill Robbins does not notice this paradox and claims that Levinas's ambivalence toward art is present even in "The Other in Proust." This is how Levinas finishes this essay: "But Proust's most profound teaching - if indeed poetry teaches - consists in situating the real in relation with what for ever remains other - with the other as absence and mystery. It consists in rediscovering this relation also within the very intimacy of the *I* and in inaugurating a dialectic that breaks definitively with Parmenides."[329] Jill Robbins interprets the ending of Levinas's essay in the following way:

> The hesitation is important, the qualifier is enormous. For it is not at all clear that poetry - Proust's or anyone else's *can* contain teaching. Teaching is an ethical relation, a paradigm of the ethical relation in *Totality and Infinity* - and *this* teaching that Proust's work is said to accomplish involves no less than an (impossible) break with Parmenides, philosopher of the unity of being which suppresses the beyond, namely, a break with the governing conceptuality of philosophy in the West. Levinas says that Proust teaches the ethical - if poetry *can* teach - but we know that he knows that it cannot, or we know that he has grave doubt about this possibility, because magic and ethics are incompatible, or in the terms of *Totality and Infinity*, poetic rapture interferes with the straightforwardness of ethical discourse. In short, in the Proust essay, Levinas seems to want to have it both ways. Poetry does and does not give access to the ethical.[330]

It is certainly possible to interpret the ending of "The Other in Proust" in this way and to describe it as a strange contradiction in Levinas's work. However, this contradiction is not resolved in Robbins's interpretation. It is true that Levinas's work after his essay on Proust is straightforwardly dismissive toward art, but that does not mean that the already mentioned contradiction is resolved in these works. I will attempt to connect this contradiction with the work of Maurice Blanchot in order to show how the possibility of ethics is opened in literature.

Blanchot's possibility

In *Existence and Existents*, Levinas says that the "night is the very experience of the *there is*, if the term experience were not inapplicable to a situation which involves the total exclusion of light."[331] For Levinas, the important features of the *il y a* are darkness and obscurity, and we are aware that, in "Reality and Its Shadow", artwork is described as the event of obscuring. This darkness of the *il y a* is pervasive and it is also associated with a certain kind of presence. This is the presence as/of absence. The nocturnal space of the *il y a* is filled with darkness and darkness is its content: "it is full, but full of the nothingness of everything."[332] In the space of the *il y a*, where absence is present, the initiative and power disappear and we are left with passive vigilance together with the feeling of horror.

We already saw that Blanchot adapts Levinas notion of the *il y a* to his analyses of literature. This happens in "Literature and the Right to Death."[333] The footnote near the end of this essay shows us that Blanchot read Levinas's *Existence and Existants*.[334] However, in *Existence and Existents*, Levinas claims that Blanchot's *Thomas l'obscure* begins with an excellent description of the *il y a*. In turn, Blanchot's "The Outside, the Night" is again influenced by Levinas's writings about the *il y a* and elaborates what he wrote in "Literature and the Right to Death." In *The Space of Literature*, Blanchot continues where he left off in "Literature and the Right to Death" and describes the *il y a* as the *other* night:

> But when everything has disappeared in the night, "everything has disappeared" appears. This is the *other* night. Night is this apparition: "everything has disappeared." It is what we sense when dreams replace

sleep, when the dead pass into the deep of the night, when night's deep appears in those who have disappeared. Apparitions, phantoms, and dreams are an illusion to this empty night. It is the night of Young, where the dark does not seem dark enough, or death ever dead enough. What appears in the night is the night that appears. And this eeriness does not simply come from something invisible, which would reveal itself under cover of dark and at the shadows' summons. Here the invisible is what one cannot cease to see; it is the incessant making itself seen. The "phantom" is meant to hide, to appease the phantom night. Those who think they see ghosts are those who do not want to see the night. They crowd it with the terror of little images, they occupy and distract it by immobilizing it - stopping the oscillation of eternal starting over. It is empty, it is not; but we dress it up as a kind of being; we enclose it, if possible, in a name, a story and a resemblance; we say, like Rilke at Duino, "It is Raimondine and Polyxène."[335]

In the *other* night, everything has disappeared and the invisibility and the incessant appear. In the *other* night, we have the presence as/of absence that was the important characteristic of the *il y a*. To access the inaccessible *other* night means "to accede to the outside."[336] Also, another characteristic of the *other* night is the impossibility of death: "*In* the night one can die; we reach oblivion. But this *other* night is the death no one dies, the forgetfulness which gets forgotten, In the heart of oblivion is the memory without rest."[337]

In "The Outside, the Night", Blanchot puts Tolstoy's story "Master and Man" in the context of Levinas's essay on the *il y a*, but also in the context of his description of the impossibility of death. "Master and Man" is a very short and simple story. Its main character, Vasili Andreevich Brekhunov (the master) wants to purchase some wood at a bargain price, but he and his servant Nikita get lost in the snowstorm. Brekhunov is described as a self-made man who despises passivity and who firmly believes in strength and power. When he and his servant realize that they are lost, their reactions are completely different. Nikita passively submits to his fate in the blizzard, while Brekhunov continues to fight as he did during his whole life. Nikita resigns himself to his destiny, but Brekhunov continues to push on. But, he circles aimlessly in the snowstorm and his horse eventually brings him back to the place where Nikita is dying.

This is the precise moment when Brekhunov realizes the true *horror* of his situation. Leo Shestov describes this realization in the following way:

> Around him was the boundless plain, boundless, at least, to him, and snow, cold, and wind, Nikita, already numbed by the cold, and the shivering horse. He felt unreasonable but insistent and overmastering terror. "What to do? What to do?" This is the regular question which every man asks when he finds himself in a difficult situation. It presents itself to Brekhunov, but this time it seems completely absurd. Hitherto, the question had always held the elements of its own answer, it had at least always shown him the possibility of an answer. But this time it held nothing of the sort. The question excluded all possibility of an answer; there *was nothing to be done*.[338]

Brekhunov decides to help Nikita and he brings him back to life. Finally, he lies down on him and warms him up in this way. When they are found in the morning, Brekhunov is dead but Nikita is still alive. The servant is saved by the unselfish act of a man who was nothing but selfish during his whole life.

The main problem of this short story is Brekhunov's motivation. How should we interpret Brekhunov's unselfish act? Why did he give his life to save Nikita? The majority of interpretations emphasize the Christian aspect of this story. According to these interpretations, the main topic of "Master and Man" is the notion of self-sacrifice. However, N.K. Mikhaylovsky notices the important problem of this interpretation:

> The master's death strongly reminds one of the death of St. Julian the Hospitalier in a well known legend by Flaubert, translated by Turgenev. St. Julian, too, lies down on a dying man in order to warm him, and, dying himself, also feels "an abundance of happiness, a superhuman joy." In his terminal delirium the person of the leper whom he was warming, also fuses with the higher being who, admittedly, does not call on St. Julian to join him but directly carries him off into the wide blue yonder. The master is not guilty of any of those terrible sins and evil deeds that burden St. Julian's soul, but, on the other hand, St. Julian atones for his sins by years of achievement, and his final selfless deed is merely the last link in a chain, which lends the story to the naturalness insofar as this is possible in a legend. The master, on the other hand, did not spill any blood, like St. Julian, nor did he kill his parents, yet he was a crook and probably responsible for the ruinations of dozens of people in order to advance his own well being. Let us say, all this can be atoned for by his last minutes, but it seems to me that only one of two things is possible: if the master saved his man, inadvertently, hoping to save himself by warming himself with the man's body, then this is hardly a self sacrifice, and the moral value of the master's last few minutes is not great; but if he really did forget about himself and his only thought was to save the man, then this would seem to be too sudden a turnaround, too unmotivated an act - since only a short time before he was ready to betray and abandon the man to his fate in order to save himself.[339]

Something even more important is noticed in Garry Saul Morson's succinct interpretation of "Master and Man."[340] He claims that this is a story about the disappearance of the class distinction between the master and his servant in the face of the impending death. However, this distinction not only disappears, but Brekhunov also becomes Nikita and starts to talk about himself in the third person. As the death approaches, Brekhunov loses his personality:

> He remembered that Nikita was lying under him and that he had got warm and was alive, and it seemed to him that he was Nikita and Nikita was he, and that his life was not in himself but in Nikita. He strained his ears and heard Nikita breathing and even slightly snoring. 'Nikita is alive, so I too am alive!' he said to himself triumphantly.
>
> And he remembered his money, his shop, his house, the buying and selling, and Mironov's millions, and it was hard for him to understand why that man, called Vasili Brekhunov, had troubled himself with all those things with which he had been troubled.
>
> "Well, it was because he did not know what the real thing was," he thought, concerning that Vasili Brekhunov. "He did not know, but now I know and know for sure. Now I know!" And again he heard the voice of the one who had called him before. "I'm coming! Coming!" he responded gladly, and his whole being was filled with joyful emotion. He felt himself free and that nothing could hold him back any longer.[341]

Blanchot explains Brekhunov's gesture in the following way:

> It is a nocturnal gesture. It does not belong to the category of habitual acts, it is not even an inhabitual action. Nothing is accomplished by it. The intention that

first made him act - to warm Nikita, to warm himself close to the Sun of the Good has evaporated. The gesture is without purpose, without significance; it has no reality. "He lies down to die." Brekhunov, the decisive, enterprising man, even he can lie down only to die. It is death itself which all at once bends this robust body and lays it down in the white night. And this night does not frighten him; he does not refuse it or draw back from it, On the contrary, he hurries joyfully to meet it. But as he lies down in the night, it is, all the same upon Nikita that he lies, as if the night were still the hope and future of a human form, as if we could not die except by entrusting our death to someone else, to all the others, that it might await in them the icy depths of the future.[342]

At the beginning of this passage, Blanchot seemingly refuses to assign any meaning to Brekhunov's gesture. However, this gesture will attain meaning if we perceive it in the context of "Death as Possibility." This essay enables us to interpret Brekhunov's gesture as a desperate and futile attempt to stop the approach of the impersonal other night. There is no *je* in death, only an impersonal *il* and also an endless passivity of dying. According to Alain P. Toumayan, "Brekhunov's experience is an 'expérience limite', the experience of a most radical otherness..."[343] Blanchot's interpretation of this story is important because he claims, unlike Levinas, that the *other* night leads us into pure exteriority; it offers the experience of fundamental alterity. If this is the case then literature is capable to open the possibility of ethics. In Blanchot's interpretation, literature becomes the exposure to the strange and paradoxical presence of the Other who calls into question the supposed dominance of the subject.

In order to support this thesis, I will proceed with the interpretation of "The Outside, the Night." After Tolstoy,

Blanchot turns to Kafka and to his famous story "The Burrow." Most critics think that Kafka's story remained unfinished. It begins with the completion of the burrow that becomes a supposedly perfectly safe hiding place. However, although the narrator states that the burrow is perfect, during the course of the story it will become clear that it has one crucial flaw. The beast needs to go outside to replenish its reserves of food and the air comes into the burrow through the entrance. The entrance is the weak point of the burrow because it is also the place of entry for potential enemies.

After this realization, the beast is woken up by the strange and almost inaudible noise. This sound is pervasive and it can be heard anywhere in the burrow. Because of that, the beast is overwhelmed with the feeling of horror. The sound becomes more and more audible and it is slowly approaching. The beast starts to contemplate the possible encounter with the author of this noise and at that point Kafka's story stops.

As in the case of the myth of Orpheus, Blanchot's interpretation contains a surprising insight. Joseph Libertson correctly notices that "Blanchot treats the problem of the burrow as though there were no entrance, no irony of the troublesome and irreducible imperfection of the burrow's closure. The barely perceptible noise which comes to signify the approach of another animal is interpreted by Blanchot in the terms of proximity, as a necessary consequence of the very invulnerability of the burrow."[344] Therefore, in Blanchot's interpretation of the story, the threat does not come from the outside but from the burrow itself. Blanchot says:

> The more the burrow seems solidly closed to the outside, the greater the danger that you be closed in with the outside, delivered to the peril without any means of

> escape. And when every foreign threat seems shut out of this perfectly closed intimacy, then it is intimacy that becomes menacing foreignness. Then the essence of danger is at hand.[345]

Blanchot claims that the beast hears the approach of the *other* night. This *other* night is the inaccessible and inapproachable alterity. Dora Diamant reports that "The Burrow" was finished and that its ending contained the death of the narrator in the fight with the rival beast. According to Blanchot, this is impossible and the so called "decisive" combat can never happen. Kafka's story is about the approach of something that can never become actually present:

> What the beast senses in the distance -- that monstrous thing which eternally approaches it and works eternally at coming closer -- is itself. And if the beast could ever come into this thing's presence, what it would encounter would be its own absence: itself, but itself become the other, which it would not recognize, which it would not meet. The other night is always the other, and he who senses it becomes the other. He who approaches it departs from himself, is no longer he who approaches but he who turns away, goes hither and yon. He who, having entered the first night, seeks intrepidly to go toward its profoundest intimacy, toward the essential, hears at a certain moment the other night -- hears himself, hears the eternally reverberating echo of his own step, a step toward silence, toward the void. But the echo sends this step back to him as the whispering immensity, and the void is now a presence coming toward him.[346]

The most valuable insight in Blanchot's interpretation of Kafka's story is that the approach of alterity does not happen from the outside, but from the inside (from within the burrow). Joseph Libertson describes this approach in the following way:

To dig the burrow is to go to meet the other beast - to approach the Other. Proximity is interiority "in the exterior" as well as pre-originary "outside-inside." Thus, while the other beast is paradoxically "known" to the protagonist in *oubli,* it is also true that the protagonist's being is not exhausted by the proposition of his solitude in the burrow. "Where I am alone, I am not alone." It is perhaps for this reason that Kafka places him at repeated moments outside the burrow, close to the throng of animal traffic past the hidden entrance. Interiority must oversee itself from the exterior - from the perspective of its involvement with alterity. The other beast is "known" in another way as well. If it were to arrive - which it cannot (this impossibility is, to paraphrase Blanchot, both its "privation" and its "domination", since its approach is more compelling than any arrival) - it would look like the protagonist. It would in fact be the protagonist, but the protagonist "become other."[347]

This approach of the absolutely Other that comes from the inside can also be described with the help of some important passages from "Reality and Its Shadow." In this essay, Levinas claims that the temporality of the artwork is the temporality of the *meanwhile*. In the section dedicated to this notion,[348] Levinas claims that every artwork is essentially a statue, because it stops the flow of time. However, he also adds that the artwork is not just a simple stoppage of time, but also a delay of time behind itself. In the artwork, the eternal present becomes "an impersonal and anonymous instant." Because of that, the characters in a literary work are essentially prisoners. In the crucial passage, Levinas identifies the *meanwhile* as the time of dying:

> What is unique and poignant in this instant is due to the fact that it cannot pass. In dying, the horizon of the future is given, but the future as a promise of a new present is refused; one is in the interval, forever an interval. The

characters of certain tales by Edgar Allan Poe must have found themselves in this empty interval. A threat appears to them in the approach of such an empty interval; no move can be made to retreat from its approach, but this approach can never end. This is the anxiety which in other tales is prolonged like a fear of being buried alive. It is as though death were never dead enough, as though parallel with the duration of the living ran the eternal duration of the interval - the *meanwhile*.[349]

The temporality of the artwork is connected with dying and the *meanwhile* is the interval that never passes. As we already know, death cannot happen to me, because there is no "I" in dying. However, what we learn from this connection between the meanwhile and art is that death cannot happen in the present and therefore it can never become actually present.

In Blanchot's work, the *meanwhile* is described as the time of time's absence. He agrees with Levinas that the *meanwhile* is the temporality of art and says that literature is the realm where the time of time's absence rules. Literature is the realm of the interminable and incessant. However, Blanchot's writings again offer an important addition to Levinas's remarks on art and its temporality. The alterity that comes from the inside leads the writer into the region of the interminable and the incessant:

> When to write is to discover the interminable, the writer who enters this region does not leave himself behind in order to approach the universal. He does not move toward a surer world, a finer or better justified world where everything would be ordered according to the clarity of the impartial light of day. He does not discover the admirable language which speaks honorably for all. What speaks in him is the fact that, in one way or another, he is no longer himself; he isn't anyone any

more. The third person substituting for the "I": such is the solitude that comes to the writer on account of the work. It does not denote objective disinterestedness, creative detachment. It does not glorify consciousness in someone other than myself or the evolution of a human vitality which, in the imaginary space of the work of art, would retain the freedom to say "I." The third person is myself become no one, my interlocutor turned alien; it is my no longer being able, where I am, to address myself and the inability of whoever addresses me to say "I"; it is his not being himself.[350]

Blanchot agrees with Levinas that the temporality of the artwork is the temporality of the meanwhile. However, the encounter with the absolutely other (that does not come from the outside, but from the inside) lies at the basis of this temporality. Therefore, the temporality of the meanwhile is not just the temporality of dying and artwork, but also the temporality of the absolutely other.[351]

In the essay "The Trace of the Other", written three years after the publication of *Totality and Infinity*, Levinas revises some of his positions. This revision happens with the help of the notion of *trace* which "obliges with regard to the infinite, the absolutely other."[352] He thus poses the question: "Does there exist signifyingness of signification which would not be equivalent to the transmutation of the other into the same? Can there be something as strange as the experience of the absolutely exterior, as contradictory in its terms as heteronomous experience?"[353]

Levinas answers that the work is capable of offering the experience of the absolutely exterior and he adds that "a work is thus a relationship with the other who is reached without showing himself touched."[354] It is precisely in these terms that

Blanchot also describes the quest of Orpheus and his travel in the Underworld. Levinas also claims that that the relationship with the other is a relationship with the radical absence and that this absence actually prevents the transmutation of the other into the Same. The experience of radical absence is the necessary condition for the encounter with the other. The search for this absence that can never become presence lies at the basis of Orpheus's quest and it enables his relationship with the absolute alterity.

However, the important characteristic of this encounter is a strange temporality that does not correspond with our linear understanding of time. We must bear in mind that Orpheus can turn toward Eurydice (and consequently lose her), because his song, in which she is already lost, enables him to descend into the Underworld. The encounter with the other can happen because it has always already happened. This complicated and paradoxical temporal structure that contains a moment of encounter that must always precede itself is the main topic of Blanchot's essay "Encountering the Imaginary."

Blanchot begins with the question about the nature of the song of the Sirens. The song is described in two ways. First, as an inhuman song and as something that lies outside of the human realm. According to the second interpretation, the otherness of this song does not come from the outside, but from the inside. Blanchot writes:

> But, say others, the enchantment was stranger than that: it did nothing but reproduce the habitual song of men, and because the Sirens, who were only animals, quite beautiful because of the reflection of feminine beauty, could sing as men sing, they made the song so strange that they gave birth in anyone who heard it a suspicion

of the inhumanity of every human song. Is it through despair, then that men passionate for their own song came to perish? Through a despair very close to rapture. There was something wonderful in this real song, this common secret song, simple and everyday, that they had to recognize right away, sung in an unreal war by foreign, even imaginary powers, song of the abyss, that, once heard, would open an abyss in each word and would beckon those heard it to vanish into it.[355]

Blanchot then retells Ulysses's encounter with the Sirens and he offers his unique interpretation of this event. Alain P. Toumayan explains that Blanchot's interpretation of Ulysses's encounter with the Sirens offers "a clear, symmetrical reversal of the story of Orpheus."[356] At the first glance, it seems that Ulysses, unlike Orpheus, has won. His cunning enabled him to conquer the Sirens. How is this victory achieved? Blanchot claims that it is achieved through the passage from *je* to *il* that entails a temporal paradox: "To hear the Song of the Sirens, he had to stop being Ulysses and become Homer, but it is only in Homer's narrative that the actual meeting occurs in which Ulysses becomes the one who enters into that relationship with the power of the elements and the voice of the abyss."[357]

Basically, in his retelling of the myths of Orpheus and Ulysses, Blanchot explores the possibility that was already opened in Levinas's essay "Reality and Its Shadow." In this essay, Levinas notices the strange temporality of the work of art but, unlike Blanchot, he claims that this temporality is "something inhuman and monstrous."[358] This temporality is, as we already mentioned, identified as the time of dying. Precisely because death is something that cannot happen to me, because it includes passivity and a passage from *je* to *il*, Levinas will insist that art is irresponsible and therefore also unethical.

Blanchot's essays, on the other hand, tell us about the encounter with alterity. It includes the passage from *je* to *il* and its temporality is not linear. Again, we will repeat the words of John Gregg in order to describe Ulysses encounter with the Sirens (and the encounter between Ahab and Moby Dick): it is the encounter "that always already has had to have taken place in order to occur."[359] This encounter introduces an interval or the delay in time itself. Precisely this brings back to the temporality of the *meanwhile* and substantiates the thesis that the *meanwhile* is both the time of the artwork and the time of the Other.[360] If this is the case then literature is not unethical, but actually opens the possibility of ethics.

CONCLUSION:
LITERATURE AND THE POSSIBILITY OF ETHICS

Orpheus was an important member of Jason's crew and his singing enabled them to overcome the insurmountable obstacle during their return home after they recovered the Golden Fleece. His singing and lyre playing saved Jason and the Argonauts from the Sirens. The song of Orpheus was stronger than the song of the Sirens; by echoing their song Orpheus managed to confuse the Sirens and to significantly reduce their allure.

In the 12th book of *The Odyssey*, Circe warns Ulysses about the Sirens. Orpheus is already dead and torn to pieces and Ulysses is aware that he must follow Circe's advice in order to survive the encounter with the Sirens. He does not possess the power of Orpheus, but he is the master of cunning and trickery. Therefore, he orders his men to stuff their ears with beeswax so that they cannot hear the enchanting song. This simple trick enables them to pass safely. However, Ulysses is a curious man and wants to hear the alluring song of the Sirens, so he also orders his sailors to tie him to a mast. This way he was able to hear the song, but also to remain relatively safe. I say "relatively safe" because, after surviving the Encounter, he is drawn into another song that is entitled *The Odyssey*.[361]

As we already know, the first essay in Blanchot's *The Book to Come* is devoted to Ulysses's encounter with the Sirens.[362] This encounter offers "a clear, symmetrical reversal of the story of Orpheus."[363] and it functions as another example of the fundamental experience of literature.[364] In Blanchot's retelling, both stories speak about the (im)possibility of literature. On this basis, I will use Ulysses's encounter with the Sirens to illuminate (and underline) the main points of this study.

Blanchot's essay poses the important question: who is the narrator of this encounter? The answer to this kind of question is often guided by *a common sense reductiveness*. As we already saw in the case of Dejan Ilić's attempts to interpret *Infinitive*, this perspective emphasizes the role of the author. According to this usual account, narration serves its author as a means for achieving understanding. The author is the master of narration. In this conception, language is understood as the written (or oral) expression of what needs to be communicated. The starting point of this conception is the understanding of an author as someone who straightforwardly expresses what troubles him or what happened to him. Also, an understanding of truth as correspondence is crucial for this conception. The author and the narrator are usually joined in one person and the narration is organized on the principle of fidelity; either it is a fidelity to the event that actually happened or fidelity to the idea that the author managed to successfully transcribe in the work of art.

"Encountering the Imaginary" shows all the limitations of this kind of approach to literature. In his essay "Blanchot, Narration, and the Event", Lars Iyer correctly notices that Blanchot's essay poses the following questions: "What if the identity of the teller is given in the articulation of the tale?

What if there would be not only no tale without a teller, but no teller without a tale? What if tale and teller were bound up in an interdependence that is far more complex than hitherto supposed?"[365]

Like Borges, Blanchot also amalgamates the figures of Ulysses and Homer together and claims that *The Odyssey* was written by Ulysses who managed to survive his encounter with the Sirens.[366] In order to give an account of his experience, he had to become Homer. Ulysses's victory is only apparent because the song of the Sirens ultimately wins. The passage from *je* to *il* is the fate that befalls Ulysses. Lars Iyer writes:

> Yes, Ulysses is a cowardly figure who seeks to preserve himself against his disappearance, but he really does "fall" or "disappear" nonetheless; the encounter with the Sirens overcomes his mastery. Although we can imagine Ulysses regaling Penelope and Telemachus with stories of his exploits, there is one tale he would be unable to recount. If Ulysses were to begin one day on a book of reminiscences, if he were, as Blanchot suggests, to become Homer himself and tell the story of his exploits by narrating the first story, an entire dimension of the encounter with the Sirens would hold itself in reserve. But it is this encounter with the Sirens that allows the author to assume the power to write. Ulysses-Homer could not begin his book without having undertaken the journey as Ulysses.
>
> It follows that for every Homer, every novelist, there is, for Blanchot, always and already a drowned Ulysses.[367]

Why drowned Ulyssses? Because, according to Geoffrey Hartmann and Kevin Hart, "literature for Blanchot indicates our relation with death; more, it discloses that death is itself divided into the negative and the neutral; and this neutral aspect of death - namely, dying - reveals that our response to the world cannot always take the form of possibility or power but is marked by a passivity beyond all usual oppositions of activity and passivity."[368] On the one hand, death can be perceived as the ultimate possibility. Our analysis of the power of naming has shown that negation can indeed enable the mastery over things. However, this mastery has its price because the real objects are annihilated in this creation of meaning. Therefore, our language enables us the creation of meaning by giving us *presence sheltered in absence.*

What is possibility on one side, turns out into the impossibility on the other. In *The Space of Literature,* by turning to Kafka, Blanchot makes this impossibility of a possibility visible. He again employs the temporal paradox from the myth of Orpheus and Ulysses's encounter with the Sirens and associates it with writing.[369] The writing and the production of narrative are associated with the impossibility of death. Blanchot claims that *my* death can never become *mine*, because it constitutes a moment that never properly arrives (it is movement toward a point that can never be attained) and my consciousness becomes dissolved into unbearable anonymity. There is a crucial connection between art and death together with a removal of me from myself. The essential experience of writing and narrating is the passage from *je* to *il* that divests me of the power to say *I*.

In his commonsensical approach, Dejan Ilić does not take into account the paradoxical construction (and temporality) of *Infinitive*. Because of that he claims that *Infinitive* is not even a literary work of art. However, precisely the opposite is the case, because Ugričić's work makes visible

both the non-coincidence of literature with itself and its (im)
possibility.[370]

Dejan Ilić equates the narrator of *Infinitive* with the
real-life figure of Sreten Ugričić. However, even at the first
glance, false quotations, erroneous attributions and deliberate
mystifications undermine any straightforward assumptions
about the narrator of *Infinitive*. Things become even more
complex when we realize that Ugričić's book is based on
the same temporal paradox as the narration about Ulysses's
encounter with the Sirens. Since *Infinitive* is a monograph, it
has its origin in *The Axiological Infinitive*. However, this origin
will always remain unattainable and infinitely absent, or, to be
more precise, it will become present as absent on the pages
of Ugričić's *Infinitive*. Therefore, we can understand *Infinitive*
as the perpetual quest for its own origin; as a work which
continually investigates its own possibility.

Sreten Ugričić and Ulysses narrate their encounter, but
in order to do so they stop being themselves. Ulysses stops
being who he is and becomes Homer and this passage from *je*
to *il* enables him to hear the song of the Sirens all over again; to
become enchanted by it, but also to lose himself and to dream
that he is capable of following it to its source. This is how he is
lured into the realm of imaginary that is governed by the time
of time's absence.[371] As Vivian Liska notices, "the complex
structure implied in the song's promise of a coming narration
of past events embedded in the very narration of these events
evokes a disrupted, nonlinear temporality."[372] Therefore, the
song of the Sirens is only a promise of a song still to come (that
might be *The Odyssey* itself).

Only in Homer's work the encounter really takes place and common sense tells us that it needs to have preceded the narration about it. However, in Blanchot's retelling, it becomes clear that the encounter can take place only as a consequence of a narration. And even when it occurs, it can only refer to the abyssal absence that constituted it. This the reason why the song of the Sirens can never become truly present. Its main characteristic is seduction and a promise of a beginning (origin) that will remain infinitely absent.[373]

Ulysses needed to become Homer in order to narrate his encounter and Henri-Alban had to become Alain-Fournier in order to tell us about what happened on June 1, 1905, on Ascension Thursday. The encounter with Yvonne de Quiévrecourt that happened on that day will become both the central event of his masterpiece *The Lost Estate,* but also the most important event of his whole life. We know that the passage from *je* to *il* was a necessary condition for the narration of this event, but we also have to illuminate who Henri-Alban actually met. He met the person who was always already irretrievably lost. She was never real, but always doubled in herself and she belonged to the realm of imaginary. She was never really present and her enchantment (and power) lies in her presence as absence.

It is true that the origin of *The Lost Estate* is the encounter that took place in Paris on June 1, 1905. However, this encounter had a paradoxical nature. The narration of *The Lost Estate* is a movement toward Yvonne, toward the origin of a narrative that can never be attained. Lars Iyer describes this movement in the following way:

> For Blanchot, Alain-Fournier's *récit* testifies in an extraordinary way to the encounter with the Sirens that

redoubles his enigmatic encounter with Yvonne. True, Alain-Fournier met Yvonne and was intrigued by her. He set out to write a work that related this encounter and this fascination. But in writing *The Lost Estate*, in recasting his adventure on an ideal plane, apparently subordinating words and sentences in order to tell his tale, Alain-Fournier removes himself yet further from her. Writing of Yvonne, he loses her anew and has to make do with a papery Yvonne, made of words. But the redoubled loss of Yvonne demands another loss, for Alain-Fournier yields himself up as a writer, that is, as the one who freely, sovereignly, would sign his name to the book that is ostensibly his. Alain-Fournier does not do so voluntarily, nor, afterwards, is it given to him to remember, at least in a straightforward and unambiguous way, the vicissitudes of literary creation. Nevertheless, the attempt to write about a marvelous moment itself requires his "disappearance" as an author. It is as if the act of narrating set a trap for him. To take up writing, to narrate an encounter, is to give oneself up as a lure to the trap that threatens to snap shut. That the author escapes it, recovering in order to finish a work, is not a tribute to his ingenuity. To be sure, Alain-Fournier finishes *The Lost Estate*, but his narrative depends upon the other journey he was compelled to undertake as soon as he took up his pen. He is lost, as Blanchot writes, "in a preliminary Narrative," in an event that begins when he starts to write.[374]

Blanchot uses the myth of Orpheus and Ulysses's encounter with the Sirens to tell us something about the (im)possibility of literature and this (im)possibility is associated with the passage from *je* to *il*. This loss of personality (and the inability to subsume the work of art under terms of decision and intention) leads to a strange realm that is governed by the time of time's absence. Emmanuel Levinas does not offer a coherent aesthetic theory, but he shares Blanchot's views about the paradoxical nature of literature. In some essays (e.g. "Reality and Its Shadow"), what especially interests Levinas is the relationship between ethics and aesthetics. Levinas asserts that, for the artist, even his own life looks like an adventure from the book. Even before he can be called an artist, he is always already in the realm of imaginary where he loses the power to speak in the first person. Although he agrees with Blanchot that literature is characterized by the passage from *je* to *il* and by the strange temporality of the time of time's absence (the temporality of the *meanwhile*), Levinas shows hostility toward art and he claims that its paradoxicality and (im)possibility prevents it from being ethical. In his work, precisely the passage from *je* to *il* and the time of time's absence (which Levinas terms the *meanwhile*) block the possibility of a relationship between ethics and aesthetics.

In his essay "Reality and Its Shadow", Levinas asserts that the basic procedure of art "consists in substituting for the object its image."[375] This process opens the realm of imaginary. This is how the relationship with the real object is neutralized and this neutralization is the reason why Yvonne will always remain unattainable for Alain-Fournier. For Levinas, this neutralization is the main reason for aesthetic disengagement from the world.

Levinas also claims that images, like the song of the Sirens, have the ability to fascinate and to enchant. They have this ability because they are essentially musical. Levinas uses the notion of rhythm to describe this enchantment and writes that "rhythm represents a unique situation where we cannot speak of consent, assumption, initiative or freedom, because the subject is caught up and carried away by it."[376] He understands rhythm as the passage from *je* to *il*; as the transition from oneself to anonymity in which subject ceases to experience himself as himself.

According to Levinas, participation and rhythm constitute the essential features of art and their role is to enable the passage from oneself to anonymity. Precisely this impersonal existence blocks any possibility for the appearance of ethics. This happens because the main characteristic of this impersonal existence is, for Levinas, the loss of agency which is the necessary condition for the appearance of ethics.

In "Reality and Its Shadow", Levinas also describes the temporality of the artwork as the temporality of the *meanwhile*. For Levinas, every artwork is essentially a statue because it freezes the flow of time. The temporality of artwork is not linear, but circular. The characters in the novel are stuck in the eternal present that is immune to the future. Art stops the flow of time, making it essentially inhuman. The temporality of artwork is described by both Levinas and Blanchot as the time of dying. This temporality is actually the interval that never passes:

> What is unique and poignant in this instant is due to the fact that it cannot pass. In dying, the horizon of the future is given, but the future as a promise of a new present is refused; one is in the interval, forever an interval. The characters of certain tales by Edgar Allan Poe must have found themselves in this empty interval. A threat appears to them in the approach of such an empty interval; no move can be made to retreat from its approach, but this approach can never end. This is the anxiety which in other tales is prolonged like a fear of being buried alive. It is as though death were never dead enough, as though parallel with the duration of the living ran the eternal duration of the interval - the *meanwhile*.[377]

Levinas also claims that in this time of time's absence the assumption of responsibility is impossible. Art turns time into fate and because of that "there is something wicked and egoist and cowardly in artistic enjoyment. There are times when one can be ashamed of it, as of feasting during a plague."[378]

However, in his essay "The Other in Proust",[379] Levinas offers a different perspective on art. According to this perspective, art can be ethical because it is an encounter with the absolutely other. Levinas argues that the mystery at the heart of *The Captive* is the mystery of the other:

> The story of Albertine... is the narrative of the inner life's sudden intensification brought about by an insatiable curiosity about the alterity of the other, at once empty and inexhaustible. The reality of Albertine is her evanescence in her very captivity - a reality made up of nothingness. She is a prisoner, though she has already disappeared, and she has disappeared though a prisoner - since despite the strictest surveillance she retains a dimension of secrecy. The objective facts Proust is able to gather about her after her death do not dispel the doubt that surrounded her when her lies disguised her fugues. When she is no longer there to defend her absence, when evidence abounds, leaving no room for doubt, the doubt remains intact. Albertine's nothingness uncovers her total alterity.[380]

The passage from *je* to *il* and the paradoxical temporality of the time of time's absence are necessary for a non-totalizing encounter with the other. In the story about the relationship between the narrator of *Remembrance of Things Past* and Albertine, we can also recognize the already described figures of Alain-Fournier and Yvonne. What enchants Alain-Fournier and Marcel is the infinite absence of Yvonne and Albertine. Yvonne and Albertine were never actually present, but always already doubled in themselves and therefore situated in the realm of imaginary that is governed by the time of time's absence. However, precisely because they are situated in the realm of imaginary they are capable of remaining absolutely other.

Therefore, an essential ambiguity is produced by the substitution of the object by its image. This substitution possesses a strange temporality and in Levinas's essay on Proust it is not perceived as something negative, but as something that opens the possibility of ethics (it allows Albertine to remain unattainable and absolutely other).

Both Blanchot and Levinas agree that the passage from *je* to *il* is visible in Proust's work. Levinas writes about the self-reflexivity of Proust's experience in his essay and this is how Blanchot describes it in "The Experience of Proust":

> Where is this experience produced? In what "time"? In what world? And who is the person who has experienced it? Is it Proust, the actual Proust, the son of Adrien Proust? Is it Proust already become become a writer and telling in the fifteen volumes of his grandiose work about how his calling was formed [...]? Not at all as we know. None of these Prousts is at issue. The dates, if they were necessary, would prove it, since this revelation to which *Le temps retrouvé* alludes to us to the decisive event that will set in motion the work that is not yet written, takes place - in the book - during the war, at a time when *Swann* is already published and when a large part of the work is composed. Is Proust not telling the truth then? But he does not owe us this truth and he would certainly be unable to tell it to us. He could only express it, make it real, concrete and true, by projecting it into the very time of which it is the implementation, whence the work draws its necessity: the time of the narrative, when,

> although he says "I", it is no longer the real Proust or the writer Proust who has the ability to speak, but their metamorphosis into that shadow that is the narrator turned into a "character" of the book, the one who in the story writes a story that is the work itself, and produces in his turn other metamorphoses of himself that are the different "I's" whose experiences he recounts. Proust has become elusive, because he has become inseparable from the quadruple metamorphosis that is only the movement of the book toward the work.[381]

The passage from *je* to *il* proves to be crucial because it is not a simple division within the "I", but something more profound that shatters the linear conception of time. In the passage from *je* to *il*, "I" can become the other within the self and this metamorphosis is necessary for the ethical encounter with the absolutely other. Therefore, the encounter with the other is doubled in itself and this doubling enables the emergence of ethics. This is the reason why the non-totalizing encounter with the other can be described as an encounter "that always already has had to have taken place in order to occur."[382]

This brings us back to the story about Ulysses. *The Odyssey* is a narrative about the return home and it is usually described as inherently conservative (a story about self-identity). In Levinas's terms, Ulysses's journey home could be described as the identification of the same in the I. Ulysses wants to become who he already is - the king of Ithaca. According to this usual interpretation, if there is any alterity in this story, it is only "spurious alterity."

However, if we again use Levinas's terms, we will notice that Blanchot interprets this story as "a movement of the same unto the other which never returns to the same."[383] This interpretation opens the possibility of a relationship between literature and ethics. Although Ulysses seemingly defeated the Sirens, he had to go through the passage from *je* to *il* and to become Homer in order to give us the account of his "victory." In Blanchot's retelling of Ulyses's encounter with the Sirens, the passage from *je* to *il* and the secret law of narrative (temporal inversion) become necessary conditions for the introduction of fundamental alterity.

NOTES

1   See Sreten Ugričić, *Infinitiv*, Stubovi kulture, Beograd, 1997, pp. 53-60. All translations from this book will be mine.

2   Aristotle, *On Rhetoric: A Theory of Civic Discourse* (translated by George A Kennedy), Oxford University Press, New York and Oxford, 2007, p. 76 (1366b). The translation of W. Rhys Roberts is perhaps a little bit clearer: "The Noble is that which is both desirable for its own sake and also worthy of praise; or that which is both good and also pleasant because good. If this is a true definition of the Noble, it follows that virtue must be noble, since it is both a good thing and also praiseworthy." See Aristotle, *Rhetoric* (translated by W. Rhys Roberts), Dover Publications, New York, 2004.

3   See Jorge Luis Borges, *The Book of Imaginary Beings*, Cape, London, 1970.

4   John Burnett, *Early Greek Philosophy*, A. & C. Black, London, 1920, p. 302.

5   Patricia Hurd, *Anaxagoras of Clazomenae: Fragments and Testimonia*, University of Toronto Press Incorporated, Toronto, 2007, p. 75.

6   See Sigmund Freud, *The Interpretation of Dreams*, MacMillan, New York, 1927.

7   See Jorge Luis Borges, "Pierre Menard, Author of the *Quixote*", in: *Labyrinths: Selected Stories and other Writings*, New Directions Publishing Corporation, New York, 1964, pp. 49-56.

8   Jorge Luis Borges, *The Aleph and Other Stories 1933-1969*, Bantam Books Inc., New York, 1971, pp. 167-168. About this quotation Emir Rodriguez Monegal writes: "More important than the success of the hoax is the fact that Borges had finally discovered a format for his future fiction which was unmistakably original. It was a combination of fiction and essay – two literary genres that convention had generally kept apart but that in Borges's peculiar view of

reality were bound to mesh. By pretending that a story has already been told in a published book, Borges could offer, instead of a retelling of the story, a critique of it. The narrative discourse was submerged, masked under the critical discourse. Fiction became truth because what was invented was not the fact that the story may have happened (a commonplace task in disguising fiction but that the story pre-existed its telling). By pretending that the story had already been invented, Borges again claimed the rights of a reader, not of an author." Emir Rodriguez Monegal, *Jorge Luis Borges: A Literary Biography*, E.P. Dutton, New York, 1978, p. 265.

9   François Truffaut, *Hitchcock,* 1978, Paladin, London, pp. 157-158.

10 Slavoj Žižek, *The Sublime Object of Ideology*, Verso, London and New York, 2008, pp. 183-184.

11 Dejan Ilić, "Postoje tri Eudoksa: prvi je ovaj naš", in: *Reč*, vol. 4, no. 40 (1997), pp. 177-180. All translations from this text will be mine.

12 Dejan Ilić, "'Čudotvorni' performativ", in: *Reč*, vol. 5. no. 42 (1998), pp. 143-148. All translations from this text will be mine.

13 See Martin Heidegger, "The Nature of Language", in: *On the Way to Language*, Harper & Row Publishers Inc., New York, 1982, p. 58.

14 After Dejan Ilić published his review, Sreten Ugričić replied to him in his text "About Himself." I did not use the argumentation from Ugričić's text because I was more interested in the general perspective of Ilić's texts. What also interested me were the consequences of this perspective. This chapter is constructed as a dialogue with Dejan Ilić about the basic assumptions for the interpretation of literature. For another perspective on the whole problem of *Infinitive* see: Sreten Ugričić, "O sebi", in: *Reč*, vol. 5, no. 41 (1998), pp. 157-166.

15 Dejan Ilić, "'Čudotvorni' performativ", in: *Reč*, vol. 5, no. 42 (1998), p. 143.

16 The third chapter of this book will provide another perspective on the problem of the cause of a work.

17 W.K Wimsatt and M.C. Beardsley, "The Affective Fallacy", in: David Lodge (ed.), *20th Century Literary Criticism: A Reader*, Longman, London, 1972, pp. 345-359.

18 Jacques Derrida, "Signature, Event, Context", in: *Limited Inc*, Northwestern University Press, Evanston, 1988, p. 8.

19 See Plato, *Phaedrus*, Oxford University Press, Oxford and New York, 2002, pp. 68-69. A very important analysis of this this story can be found in: Jacques Derrida, "Plato's Pharmacy", in: *Dissemination*, The University Of Chicago Press, Chicago, 1981, pp. 65-173.

20 John Searle, "Reiterating the Differences: A Reply to Derrida", in: *Glyph*, vol. 1 (1977), p. 201.

21 *Ibid*, p. 201.

22 "I am ready to agree with the ones who claim that to understand some text means to understand what the author wanted to say. And, furthermore, that language gives the author the options to actualize and to record with words what he wants to say, and that the reader is capable of understanding what the author wrote. Starting from this position, as I did before, I wrote about Sreten Ugričić's book Infinitive." See Dejan Ilić, "'Čudotvorni' performativ", in: *Reč*, vol. 5, no. 42 (1998), p. 143.

23 John Searle, "Reiterating the Differences: A Reply to Derrida", in: *Glyph*, vol. 1 (1977), p. 201.

24 Jacques Derrida, "Limited Inc a b c...", in: *Limited Inc*, Northwestern University Press, Evanston, 1988, p. 62.

25 *Ibid*, p. 62.

26   *Ibid*, p. 62.

27   This sentence of Nietzsche is also examined in: Jacques Derrida, *Spurs: On Nietzsche's Styles*, University of Chicago Press, Chicago,1978. I will come back to this question in the second chapter of this book in relation to the sentence of Kafka's novel *The Castle*: "The head clerk called."

28   It is not impossible to use the metaphor of a line in this case, but we will need the one from "The Death and the Compass". At the very end of this story, after he finished listening to Scharlach's explanation about his trap Lönnrot points to the flaw in the construction of Scharlach's murderous maze: "'In your labyrinth there are three lines too many,' he said at last. 'I know of one Greek labyrinth which is a single straight line. Along that line so many philosophers have lost themselves that a mere detective might well do so, too. Scharlach, when in some other incarnation you hunt me, pretend to commit (or do commit) a crime at A, then a second crime at B, eight kilometers from A, then a third crime at C, four kilometers from A and B, half-way between the two. Wait for me afterwards at D, two kilometers from A and C, again halfway between both. Kill me at D, as you are now going to kill me at Triste-le-Roy.' 'The next time I kill you,' replied Scharlach, 'I promise you that labyrinth, consisting of a single line which is invisible and unceasing.'" See Jorge Luis Borges, "Death and the Compass", in: *Labyrinths: Selected Stories and other Writings*, New Directions Publishing Corporation, New York, 1964, p. 94.

29   Maurice Blanchot, "Literature and the Right to Death", in: *The Work of Fire*, Stanford University Press, Stanford, 1995, pp. 300-344.

30   *Ibid*, p. 303.

31   *Ibid*, p. 303.

32   Jorge Luis Borges, "My Books", in: *The Book of Sand*, Penguin, Harmondsworth, 1979, p. 178.

33 Maurice Blanchot, "Literature and the Right to Death", in: *The Work of Fire*, Stanford University Press, Stanford, 1995, p. 369.

34 Dejan Ilić, "'Čudotvorni' performativ", in: *Reč*, vol. 5, no. 42 (1998), p. 143.

35 This is the reason why Montaigne in his *Essays* writes: "Et il y a autant de différence entre nous et nous-mêmes qu'entre nous et un autre." See Michel de Montaigne, *Essais - Livre II*, Guy de Pernon/numlivres.fr, 2010, p. 26 (epub). Also, Jean-François Lyotard draws our attention to something very important in his work *The Differend: Phrases in Dispute* (fragments 51 and 52): "When I speak of the 'subject of uttering' in a phrase, the addressor instance of this phrase is placed in the situation of the referent instance of the current phrase. Each bear the same proper name (if they are named). The two phrase universes are not equivalent, however. For example, I relate that Kant writes of the French Revolution that it aroused the enthusiasm of its spectators. 'Kant' is the 'subject of uttering' in the phrase 'The French Revolution aroused the enthusiasm of its spectators', but he is the referent (or 'subject of the utterance') in the phrase (in which 'I' am the 'subject of uttering'): 'Kant states that the French Revolution (etc.) .' If Kant were not the subject of the utterance in 'my' phrase (the second one), how could I say that he is the subject of the uttering in the first? The name he bears is a received one (though not necessary from 'me'), and it may be that every proper name is a received one. The conversion of a proper name from the position of "subject of the uttering" to that of "subject of the utterance" is equivalent to its displacement from the situation of addressor in the universe of a current phrase 'p' to that of a referent in the universe of a current phrase 'q'. This conversion requires at least two phrases, and these seem like they should be successive. The someone else can bear the same name. For example, the author of 'The Conflict with the Faculty of Law' signs the phrase about the French Revolution with the name 'Kant'. Phrase (1) is: 'The French Revolution aroused the enthusiasm of peoples'; the signature-phrase (2) is: 'Kant states that the

French Revolution (etc.)." It is observed that the addressor of phrase (2) remains unnamed: who speaks? It could be 'Kant' or someone else, but there needs to be phrase (3) to name him (of the type: 'Kant' (or x) states that 'Kant states that the French Revolution (etc.)." In any case, what seems important is that at least two phrases be linked together, such as the second assigns to the first an addressor left unnamed in the first and placed in the situation of referent in the second." See Jean-François Lyotard, *The Differend: Phrases in Dispute*, University of Minnesota Press, Minneapolis, 1988, p. 34.

36 In my research relating to this text, the following work was very helpful: Novica Milić, "Od Pjera Menara do Don Kihota", in : *PH5- godišnjak za poetička i hermeneutička istraživanja*, Čigoja, Beograd, 2001, pp. 154-214. This text led me to other interesting literature that I used in the construction of my analysis: Enrique Sacerio-Gari: "Towards Pierre Menard", in: *Modern Language Notes*, vol. 95, no. 2 (March 1980), pp. 460-471, John T. Irwin, "Mysteries We Reread, Mysteries of Rereading: Poe, Borges, and Analytic Detective Story", in: *Modern Language Notes*, vol. 101, no. 5 (December 1986), pp. 1168-1215, Roberto González Echevarría, "Borges and Derrida", in: Harold Bloom (ed.), *Jorge Luis Borges*, Chelsea House Publishers, New York, 1986, pp. 227-234, Ion T. Agheana, "Borges 'Creator' of Cervantes. Cervantes 'Precursor' of Borges", *Revista de Estudios Hispanicos* (Universidad de Puerto Rico), IX, 1982, pp. 17-22.

37 In his "Preface" to the First Edition of *A Universal History of Iniquity* Borges wrote: "I sometimes think that good readers are poets as singular, and as awesome, as great authors themselves... Reading, meanwhile, is an activity subsequent to writing—more resigned, more civil, more intellectual." Jorge Luis Borges, *A Universal History of Iniquity*, in: *Collected Fictions*, Penguin Books, London and New York, 1998, p. 3.

38 Jorge Luis Borges, "Pierre Menard, Author of the *Quixote*", in: *Labyrinths: Selected Stories and Other Writings*, New Directions Publishing Corporation, New York, 1964, pp. 52-53.

39 Jorge Luis Borges, "The Wall and the Books", in: *Selected Non-Fictions,* Penguin Books, London and New York, 2000, p. 346. It can be useful to compare Borges and Derrida at this point: "But is it by chance that the book is, first and foremost, volume? And that the meaning of meaning (in the general sense of meaning and not in the sense of signalization) is infinite implication, the indefinite referral of signifier to signifier? And that its force is a certain pure and infinite equivocality which gives signified meaning no respite, no rest, but engages it in its own economy so that it always signifies again and differs? Except in the *Livre irréalisé* by Mallarmé, that which is written is never identical to itself." Jacques Derrida, *Writing and Difference*, Routledge, London and New York, 2007, p. 29.

40 "I only show that I have understood an author when I can act in his spirit; when, without diminishing his individuality, I can translate him and transform him in many ways." Cited in: Daniel Balderston, *Out of Context: Historical Reference and the Representation of Reality in Borges*, Duke University Press, Durham, 1993, p. 21.

41 Miguel de Cervantes Saavedra, *The Ingenious Hidalgo Don Quixote de la Mancha*, Penguin Books, London, 2001, p. 11. In his text about *Don Quixote*, Bruce W. Wardropper makes an interesting observation: "I like to think that some of the inspiration for *Don Quixote* may have come from yet another example of spurious history: Miguel de la Luna's *Historia Verdadera del rey don Rodrigo, compuesta por Albucácim Tárif.* Part I of this *true history* appeared in Granada in 1592 and part II in 1600, 'tres años antes y cinco después del falso hallazgo de los libros plúmbeos que problaron de mártires fantásticos el Sacro Monte de aquella ciudad', comments Menéndez Pidal significantly. Miguel de Luna, the official Arabic interpreter to Phillip II, had the gall to dedicate to his sovereign this egregious example of intellectual dishonesty. He claimed to be merely a translator of a work written in the eighth century by Albucácim Tárif, a Moor alleged to have had access to King Roderick's archives and to letters written by Florinda and Don Pelayo. To give his work the air of authenticity Luna entered into the margins the alleged Arabic original

of words he had supposedly found difficult to translate. Given the fraudulent nature of his undertaking, he comes perilously close to blasphemy when in his preface he has Albucácim invoke God's help: 'solo Dios criador, y sumo hazedor de todas las cosas criadas en este mundo..., a quien humilmente suplico me dè aliento para que sin genero de inuencion pueda contar con verdad clara, y abierta la historia del sucesso de la guerra de España.' God is called upon to ber witness to the truth of this fake history.... I cannot, of course, prove that Cervantes saw in Albucácim the progenitor of Cide Hamete Benengeli, but the point is that, at the time he was composing *Don Quixote,* such liberties were being taken with history. Cervantes does with pleasant irony what Luna does with deadly seriousness of a forger. Bruce W. Wardropper, "*Don Quixote*: Story or History?", in: *Cervantes's 'Don Quixote': A Casebook,* Oxford University Press, Oxford, 2005, pp. 151-152.

42   Miguel de Cervantes Saavedra, *The Ingenious Hidalgo Don Quixote de la Mancha*, Penguin Books, London, 2001, p. 73.

43   *Ibid*, pp. 74-75.

44   Miguel de Cervantes Saavedra, *The Ingenious Hidalgo Don Quixote de la Mancha*, Penguin Books, London, 2001, p. 76.

45   Jacques Derrida, "Limited Inc a b c...", in: *Limited Inc*, Northwestern University Press, Evanston, 1988, p. 49.

46   See Michel Foucault, "What is an Author?", in: Paul Rabinow (ed.), *The Foucault Reader*, Pantheon Books, New York, 1984, pp. 101-120.

47   *Ibid,* p. 108.

48   Michel Sanouillet and Elmer Peterson (eds.), *The Writings of Marcel Duchamp*, Da Capo Press, New York, 1989, p. 5.

49 Michel Foucault, "What is an Author?", in: Paul Rabinow (ed.), *The Foucault Reader*, Pantheon Books, New York, 1984, p. 112.

50 Can we really believe, without any trace of doubt, in the presented informations about Sreten Ugričić? All these fake quotations, false attributions and deliberate mystification seriously undermine any straightforward assumptions about the author and the narrator of *Infinitive*.

51 Giorgio Agamben, "Author as Gesture", in: *Profanations*, Zone Books, New York, 2007, pp. 71-72.

52 See Dejan Ilić, "Postoje tri Eudoksa: prvi je ovaj naš", in: *Reč*, vol. 4, no. 40 (1997), p. 177.

53 Sreten Ugričić, *Infinitiv*, Stubovi kulture, Beograd, 1997, p. 7.

54 *Ibid*, p. 218.

55 Dejan Ilić, "Postoje tri Eudoksa: prvi je ovaj naš", in: *Reč*, vol. 4, no. 40 (1997), p. 177.

56 Dejan Ilić, "'Čudotvorni' performativ", in: *Reč*, vol. 5, no. 42 (1998), p. 145.

57 For example, in his text "The Limits of Interpretation", Dejan Ilić claims that M. H. Abrams is right when he says that an interpretation of some literary work is correct if it is consistently formulated and founded on true interpretative statements. After the analysis of Ilić's essays the only conclusion is that he understands truth as *adaequatio*. But, in the case of *Infinitive*, we can ask the following question: correspondence or accordance with what? See Dejan Ilić, *Osam i po ogleda iz razumevanja*, Fabrika knjiga, Beograd, 2008, pp. 9-46. In contrast to this, Martin Heidegger writes at the beginning of *Being and Time*: "Furthermore, because logos lets something be seen, it can therefore be true or false. But everything depends on staying clear of any concept of truth construed in the sense of 'correspondence' or 'accordance.' This idea is by

no means the primary one in the concept of *alētheia*. The 'being true' of logos as *alētheuein* means: to take beings that are being talked about in *legein* as *apophainesthai* out of their concealment; to let them be seen as something unconcealed (*alēthes*); to discover them. Similarly, 'being false', *pseudesthai*, is tantamount to deceiving in the sense of covering up: putting something in front of something else (by way of letting it be seen) and thereby passing it off as something it is not." Martin Heidegger, *Being and Time*, State University of New York Press, Albany, 1996, p. 29.

58 Jacques Derrida, "Signature, Event, Context", in: *Limited Inc*, Northwestern University Press, Evanston, p. 18.

59 Jacques Derrida, "The Law of Genre", in: *Acts of Literature*, Routledge, New York and London, 1992, pp. 221-252.

60 See also Jacques Derrida, "Before the Law", in: *Acts of Literature*, Routledge, New York and London, 1992, pp. 181-220.

61 Dejan Ilić, "Postoje tri Eudoksa: prvi je ovaj naš", in: *Reč*, vol. 4, no. 40 (1997), p. 177.

62 Maurice Blanchot, "The Song of the Sirens", in: *The Station Hill Blanchot Reader*, Station Hill, Barrytown, 1999, pp. 443-450.

63 See Leslie Hill, "The (Im)Possibility of Literature", in: *Blanchot – Extreme Contemporary*, Routledge, London and New York, 1997, pp. 53-102. Can we follow Blanchot and claim that the author (or maybe we should call him narrator) of *Infinitive* only encounters *The Axiological Infinitive* on the pages of *Infinitive*? But, also this encounter is what enables him to write *Infinitive*. This (im)possibility of the encounter will be the main topic of my third chapter.

64 See Sreten Ugričić, *Infinitiv*, Stubovi kulture, Beograd, 1997, pp. 201-207.

65 Maurice Blanchot, "The Original Experience", in: *The Space of Literature,* University of Nebraska Press, Lincoln, 1989, p. 244.

66 Dejan Ilić, "Postoje tri Eudoksa: prvi je ovaj naš", in: *Reč,* vol. 4, no. 40 (1997), pp. 178, 179.

67 Dejan Ilić, "'Čudotvorni' performativ", in: *Reč,* vol. 5, no. 42 (1998), p. 145.

68 Franz Kafka, *Blue Octavo Notebooks,* Exact Change, Cambridge, 1991, p. 15.

69 Maurice Blanchot, "Kafka and the Work's Demand", in: *The Space of Literature,* University of Nebraska Press, Lincoln, 1989, p. 80.

70 Dejan Ilić, "'Čudotvorni' performativ", in: *Reč,* vol. 5, no. 42, (1998), p. 143.

71 "*L'Infinitif* 'n'illustre que l'idée, pas une action effective, dans un hymen (d'où procède le Rêve), vicieux mais sacré, entre le désir et l'accomplissement, la perpetration et son souvenir: ici devançant, là remémorant, au futur, au passé, **sous une apparence fausse de present**. Tel opère *L'Infinitif,* dont le jeu se borne à une allusion perpétuelle sans briser la glace: il installe, ainsi, un milieu, pur, de fiction." Stéphane Mallarmé, *Mimique,* dans: *Œuvres completes,* Éditions Gallimard, Paris, 1945, p. 310. In the spirit of *Infinitive,* translation and the original were modified by me. See also Jacques Derrida, "The Double Session", in: *Dissemination,* University of Chicago Press, Chicago, 1981, pp. 173-285.

72 ... *l'espace vide, le milieu entre la matière et le néant sans appartenir ni à l'un ni à l'autre.* Blaise Pascal, *Œuvres de Blaise Pascal,* Chez Lefèvre, Libraire, Paris, 1819, p. 122.

73 Wolfgang Hildesheimer, *Marbot: A Biography,* J. M. Dent & Sons Ltd, London and Melbourne, 1983.

74 *Ibid,* p. 40.

75   *Ibid*, p. 232.

76   Dorrit Cohn, "Breaking the Code of Fictional Biography: Wolfgang Hildesheimer's *Marbot*", in: *The Distinction of Fiction*, The Johns Hopkins University Press, Baltimore and London, 1999, p. 79.

77   Käte Hamburger, "Authenticity as Mask: Wolfgang Hildesheimer's *Marbot*", in: Ann Fehn, Ingeborg Hoesterey and Maria Tatar (ed.), *Neverending Stories: Toward a Critical Narratology*, Princeton University Press, Princeton, 1992, p. 97.

78   J. P. Stern, "Sweet Sin", in: *London Review of Books*, vol. 4, no. 14, August 5, 1982.

79   *London Review of Books*, vol. 4, no. 17, September 16, 1982.

80   *Ibid*

81   Jean-Marie Schaeffer, *Why Fiction?*, University of Nebraska Press, Lincoln, 2010.

82   Käte Hamburger, "Authenticity as Mask: Wolfgang Hildesheimer's *Marbot*", in: Ann Fehn, Ingeborg Hoesterey and Maria Tatar (ed.), *Neverending Stories: Toward a Critical Narratology*, Princeton University Press, Princeton, 1992, pp. 87-97.

83   Dorrit Cohn, "Breaking the Code of Fictional Biography: Wolfgang Hildesheimer's *Marbot*", in: *The Distinction of Fiction*, The Johns Hopkins University Press, Baltimore and London, 1999, pp. 79-95.

84   Unfortunately, the situation is not as simple as Schaeffer suggests. Käte Hamburger speaks about "largely panegyric press criticism of Marbot" and also explains that the press was completely aware of the fictional nature of Marbot's biography. See Käte Hamburger, "Authenticity as Mask: Wolfgang Hildesheimer's *Marbot*", in: Ann Fehn, Ingeborg Hoesterey and Maria Tatar (ed.), *Neverending Stories:*

Toward a Critical Narratology, Princeton University Press, Princeton, 1992, pp. 95, 97. In her text, Judith Ryan speaks not about the deception, but of mystification and offers a brief history of Marbot's reception. She also mentions Hildesheimer's reaction after J.P. Stern's review of *Marbot*. According to Judith Ryan, this brief history of Marbot's reception looks like this: "*Marbot*'s artful erudition challenges the reader to match his wits with the author, and this feature, along with the work's reception history, places it within the tradition of mystification. To all appearances, many readers mistook the novel for a factual narrative. Johannes Kleinstück's review of *Marbot* for the newspaper *Die Welt* treats the text as if it were the biography of the historical individual. In the United States, the Daedalus book catalogue initially grouped *Marbot* among its biographies and only later corrected the error, replacing the title under the heading of fiction…In a review for the weekly news magazine *Der Spiegel,* Peter Wapnewski took care to mention that while the biography seems convincing, it is in point of fact not true. John Simon's review for *The New York Times Book Review* begins with the phrase, 'Wolfgang Hildesheimer's *Marbot: A Biography* is a marvellous hoax […].' At the end of a review for *The Boston Sunday Globe,* Arthur Hepner concludes, 'It is all a very neat and meticulously researched tale […]. Only the whole thing is a fraud. […] That the ruse comes off so persuasively is a tribute to Hildesheimer's own inventive powers.' None of those reviewers were deceived for very long . However, their remarks suggest that for each of them, reading *Marbot* involved an experience of deception which preceded a clearer understanding of the text. It appears that booksellers, and presumably readers, continued to be mystified by *Marbot.* In an article published in 1998 on imagined artists, Paul Mattick wrote that '*Marbot* still shows up regularly in the biography section in used bookshops.' […] A year before *Marbot* appeared in print, Hildesheimer published signed articles about the project in several newspapers. These pieces announced the biography's subject to be an apocryphal figure. The article that appeared in the most prominent paper, the widely circulated Hamburg weekly *Die Zeit*, began with headlines that frankly describe the narrative as a 'falsified biography'. That deception was meant to be short-lived is evident in another curious incident from the next's reception history. In an article on *Marbot* for the *London Review of Books,* J.P. Stern, as I have noted, treats the text as an historical biography, before finally suggesting in the very last sentence that he is playing Hildesheimer's game. Hildesheimer, deceived by Stern's review, then wrote to the *London Review of Books*, 'to correct what he thought was Stern's mistaken belief in the reality of *Marbot*.' See Judith Ryan, "Fictionality, Historicity, and Textual Authority: Pater, Woolf, Hildesheimer", in: Ann Fehn, Ingeborg Hoesterey and Maria Tatar (ed.), *Neverending Stories: Toward a Critical Narratology*, Princeton University Press, Princeton, 1992. pp. 80-81.

85 Richard Littlejohns, "In No-man's-land beyond Biography: Dr Cake, Mozart and Other Cases", in: Nigel Harris and Joanne Sayner (eds.), *The Text and Its Context*, Peter Lang AG, Bern, 2008, p. 155.

86 Dorrit Cohn, "Breaking the Code of Fictional Biography: Wolfgang Hildesheimer's *Marbot*", in: *The Distinction of Fiction*, The Johns Hopkins University Press, Baltimore and London, 1999, pp. 92-93.

87 *Ibid*, p. 93.

88 *Ibid*, p. 84.

89 See Brian McHale, "From Modernist to Postmodernist Fiction: Change of Dominant", in: *Postmodernist Fiction*, Routledge, London and New York, 1987, pp. 3-25.

90 Dorrit Cohn, "Breaking the Code of Fictional Biography: Wolfgang Hildesheimer's *Marbot*", in: *The Distinction of Fiction*, The Johns Hopkins University Press, Baltimore and London, 1999, p. 85.

91 See Steven Connor, "Postmodernism and Literature", in: *The Cambridge Companion to Postmodernism*, Cambridge University Press, London and New York, 2004, pp. 62-81.

92 Maurice Blanchot, *Infinite Conversation*, University of Minnesota Press, Minneapolis and London, 1993, p. 381. The myth of Orpheus will prove to be extremely important for the understanding of *Infinitive* and *Marbot*. I will devote more attention to this myth in the final section of this chapter and also in the second section of the third chapter.

93 See Sreten Ugričić, "O sebi", in: Reč, vol. 5, no. 41 (1998), pp. 157-166.

94 Käte Hamburger, "Authenticity as Mask: Wolfgang Hildesheimer's *Marbot*", in: Ann Fehn, Ingeborg Hoesterey and Maria Tatar (ed.), *Neverending Stories: Toward a Critical Narratology*, Princeton University Press, Princeton, 1992, pp. 95-96. The observations from the quoted passage will become very important in the second and third section of this chapter. The important relation between fiction and truth is raised in Käte Hamburger's text and I will try to approach it with the help of Martin Heidegger and Maurice Blanchot. However, we need to note that this question is only raised in Käte Hamburger's text and that she does not provide an adequate answer to it. Unlike Schaeffer, she is reluctant to claim that *Marbot* is a simple hoax, but she is perfectly content to describe it as "a theoretical paradox." The topic of my work are precisely the consequences of this "theoretical paradox."

95 Aristotle, *The Poetics* (translated by Simon Butcher), Macmillan and Co., London, 1922, p. 43.

96 Can we really say that the true is the actual? Is this enough? Martin Heidegger writes: "The true is the actual. Accordingly, we speak of true gold in distinction from false. False gold is not what it actually appears to be. It is merely a 'semblance' and thus is not actual. Accordingly, we speak of true gold in distinction from false. False gold is not what it actually appears to be. It is merely a 'semblance' and thus is not actual. What is not actual is taken to be the opposite of actual. But, what merely seems to be gold is nevertheless something actual. Accordingly, we say more precisely: actual gold is genuine gold. Yet

both are 'actual' the circulating counterfeit no less than genuine gold. What is true about genuine gold thus cannot be demonstrated merely by its actuality. The question recurs: what do 'genuine' and 'true' mean here?" Martin Heidegger, "On the Essence of Truth", in: *Pathmarks*, Cambridge University Press, Cambridge and New York, 1998, p. 137.

97 Friedrich Nietzsche, "On Truth and Lies in a Nonmoral Sense", in: *The Nietzsche Reader*, Blackwell Publishing Ltd., Oxford, 2006, p. 116.

98 Hayden White, *Tropics of Discourse*, The Johns Hopkins University Press, Baltimore and London, 1978, p. 55.

99 Friedrich Nietzsche, *The Will to Power*, Vintage Books, New York, 1968, pp. 265-266.

100 Paul de Man, *Allegories of Reading*, Yale University Press, New Haven and London, 1979, pp. 107-108.

101 Sreten Ugričić, *Infinitiv*, Stubovi kulture, Beograd, 1997, p. 99. The translation of this story is mine.

102 *Ibid*, pp. 93-114.

103 See Otto Pöggeler, "The Seminality of Art", in: *Martin Heidegger's Path of Thinking*, Humanities Press International, New Jersey, 1987. pp. 167-174.

104 See Friedrich von Hermann, *Heideggers Philosophie der Kunst*, Klostermann, Frankfurt am Main, 1994. My intention is not to get into details of this discussion simply because it is not relevant for the questions posed in my work. On the other hand, I wanted to inform my readers about two perspectives on the role of "The Origin of the Work of Art" in Heidegger's philosophy. Brief summary of Pöggeler-von Hermann debate can be found in: Nebojša Grubor, *Hajdegerova filozofija umetnosti* (*Heidegger's Philosophy of Art*), Mali Nemo, Pančevo, 2005.

105 See Timothy Clark, "Heidegger's Dream of Singularisation", in: *The Poetics of Singularity: The Counter-Culturalist Turn in Heidegger, Derrida, Blanchot and Later Gadamer*, Edinburgh University Press, Edinburgh, 2005, pp. 32-60.

106 Martin Heidegger, *Elucidations of Hölderlin's Poetry*, Humanity Books, New York, 2000, p. 21.

107 We have to bear in mind that Heidegger's path of thinking is not an ordinary path. In the "Translator's Forward" to *Off the Beaten Track* it is explained that *Holzweg* has a double meaning. On the one hand, its is a timber path that leads to a clearing in the forest where the woods are cut. On the other, it is a path that leads to a dead end; it can take us to a place that is overgrown and which leads nowhere. In a popular German idiom, states the translator, to be *on a Holzweg* means to be lost, to be on the wrong track or in a *cul-de-sac*.

108 Consider the following passages from Hildesheimer's "Preface" to *Mozart*: "No attempt to penetrate the essence of Mozart's genius can entertain the question of success or failure. It can at best lead to convictions which, however firm, must not be mistaken for certainty. The limits to potential understanding are everywhere. If one illuminating factor seems to make them recede, they reappear all the more solidly on its dark opposite side. The task comes to be its own justification and to provide enrichment in itself, though fortified by a hope that others may also be enriched. The more facts brought to light, the more puzzling their undiscovered circumstances and motivations: Mozart's reactions to the external and internal conditions of his life as revealed in the documents are not illuminated by his works. Moreover, they are obscured, unconsciously, but systematically, and sometimes by Mozart himself..." "His autobiographical statements clarify only the fact that he is withdrawing from us, hiding behind his music, and the music, too, in its deepest meaning, is inaccessible to us, allowing no understanding outside music itself." See Wolfgang Hildesheimer, *Mozart,* J. M. Dent and Sons Ltd, London, 1983. pp. 4, 12.

109 Hayden White's main works are: Hayden White, *Metahistory: Historical Imagination in Nineteenth Century Europe*, The Johns Hopkins University Press, Baltimore and London, 1975; Hayden White, *The Content of the Form: Narrative Discourse and Historical Representation*, The Johns Hopkins University Press, Baltimore and London, 1990; Hayden White, *Tropics of Discourse: Essays in Cultural Criticism*, The Johns Hopkins University Press, Baltimore and London, 1985. Brief summary of his main ideas can be found in: Kuisma Korhonen, "General Introduction: The History/Literature Debate", in: Kuisma Korhonen (ed.), *Tropes for the Past: Hayden White and the History/ Literature Debate*, Rodopi, Amsterdam and New York, 2006, pp. 9-20. In this chapter, I also used the helpful text from *A Poetics of Postmodernism*. See Linda Hutcheon, "Historicizing the Postmodern: The Problematizing of History", in: *A Poetics of Postmodernism: History, Theory, Fiction,* Routledge, New York and London, pp. 87-101.

110 Hayden White, "The Burden of History", in: *Tropics of Discourse: Essays in Cultural Criticism*, The Johns Hopkins University Press, Baltimore and London, 1985, p. 46.

111 I would like to remind my readers that Stewart Greenchurch understands infinitive as the highest value and the only criterion of evaluation. Infinitive is neither good nor bad, it is – a pure axiological openness. The measure of all values must remain outside all empirical evaluation. If it was not the case, if it was possible to, for example, criticize that measure of all measures, that would mean that there is another and higher value. Hence, to determine or to divulge the infinitive means to lose it. Because of that, Sreten Ugričić's book is about the invisible philosopher and his invisible work. The relationship between the book of Stewart Greenchurch and Ugričić's book is similar to the relationship between the infinitive and meta-definitive.

112 When he analyses the work of Jacob Burckhardt, Hayden White comes very close to Greenchurch's assertion, but, for some reasons, he never proceeds as far as Greenchurch.

Compare this passage with Greenchurch's statement that emplotment is definitive of narrative, while sense is infinitive: "Like his contemporaries in art, Burckhardt cuts into the historical record at different points and suggests different perspectives on it, omitting, ignoring, or distorting as his artistic purpose requires. His intention was not to tell the whole truth about Italian Renaissance, but one truth about it, in precisely the same way that Cézanne abandoned any attempt to tell the whole truth about the landscape. He had abandoned the dream of telling a story because he had long since abandoned the belief that history had any other inherent meaning or significance. The only 'truth' that Burckhardt recognized was that which he had learned from Schopenhauer - namely, that every attempt to give form to the world, every human affirmation attained to a worth of its own insofar as it succeeded in imposing upon the chaos of the world a momentary form." See Hayden White, "The Burden of History", in: *Tropics of Discourse: Essays in Cultural Criticism*, The Johns Hopkins University Press, Baltimore and London, 1985, p. 44.

113 See Martin Heidegger, *Being and Time*, State University of New York Press, Albany, 1996, pp. 196-211. I also used Michael Gelven, "Care, Reality and Truth", in: *A Commentary on Heidegger's Being and Time*, Northern Illinois University Press, DeKalb, pp. 111-135, and Richard Polt, "Reality and Truth", in: *Heidegger: An Introduction*, Cornell University Press, New York, 1999, pp. 80-84.

114 Martin Heidegger, *Being and Time*, State University of New York Press, Albany, 1996, p. 198.

115 *Ibid*, p. 200-201.

116 A very useful clarification of this example can be found in Paul Gorner, "Truth", in: *Heidegger's Being and Time: An Introduction*, Cambridge University Press, Cambridge, 2007, pp. 94-104. I also used Mark A. Wrathall, "Unconcealment", in: *Heidegger and Unconcealment: Truth, Language, History*, Cambridge University Press, Cambridge, 2010. pp. 11-34.

117 Richard Polt, *Heidegger: An Introduction*, Cornell University Press, New York, 1999, p. 82

118 This simplified approach to literary works can be found in the works of Martha Nussbaum. She does not take into account the textual nature of literary works and her interpretations are based on the simplistic assumption that the situations and characters in literature are somehow actually present. She ignores its textual nature and insists on reading through literature to *a life beyond the text*. See Martha Nussbaum *Love's Knowledge: Essays on Philosophy and Literature*, Oxford University Press, Oxford, 1990. Robert Eaglestone offers an excellent presentation (and critique) of Nussbaums's approach. See Robert Eaglestone, "The Dialogue Between Perception and Rule: Martha Nussbaum", in: *Ethical Criticism: Reading After Levinas*, Edinburgh University Press, Edinburgh, 1997. pp. 35-60.

119 Jean-François Lyotard, *The Differend: Phrases in Dispute*, University of Minnesota Press, Minneapolis, 1988, p. 61.

120 *Ibid,* p. 62.

121 Why did I choose this difficult example? In order to discern what is happening in it one needs to have not only the knowledge of Kant's *The Critique of Pure Reason,* but also of Jean-François Lyotard's philosophy. Also, in the chapter "They Said About *The Axiological Infinitive*", some other fragments from *The Differend* are quoted. These fragments are reworked in order to include the references to Stewart Greenchurch. "They Said About *The Axiological Infinitive*" has the ability to function as a rich reservoir of the potential interpretations of *Infinitive*. In this chapter of *Infinitive*, not only Lyotard, but Derrida, Said, Rorty, Rawls and Ricœur are "speaking" about Stewart Greenchurch and about the importance of his work. It is impossible to cover all relations between *Infinitive* and these theoreticians in a single work. Therefore, I had to make a decision and to present only one possible aspect of the relation between *Infinitive* and *The Differend.* Basically, I chose one aspect that can illuminate one of my main arguments - how the immediacy of the given is not immediate. The importance

of this example will be fully comprehended when we come to the Chapter 3 of this work. In this chapter, especially in the part about *The Lost Estate*, I will present the example that will clearly show how the immediacy of the given is not immediate. For the alternative relations between *Infinitive* and *The Differend* compare Lyotard's fragments 47, 57, 65 and 92 with Sreten Ugričić, *Infinitiv*, Stubovi kulture, Beograd, 1997, pp. 165-167.

122 Martin Heidegger, "On the Essence of Truth", in: *Pathmarks,* Cambridge University Press, Cambridge, 1998, pp. 136-154. In the interpretation of this text I also used: William J. Richardson, "On the Essence of Truth", in: *Heidegger: Through Phenomenology to Thought,* Martinus Nijhoff, The Hague, 1967, pp. 211-254, and Lee Braver, "On the Essence of Truth", in: *Heidegger's Later Writings: A Reader's Guide,* Continuum, London and New York, 2009, pp. 25-39.

123 Martin Heidegger, *Being and Time,* State University of New York Press, Albany, 1996, p. 205.

124 *Ibid,* p. 204.

125 William J. Richardson, *Heidegger: Through Phenomenology to Thought,* Martinus Nijhoff, The Hague, 1967, p. 211.

126 Martin Heidegger, "On the Essence of Truth", in: *Pathmarks,* Cambridge University Press, Cambridge, 1998, p. 142.

127 *Ibid,* p. 144.

128 *Ibid,* pp. 145-146.

129 Martin Heidegger, *Being and Time,* State University of New York Press, Albany, 1996, p. 129.

130 William J. Richardson, *Heidegger: Through Phenomenology to Thought,* Martinus Nijhoff, The Hague, 1967, p. 221.

131 Martin Heidegger, *Being and Time,* State University of New York Press, Albany, 1996, p. 4.

132 Martin Heidegger, "The Origin of the Work of Art", in: *Off the Beaten Track,* Cambridge University Press, Cambridge, 2002, pp. 1-56.

133 Martin Heidegger, *Being and Time*, State University of New York Press, Albany, 1996, pp. 64-65.

134 Are these really peasant shoes? For example, Meyer Schapiro claims that shoes in question are not Van Gogh's own shoes. See Meyer Schapiro, "The Still Life as a Personal Object - A Note on Heidegger and Van Gogh" and "Further Notes on Heidegger and Van Gogh", in: *Theory and Philosophy of Art: Style, Artist, and Society, Selected papers 4*, New York, George Braziller, 1994, pp. 135-142; 143-151. An interesting addition to this discussion can be found in the work of Jacques Derrida. He claims that both Heidegger and Schapiro are wrong in respect to the attribution of the shoes. See Jacques Derrida, "Restitutions of the Truth in Pointing [*pointure*]", in: *The Truth in Painting*, The University of Chicago Press, Chicago, 1987, pp. 255-382.

135 Martin Heidegger, "The Origin of the Work of Art", in: *Off the Beaten Track,* Cambridge University Press, Cambridge, 2002, p. 14.

136 See Stendhal, *The Red and the Black: A Chronicle of the Nineteenth Century*, Oxford University Press, Oxford, 1998, p. 371. According to this *credo* of realism, art mirrors reality. However, is it really as simple as that? For example, what is represented in the works of Stendhal? Erich Auerbach claims that Stendhal does not represent the reality itself, but that modern consciousness of reality found its literary form in his work. The main theme of Stendhal's works is *temporal concentration* - a perpetual change of circumstances that shapes human destiny. Stendhal deals with the reality that presents itself to him, but what presents itself to him and what he tries to catch is precisely something uncatchable - a state of flux and

constant change. Erich Auerbach writes: "But the reality which he encountered was so constituted that, without permanent reference to the immense changes of the immediate past and without a premonitory searching after the imminent changes of the future, one could not represent it; all the human figures and all the human events in his work appear upon a ground politically and socially disturbed." (I would just like to add just one thing to this: not just politically and socially, but essentially disturbed. This is why I claim that, long before Proust, the real theme of Stendhal's work is not reality, but time). See Erich Auerbach, "In the Hôtel de la Mole", in: *Mimesis: The Representation of Reality in Western Literature*, Princeton University Press, Princeton, 2003, p. 463.

137 Martin Heidegger, "The Origin of the Work of Art", in: *Off the Beaten Track,* Cambridge University Press, Cambridge, 2002, p. 30.

138 In the first chapter, I noted that Stewart Greenchurch claims that works of art are capable of taking the role of infinitive. When they do so, they become definitives that can be interpreted as infinitive. Therefore masterpieces of art are meta-definitives. Their meaning cannot be defined once and for all because of their *permanent ontological reserve of meaning.* Again, the story of Jorge Luis Borges "Pierre Menard, Author of the *Quixote*" can function as the perfect example in this case.

139 See Gianni Vattimo, "The Work of Art as the Setting to Work of Truth", in: *Art's Claim to Truth*, Columbia University Press, New York, 2008, pp. 151-160.

140 Otto Pöggeler, "The Seminality of Art", in: *Martin Heidegger's Path of Thinking,* Humanities Press International, New Jersey, 1987. p. 171.

141 Christopher Fynsk, *Heidegger: Thought and Historicity*, Cornell University Press, Ithaca and London, 1993, p. 150.

142 Martin Heidegger, "The Origin of the Work of Art", in: *Off the Beaten Track,* Cambridge University Press, Cambridge, 2002, p. 44.

143 *Ibid,* p. 46.

144 Martin Heidegger, "What are Poets For?", in: *Poetry, Language, Thought*, HarperCollins, New York, 1971, p. 129.

145 This is also evident in *Being and Time* when Heidegger writes about discourse. See Martin Heidegger, "Dasein and Discourse: Language", in: *Being and Time*, State University of New York Press, New York, pp. 150-156. Again, Richard Polt's explanation of this chapter can be very instructive: "Attunement and understanding are always working together to reveal the world, granting it intelligibility. Heidegger describes discourse (rather vaguely) as the articulation and expression of this intelligibility. It does not seem that he intends to identify discourse with speaking; rather, discourse is the fundamental way in which patterns of meaning are manifested to us. This is the ontological precondition for language, and it naturally leads to language: 'to significations, words accrue'. As an entity with discourse, I am capable of noticing how the world is articulated - that is, how it involves articulations, joints, that differentiate and unite in it patterns of meaning. For instance, I may be in a nervous mood (attunement) as I approach my garden which is intelligible to me because I am capable of gardening (understanding). The garden now shows up for me, is manifest to me, as a set of annoying, urgent tasks - and these tasks fall into meaningful patterns (discourse). Discourse makes it possible for me to share my situation with others in language. I can say, 'My garden is getting overrun by weeds!' and the garden will be manifest to others. I can reveal the garden to others because as Dasein, I am characterized by discourse; I am able to deal with patterns of meaning." Richard Polt, *Heidegger: An Introduction*, Cornell University Press, New York, 1999, p. 74.

146 Karsten Harries, *Art Matters: A Critical Commentary on Heidegger's "The Origin of the Work of Art"*, Springer, New York, 2009, p. 171.

147 Walter Biemel offers another explanation with the example of Greek temple from "The Origin of the Work of Art": "Without a doubt Greek architecture supposes a determinate conception of the essence of the gods and of the relationship of man to the gods. If the divine had not first been said in language, it would have been meaningless, even impossible, to erect memorials to the gods. In these memorials, sacred woods and temples, a certain measure is revealed, an order having an effect on the lived self-understanding of the Greek man and influencing him by forming him." See Walter Biemel, "Poetry and Language in Heidegger", in: Joseph J. Kockelmans (ed.), *On Heidegger and Language*, Northwestern University Press, Evanston, 1972, p. 78.

148 We need to be careful with the word "poetry". In German original the word is *Dichtung*. For example, Timothy Clark does not think that *poetry/poesy* difference is strong enough and he does not translate *Dichtung*. *Dichtung* is used in a very broad sense, and, in his chapter on Heidegger, Clark says: "Let us now turn to *Dichtung* (poetising) itself in Heidegger's conception, considered as a mode of language that he relates closely, with certain forms of thinking, to the essential force of language as saying (*Sage*) and hence not simply to be correlated with 'fiction' or 'poetry'. How does Heidegger distinguish between *Dichtung* and the realm of letters generally? *Dichtung* is far from being 'poetry'. It is rather a new notion of the poetic as at sway in the being of language: 'Language itself is poetry in the essential sense.'" See Timothy Clark, *Derrida, Heidegger, Blanchot: Sources of Derrida's notion and practice of literature*, Cambridge University Press, Cambridge, p. 29. Also, in this work, I am using Heidegger's writings about poetry in order to provide an interpretation of *Infinitive* and *Marbot*. Is this correct? These works do not belong to the genre of "poetry" and its form is not "poetic". These are works that are written in prose. Considering this opposition between poetry and prose we just need to remember what

Heidegger says: "The opposite of what is purely spoken, the opposite of the poem, is not prose. Pure prose is never 'prosaic.' It is as poetic and hence as rare as poetry." Martin Heidegger, "Language", in: *Poetry, Language, Thought*, HarperCollins, New York, 1971, p. 206.

149 Martin Heidegger, "Hölderlin and the Essence of Poetry", in: *Elucidations of Hölderlin's Poetry*, Humanity Books, New York, 2000, pp. 51-65.

150 Walter Biemel writes:"Thus, what Heidegger stated previously in regard to art as poetry (taken in a broad sense) he now concretizes with the help of the example of naming. Through naming, beings first become accessible as beings; it is the condition necessary for them to be recognized and used as determinate beings. This becoming accessible of beings as beings, this uncovering of their beingness, is unconcealment. This must not be understood as if beings were present before but in a state of concealment; unconcealment means, rather, the entering into Being as appearance. Through unconcealment there is being for man; being is integrated into the project of world." Walter Biemel, "Poetry and Language in Heidegger", in: Joseph J. Kockelmans (ed.), *On Heidegger and Language,* Northwestern University Press, Evanston, 1972, p. 76.

151 Martin Heidegger, "Hölderlin and the Essence of Poetry", in: *Elucidations of Hölderlin's Poetry*, Humanity Books, New York, 2000, p. 58.

152 Martin Heidegger, "The Nature of Language", in: *On the Way to Language*, Harper & Row Publishers Inc., New York, 1982, p. 60.

153 *Ibid*, p. 62.

154 J.L. Austin, *How to Do Things with Words*, Clarendon Press, Oxford, 1962, p. 1.

155 *Ibid*, p. 5.

156 Shoshana Felman, *The Scandal of Speaking Body: Don Juan with J.L. Austin or Seduction in Two Languages*, Stanford University Press, Stanford, 2002, pp. 7-8.

157 Jonathan Culler, "Philosophy and Literature: The Fortunes of Performative", in: *Poetics Today*, The Porter Institute for Poetics and Semiotics, Tel Aviv, vol. 21, no. 3 (Fall 2000), pp. 511-512.

158 Paul Valéry, "Concerning *Le cimetière marin*", in: *The Art of Poetry*, Pantheon Books, New York, 1958, p. 147.

159 Martin Heidegger, *On the Way to Language*, Harper & Row Publishers Inc., New York, 1982, p. 134. See also Walter Biemel, "Poetry and Language in Heidegger", in: Joseph J. Kockelmans (ed.), *On Heidegger and Language*, Northwestern University Press, Evanston, 1972, p. 88.

160 Jean-François Lyotard writes: "'Every phrase is.' Is everything which is, a phrase? *Is* is not which *is*. Nor is *is*, for that matter, *is real*. It cannot be said that *Every phrase is real*. Even less so, that *Everything rational is real*. Reality is a property of a referent that remains to be established (Referent Section), it is not. This includes the reality of a phrase. That everything real is rational, yes, that can be said if *rational* signifies: in conformity with the procedure for establishing the reality of a referent. In *Every phrase is*, every phrase signifies *everything which happens*; *is* signifies *there is, it happens*. But *It happens* is not what happens, in the sense that *quod* is not *quid* (in the sense that presentation is not situation). *Is* does not therefore signify *is there*, and even less so does it signify *is real*. *Is* does not signify anything, it would designate the occurrence 'before' the signification (the content) of the occurrence. It would designate it, but it does not designate it, since by designating it it situates it ("before" signification) and thereby occults *nun* in *hústeron próteron* (Aristotle Notice). Rather *is* would be: *Is it happening?* (the *it* indicating an empty place to be occupied by a referent). See Jean-François Lyotard, *The Differend: Phrases in Dispute*, University of Minnesota Press, Minneapolis, 1988, p. 79.

161 See Martin Heidegger, "The Nature of Language", in: *On the Way to Language*, HarperCollins Publishers, New York, 1971, p. 86.

162 Martin Heidegger, *On the Way to Language*, HarperCollins Publishers, New York, 1971, p. 88.

163 See Martin Heidegger, "Language", in: *Poetry, Language, Thought*, HarperCollins, New York, 1971, pp. 185-208.

164 *Ibid*, pp. 195-195.

165 *Ibid*, p. 196.

166 Gerald L. Bruns provides an interesting answer to this question: "Already in *Sein und Zeit* Heidegger had characterized discourse (*Rede*) nonsubjectively (or, say, passively) so that even 'keeping silent' could be counted as a mode of discourse. And at a crucial point he characterized discourse as a call (*Ruf*). the call does not originate with the subject, rather the subject is exposed to the call. Conscience is an event of calling; it is a mode of responsibility. The call is nonsubjective. In *Sein und Zeit* this nonsubjectivity is obscured by the central place occupied by Dasein, where conscience becomes Dasein's responsibility to itself, a call that summons (*ruft*) Dasein's Self from its lostness in the 'they' (*Das Man*). But the call itself is nonidentical (*neutral*): the caller maintains itself in conspicuous indefiniteness. If the caller is asked about its name, status, origin, or repute, it not only refuses to answer, but does not even leave the slightest possibility of one's making it into something with which one can be familiar when one's understanding of Dasein has a 'worldly' orientation. The caller is absolutely other: not another subject, nor anything that can be objectified. The call as discourse belongs to the Outside." See Gerald L. Bruns, *Maurice Blanchot: The Refusal of Philosophy*, The Johns Hopkins University Press, Baltimore and London, 1997, pp. 105-106.

167 Martin Heidegger, *Being and Time,* State University of New York Press, Albany, 1996, p. 252. Gerald L. Bruns

writes the following about the connection between "calling" and "naming": "Naming as calling in any event is dark or uncanny saying in the manner of archaic word or fragment, the enigma, and the poem in its earthly character of withdrawal, reserve, dissembling, *dichte*, opacity - poetry as the other of predication and the determination of meaning. Imagine a naming that leaves things nameless or unsignified, lets them go as if off their own, otherwise than being. In the 'Letter on Humanism', which is about being homeless in an utterly familiar place, Heidegger says: 'if man is to find his way once again in nearness of Being he must first learn to exist in the nameless.'" Gerald L. Bruns, *Heidegger's Estrangements: Language Truth and Poetry in the Later Writings,* Yale University Press, New Haven and London, 1989, pp. 72-73.

168 Martin Heidegger, "Language", in: *Poetry, Language, Thought*, HarperCollins, New York, 1971, p. 197.

169 Emmanuel Levinas, *Proper Names,* Stanford University Press, Stanford, 1996, pp. 134, 136. Is it maybe possible to perceive Sreten Ugričić's *Infinitive* as the event of this difference?

170 Blanchot formulates this in the following way: "When we speak, we gain control over things with the satisfying ease. I say, 'This woman,' and she is immediately available to me, I push her away, I bring her close, she is everything I want her to be, she becomes the place in which the most surprising sorts of transformations occur and actions unfold: speech is life's ease and security. We cannot do anything with an object that has no name." Maurice Blanchot, "Literature and the Right to Death", in: *The Work of Fire*, Stanford University Press, Stanford, 1995, p. 322.

171 *Ibid*, pp. 322-323.

172 *Ibid*, p. 327.

173 Maurice Blanchot, "The Language of Fiction", in: *The Work of Fire*, Stanford University Press, Stanford, 1995, pp. 74-84.

174 See Timothy Clark, "Blanchot: The Literary Space", in: *Derrida, Heidegger, Blanchot: Sources of Derrida's Notion and Practice of Literature*, Cambridge University Press, Cambridge, 1992, pp. 64-107.

175 Maurice Blanchot, "The Language of Fiction", in: *The Work of Fire*, Stanford University Press, Stanford, 1995, p. 76.

176 *Ibid*, p. 77.

177 For example, Blanchot writes: "In poetry we are no longer referred back to the world, neither to the world as shelter nor to the world as goals. In this language the world recedes and goals cease; the world falls silent; beings with their preoccupations, their projects, their activity are no longer ultimately what speaks. Poetry expresses the fact that beings are quiet. But how does this happen? Beings fall silent, but then it is being that tends to speak and speech that wants to be. The poetic word is no longer someone's word. In it no one speaks, and what speaks is not anyone. It seems rather that the word alone declares itself. Then language takes on all of its importance. It becomes essential. Language speaks as the essential, and that is why the word entrusted to the poet can be called the essential word. This means primarily that words, having the initiative, are not obliged to serve to designate anything or give voice to anyone, but that they have their ends in themselves. From here on, it is not Mallarmé who speaks, but language which speaks itself: language as the work and the work as language." See Maurice Blanchot, "Approaching Literature's Space", in: *The Space of Literature*, University of Nebraska Press, Lincoln and London, 1989, p. 41.

178 Gustave Flaubert, *The Letters of Gustave Flaubert: 1830-1857*, Belknap Press, Cambridge, 1980, p. 154. The quotation is modified.

179 Maurice Blanchot, *Encountering the Imaginary*, in: *The Book to Come*, Stanford University Press, Stanford, 2003, pp. 3-10.

180 *Ibid*, p. 6.

181 The most famous formulation of this paradox is: *Epimenides was a Cretan who made one immortal statement: "All Cretans are liars"*.

182 Maurice Blanchot, "Encountering the Imaginary", in: *The Book to Come*, Stanford University Press, Stanford, 2003, p. 7.

183 Timothy Clark, *Derrida, Heidegger, Blanchot: Sources of Derrida's Notion and Practice of Literature*, Cambridge University Press, Cambridge, 1992, p. 86.

184 Sreten Ugričić, *Infinitiv*, Stubovi kulture, Beograd, 1997, pp. 136-140.

185 "One can easily imagine a story in which Orpheus goes mad when he recognizes that Eurydice was never present to him, nor, for that matter, was he ever coincidental with himself (an Orpheus too many, as allegorized in the dismemberment scene). We might imagine him, as he goes to pieces, reasoning thus: 'If, in the 'terrifyingly ancient', nothing was ever present, and if, having barely produced itself, the event, by the absolute fall, fragile, at once falls into it, as the mark of irrevocability announces to us, it is because (whence our cold presentiment) the event that we thought we had lived was itself never in a relation of presence to us nor to anything whatsoever.' Eurydice was never there for Orpheus in the way he desired: that is precisely the weakness of his otherwise overwhelming desire (Plato called it the 'weakness of logos')." See Gerald L. Bruns, *Maurice Blanchot: The Refusal of Philosophy*, The Johns Hopkins University Press, Baltimore and London, 1997. pp. 189-190.

186 Leslie Hill, "'Affirmation Without Precedent': Maurice Blanchot and Criticism Today", in: *After Blanchot: Literature, Criticism, Philosophy*, University of Delaware Press, Newark, 2006, pp. 58-79.

187 *Ibid*, p. 65.

188 Sreten Ugričić, *Maja i ja i Maja*, Prometej, Novi Sad, 1993, p. 66.

189 Cited in: John Barth, "The Literature of Replenishment", in: *Essentials of the Theory of Fiction*, Duke University Press, Durham, 2005, p. 176.

190 Maurice Blanchot, "The Madness of the Day", in: *The Station Hill Blanchot Reader*, Station Hill, Barrytown, 1999, p. 199.

191 Samuel Becket, *Proust: And Three Dialogues with Georges Duthuit*, Calder Publications Ltd., London, 1965, p. 103. We can find something very similar to this at the beginning of Blanchot's essay "From Dread to Language": "The writer finds himself in this more and more comical condition - of having nothing to write, of having no means of writing it, and of being forced by an extreme necessity to keep writing it. Having nothing to express should be taken in the simplest sense. Whatever he wants to say, it is nothing. The world, things, knowledge, are for him only reference points across the void. And he himself is already reduced to nothing. Nothing is his material. He rejects the forms in which it offers itself to him as being something. He wants to grasp it not in an illusion but in its own truth. He seeks it as the no that is not no to this, to that, to everything, but the pure and simple no. What is more, he does not seek it; it stands apart from all investigation; it cannot be taken as an end; one cannot propose to the will that it adopt as its end something that takes possession of the will by annihilating it: it is not, that is all there is to it; the writer's 'I have nothing to say', like that of the accused, contains the whole secret of his solitary condition." See Maurice Blanchot, "From Dread to Language", in: *The Gaze of Orpheus and Other Literary Essays*, Station Hill Press, Barrytown and New York, 1981, p. 5.

192 Miguel de Cervantes Saavedra, *The Ingenious Hidalgo Don Quixote de la Mancha*, Penguin Books, London, 2001, p. 16.

193 See Antonio J. Cascardi, "*Don Quixote* and the Invention of the Novel", in: *The Cambridge Companion to Cervantes*, Cambridge University Press, Cambridge, 2002, pp. 58-79.

194 Christopher Fynsk, *Heidegger: Thought and Historicity*, Cornell University Press, Ithaca and London, 1993, p. 150.

195 See Leslie Hill, *Blanchot: Extreme Contemporary*, Routledge, London and New York, 1997.

196 Maurice Blanchot, *The Space of Literature*, University of Nebraska Press, Lincoln, 1989, p. 46.

197 Roberto Gonzales Echevaría, "Introduction", in: *Cervantes's 'Don Quixote': A Casebook*, Oxford University Press, Oxford, 2005, p. 10.

198 Pedro Calderon de la Barca, *Life is a Dream*, Nick Hern Books, London, 1998. To these lines we can also add the reworking of Edgar Allan Poe's poem "A Dream Within a Dream" that can be heard at the beginning of Peter Weir's *Picnic at Hanging Rock*: "What we see and what we seem are, but a dream/ A dream within a dream." Also, the narrator in Guy Maddin's movie *My Winnipeg* says something similar: "And because we dream of where we walk and walk to where we dream, we are always lost... befuddled."

199 Linda Hutcheon writes: "Don Quixote and Emma Bovary are literary examples of what happens when the referent of fiction is presumed to be real and operative. Emma is the most serious of realists, for she truly believes that art - even the romantic literature she reads - is a vehicle for experiences which really exist and/or can be made to exist in her world. Her belief raises the question of how both ordinary and literary language can ever correspond to the precise nature of non-verbal realities. It is not that Emma reads the wrong books, as some have suggested, but that, like Cervantes's hero, she reads believing the referents to be real. See Linda Hutcheon, *Narcissistic Narrative: The Metafictional Paradox*, Wilfrid Laurier University Press, Ontario, 1980, p. 94.

200   Antonio J. Cascardi, "*Don Quixote* and the Invention of the Novel", in: *The Cambridge Companion to Cervantes*, Cambridge University Press, Cambridge, 2002, p. 64.

201   Michel Foucault, "[Don Quixote in the Lettered World]", in: Ruth El Saffar (ed.), *Critical Essays on Cervantes*, G.K. Hall and Co., Boston, 1986, pp. 117-121.

202   *Ibid*, p. 118.

203   See Michel Foucault, *History of Madness*, Routledge, London and New York, 2006.

204   *Ibid*, p. 38.

205   Michel Foucault, "[Don Quixote in the Lettered World]", in: Ruth El Saffar (ed.), *Critical Essays on Cervantes*, G.K. Hall and Co., Boston, 1986, p. 119.

206   Jorge Luis Borges, "Partial Magic in the *Quixote*", in: *Labyrinths: Selected Stories and Other Writings*, New Directions Publishing Corporation, New York, 1964, p. 187.

207   Paul de Man, "A Modern Master", in: Jaime Alazraki (ed.), *Critical Essays on Jorge Luis Borges*, G.K. Hall and Co., Boston, 1987.

208   Jorge Luis Borges, "Tlön, Uqbar, Orbis Tertius", in: *Labyrinths: Selected Stories and Other Writings*, New Directions Publishing Corporation, New York, 1964, p. 21.

209   Jorge Luis Borges, "The Masked Dyer, Hakim of Merv", in: *A Universal History of Infamy*, E. P. Dutton & Co., New York, 1972, p. 84.

210   Paul de Man, "A Modern Master", in: Jaime Alazraki (ed.), *Critical Essays on Jorge Luis Borges*, G.K. Hall and Co., Boston, 1987, pp. 58-59.

211   Jorge Luis Borges, "Pierre Menard, Author of the *Quixote*", in: *Labyrinths: Selected Stories and other Writings*, New

Directions Publishing Corporation, New York, 1964, pp. 52-53.

212 John Barth, "The Literature of Exhaustion", in: Jaime Alazraki (ed.), *Critical Essays on Jorge Luis Borges*, G.K. Hall and Co., Boston, 1987, p. 87.

213 Cited in: John Barth, "The Literature of Replenishment", in: *Essentials of the Theory of Fiction*, Duke University Press, Durham, 2005, p. 176.

214 See Friedrich Hölderlin, "Remarks on *Oedipus*", in: *Essays and Letters on Theory*, State University of New York Press, Albany, 1988, p. 113.

215 Maurice Blanchot, *The Space of Literature*, University of Nebraska Press, Lincoln, 1982. p. 30.

216 John Blegen, "Writing the Question: About Maurice Blanchot", in: *Diacritics*, vol. 2, no. 2 (Summer, 1972), p. 15.

217 Maurice Blanchot, *The Space of Literature*, University of Nebraska Press, Lincoln, 1982. p. 54.

218 John Gregg, *Maurice Blanchot and the Literature of Transgression*, Princeton University Press, Princeton and New Jersey, 1994, pp. 49-50.

219 Alain-Fournier, *The Lost Estate*, Penguin Books, London, 2007.

220 I will offer a synopsis of this work that will enable an easier orientation through my text. The events in *The Lost Estate* are narrated by François Seurel. He is the son of the schoolteacher in Sainte-Agathe and everything starts with the arrival of a new pupil - Augustine Meaulnes. One day a schoolteacher asks for volunteers to meet his guests at the railway station, but Meaulnes drives off before the others in order to meet them. He loses his way and ends up in the old ruined manor. This manor is full of guests in strange costumes and they are gathered there for some kind of

party. He spends the night in the house and the next day he finds out that this is the celebration of Frantz de Galais's wedding. On a boat trip he meets Frantz's sister Yvonne and he is enchanted by her. Frantz suddenly comes back and tells everyone that the wedding is off and that his fiancee left him. Meaulnes finds a place in one carriage and falls asleep. When he wakes up he is already near home. This is the end of Part I. In the Part II Meaulnes tries to find a way back to the lost estate, but without any success. A new pupil with the bandaged head usurps his place as the leader of the boys. Before he leaves the school, he gives Meaulnes the address in Paris where, according to him, Yvonne usually goes. Meaulnes realizes too late that this stranger is actually Frantz who tried to kill himself after his fiancée left him. Meaulnes also leaves the school and goes to Paris, but fails to find Yvonne. This is the end of Part II. After a long time, and with a little bit of luck, Seurel finds the lost estate and Yvonne who is still unmarried. He arranges a meeting between Yvonne and Meaulnes, but for unknown reasons Meaulnes is sad. However, before the end of the meeting he proposes to Yvonne and she accepts. Five months later, they are married, but Meaulnes leaves to find Frantz's lost fiancee - Valentine (and also to set right some wrong that he did). A year passes and nothing is heard of Meaulnes. Seurel finds the notes of his friend and discovers that Meaulnes became engaged to Valentine during his time in Paris. However, when he realized who she is he left her to wander the streets of Paris. Yvonne dies after the birth of a baby girl and Seurel adopts the child. After some time, Meaulnes comes back home after he managed to reunite Frantz and Valentine. More detailed synopsis can be found in: Robert Gibson, *The Quest of Alain-Fournier*, Hamish Hamilton, London, 1953, pp. 203-207.

221 Of course, this expression is borrowed from René Wellek and Austin Warren's famous book. See René Wellek and Austin Warren, *Theory of Literature*, Lowe and Brydon, London, 1955.

222 Maurice Blanchot, *The Book to Come*, Stanford University Press, Stanford, 2003, p. 201.

223   Maurice Blanchot, "What is the Purpose of Criticism?", in: *Lautreamont and Sade*, Stanford University Press, Stanford, 2004, pp. 1-6.

224   I will focus more on this characteristic of criticism at the very end of this chapter.

225   The sentences from Chris Marker's masterpiece *La Jetée* are slightly modified.

226   This translation of Alain-Fournier's notes comes from: Robert Gibson, *The End of Youth: The Life and Work of Alain-Fournier*, Impress Books Ltd., 2005, pp. 71-72.

227   The description of this scene can be found in Alain-Fournier's notes and letters, but also in his novel. See Alain-Fournier, *The Lost Estate*, Penguin Books, London, 2007, p. 67.

228   *Ibid*, p. 74.

229   See Martin Turnell, *The Rise of French Novel*, Hamish Hamilton, London, 1979.

230   See Robert Gibson, *The Quest of Alain-Fournier,* Hamish Hamilton, London, 1953.

231   Søren Kierkegaard, *Repetition and Philosophical Crumbs,* Oxford University Press, Oxford, 2009, p. 49. This is the observation of Constantin Constantius about a young man.

232   Martin Turnell, *The Rise of French Novel*, Hamish Hamilton, London, 1979.

233   See Robert Champigny, *Portrait of a Symbolist Hero: An Existential Study Based on the Work of Alain-Fournier,* Indiana University Press, Bloomington, 1954.

234   Alain-Fournier's sister Isabelle Rivière writes: "Debout près d'une fenêtre de la grande classe, devant le rosier à demi effeuillé par la chaleur, une main assez mollement

enfoncée dans sa poche, les cheveux non plus ras, mais abondants et partagés par une raie de côté, adolescent déjà malgré l'ovale encore enfantin, c'est Frantz de Galais dans son costume aux ancres marines, le menton levé fièrement, le front brillant d'orgueilleuse jeunesse, mais la bouche puérile gonflée comme par une forte envie de pleurer - beau visage de jeune héros romantique, plein de hardiesse et de désir; mais dans les doux yeux tristes le rêve est déjà tout voilé de désespoir, l'enthousiasme alenti d'une sorte de langueur découragée..." Isabelle Rivière, *Images d'Alain-Fournier*, Emile-Paul, Paris, 1938, p. 174. The very same quotation can also be found in: Robert Champigny, *Portrait of a Symbolist Hero: An Existential Study Based on the Work of Alain-Fournier*, Indiana University Press, Bloomington, 1954, p. 32.

235 Maurice Blanchot, *The Book to Come*, Stanford University Press, Stanford, 2003, pp. 91-92.

336 This is Seurel's description of Frantz when he meets him after a couple of years: "He turned towards me a face on which his tears had drawn dirty furrows through the dust and mud, the face of an exhausted, defeated old child. There were freckles around his eyes, his chin was badly shaved and his overgrown hair was hanging down on to his dirty collar. He was shivering, with his hands in his pockets. This was no longer the princely child in rags of former times. In heart, no doubt, he was more a child than ever: imperious, capricious and easily discouraged. But such childishness was painful in a boy who was already showing signs of age. At one time, he possessed such arrogant youth that it seemed he could get away with any folly he liked. Now you were more likely to feel sorry for him, because he had failed in life, and then to resent the fact that he evidently persisted in playing this ridiculous part of the young romantic hero. And finally, despite myself, it occurred to me that our fine Frantz, with his exalted loves, must have been reduced to stealing to survive, just like his friend Ganache... All that pride had come to this!" Alain-Fournier, *The Lost Estate*, Penguin Books, London, 2007, p. 177.

237 These lines from *The Lost Estate* prove that awareness: "Almost immediately one of the children who had been on the ground came over, clasped his arm and clambered up on his knee so that he could look at the same time, while another did the same from the other side. Then it was a dream like the one he used to have. For a long time, he could imagine that he was in his own house, married, one fine evening. And that the charming stranger playing the piano, close by, was his wife..." See Alain-Fournier, *The Lost Estate*, Penguin Books, London, 2007, p. 61. Martin Turnell offers the following interpretation of Meaulnes's experience in *le pays sans nom*: "Meaulnes describes his experience at the "mysterious domain" to François who reproduces it in the third person, but it is clear that what we are really hearing is the novelist's own experience translated into highly imaginative terms." Martin Turnell, *The Rise of French Novel*, Hamish Hamilton, London, 1979, p. 232.

238 Martin Turnell, *The Rise of French Novel*, Hamish Hamilton, London, 1979, p. 233.

239 Alain-Fournier, *The Lost Estate*, Penguin Books, London, 2007, p. 45.

240 Maurice, Blanchot, *Friendship*, Stanford University Press, Stanford, 1997, p. 144.

241 *Ibid*, pp. 141-142.

242 Two examples from the work clearly show Meaulnes's estrangement from himself. After the first night at the lost estate Meaulnes leaves his room and goes for a walk. "For a moment, in the garden, Meaulnes leant against the rickety wooden fence around the fish pond: a little ice remained on the edges, thin and wrinkled like a foam. He saw himself reflected in the water, as if leaning against the sky, in his romantic student garb. And he thought he saw another Meaulnes, no longer the schoolboy who had run away in peasant's cart, but a charming fabled being, from the pages of the sort of books given as end of term prizes..." In Meaulnes's diary that is discovered

by Seurel after Yvonnne's death we can find the following description of Valentine: "This was the companion that Meaulnes, the hunter and peasant, must have wished for before his mysterious adventure." See Alain-Fournier, *The Lost Estate*, Penguin Books, London, 2007, pp. 63, 211.

243   *Ibid,* p. 12.

244   *Ibid,* p. 223.

245   Maurice Blanchot, *The Space of Literature*, University of Nebraska Press, Lincoln, 1989, p. 90.

246   This is how Seurel describes his relationship with Yvonne: "Weeks and months went by. Time past! Lost happiness! She had been the fairy, the princess and the mysterious love of all our adolescence, and it fell to me, my friend having left us, to take her arm and say the words that would assuage her grief. Those days, those conversations in the evening after the class that I took in the hillside school of Saint-Benoist-des-Champs, those walks when the only thing that we needed to discuss was the one thing about which we had both decided to say nothing - what can I say about all this? I remember nothing but the memory, already half erased, grown thin, and of two eyes with lids slowly lowered as they looked at me, as if already wishing to see no world except the one inside." Alain-Fournier, *The Lost Estate*, Penguin Books, London, 2007, p. 189. Robert Gibson points out to the variant of this passage in Alain-Fournier's notes that is even more explicit: "Yvonne, I too loved you, although I never told you so. I didn't want to tell you and you didn't guess. Now you will never know. I would have loved other girls, I'd have told you about them, and you would have consoled me. Yvonne, this is how I would have loved you... I would not have been brusque and impulsive like Meaulnes. But what am I saying? You would never have ceased to be that wonderful girl one always seeks in vain." Robert Gibson, *The End of Youth: The Life and Work of Alain-Fournier*, Impress Books Ltd., 2005, p. 319.

247 Blanchot writes: "The image, according to the ordinary analysis, is secondary to the object. It is what follows. We see, then we imagine. After the object comes the image. 'After' means that the thing must first take itself off a ways in order to be grasped. But this remove is not the simple displacement of a moveable object which would nevertheless remain the same. Here the distance is in the heart of the thing. The thing was there; we grasped it in the vital movement of a comprehensive action -- and lo, having become image, instantly it has become that which no one can grasp, the unreal, the impossible. It is not the same thing at a distance but the thing as distance, present in its absence, graspable because ungraspable, appearing as disappeared. It is the return of what does not come back, the strange heart of remoteness as the life and the sole heart of the thing. In the image, the object again grazes something which it had dominated in order to be an object -- something counter to which it had defined and built itself up. Now that its value, its meaning is suspended, now that the world abandons it to idleness and lays it aside, the truth in it ebbs, and materiality, the elemental, reclaims it. This impoverishment, or enrichment, consecrates it as image. However: does the reflection not always appear more refined than the object reflected? Isn't the image the ideal expression of the object, its presence liberated from existence? Isn't the image form without matter? And isn't the task of artists, who are exiled in the illusory realm of images, to idealize beings -- to elevate them to their disembodied resemblance?" See Maurice Blanchot, "The Two Versions of the Imaginary", in: *The Space of Literature*, University of Nebraska Press, Lincoln, 1989, pp. 255-256.

248 Robert Gibson, *The End of Youth: The Life and Work of Alain-Fournier*, Impress Books Ltd., 2005, p. 107.

249 *Ibid,* p. 107.

250 David Arkell, *Alain-Fournier: A Brief Life*, Carcanet Press Limited, Manchester, 1986, p. 35.

251 Robert Gibson, *The End of Youth: The Life and Work of Alain-Fournier*, Impress Books Ltd., 2005, p. 66.

252 Robert Champigny, *Portrait of a Symbolist Hero: An Existential Study Based on the Work of Alain-Fournier,* Indiana University Press, Bloomington, 1954, p 129.

253 *Ibid*, p. 59.

254 David Arkell, *Alain-Fournier: A Brief Life*, Carcanet Press Limited, Manchester, 1986, pp. 40-41.

255 Maurice Blanchot, *The Space of Literature*, University of Nebraska Press, Lincoln, 1989, p. 172.

256 Michel Guiomar, *Inconscient et imaginaire dans 'Le Grand Meaulnes',* Corti, Paris, 1964, p. 224. (The quoted passage is translated by Robert Gibson.)

257 Maurice Blancot, "Encountering the Imaginary", in: *The Book to Come*, Stanford University Press, Stanford, 2003, pp. 9-10. The translation of this passage is modified and, instead of Ulysses, I used the name of Alain-Fournier (together with a short reference to his Encounter in Paris). A similar technique is used in Sreten Ugričić's *Infinitive*.

258 Maurice Blanchot, *The Writing of the Disaster*, University of Nebraska Press, Lincoln, 1995, p. 72.

259 Jorge Luis Borges, "The Immortal", in: *Labyrinths: Selected Stories and Other Writings*, New Directions Publishing Corporation, New York, 1964. p. 120. The translation is modified. Borges mentions the names of Homer and Ulysses, while I am using the names of Alain-Fournier, Seurel and Meaulnes.

260 Emmanuel Levinas, "Reality and Its Shadow", in: *The Levinas Reader* (edited by Seán Hand), Basil Blackwell, Oxford, 1989, pp. 129-143.

261 Robert Eaglestone, "'Cold Splendor': Levinas's Suspicion of Art", in: *Ethical Criticism: Reading After Levinas*, Edinburgh University Press, Edinburgh, 1997, pp. 99-100.

262 Emmanuel Levinas, "Reality and Its Shadow", in: *The Levinas Reader* (edited by Seán Hand), Basil Blackwell, Oxford, 1989, p. 130.

263 Martin Heidegger, "The Origin of the Work of Art", in: *Off the Beaten Track*, Cambridge University Press, Cambridge, 2002, p. 15.

264 Emmanuel Levinas, "Reality and Its Shadow", in: *The Levinas Reader* (edited by Seán Hand), Basil Blackwell, Oxford, 1989, p. 130.

265 *Ibid*, p. 131.

266 See Seán Hand, *Emmanuel Levinas*, Routledge, London and New York, 2009.

267 Plato, *Ion*, Koninklijke Brill, Leiden and Boston, 2007.

268 Emmanuel Levinas, "Reality and Its Shadow", in: *The Levinas Reader* (edited by Seán Hand), Basil Blackwell, Oxford, 1989, p. 131.

269 *Ibid*, p. 132.

270 Otto Pöggeler, "The Seminality of Art", in: *Martin Heidegger's Path of Thinking,* Humanities Press International, New Jersey, 1987. p. 171.

271 Maurice Blanchot, "The Language of Fiction", in: *The Work of Fire*, Stanford University Press, Stanford, 1995, p. 177.

272 Emmanuel Levinas, "Reality and Its Shadow", in: *The Levinas Reader* (edited by Seán Hand), Basil Blackwell, Oxford, 1989, pp. 135-137.

273 *Ibid*, p. 132.

274 *Ibid*, p. 132.

275 *Ibid*, p. 132.

276 Josh Cohen, "'Absolute Insomnia': Interrupting Religion, or Levinas", in: *Interrupting Auschwitz: Art, Religion, Philosophy*, Continuum, New York and London, 2005, pp. 73-74.

277 See Maurice Blanchot, "The Essential Solitude", in: *The Space of Literature*, University of Nebraska Press, Lincoln, 1982, pp. 21-34.

278 *Ibid*, p. 30.

279 *Ibid*, p. 28.

280 Emmanuel Levinas, "Reality and Its Shadow", in: *The Levinas Reader* (edited by Seán Hand), Basil Blackwell, Oxford, 1989, p. 135.

281 See Maurice Blanchot, "The Two Versions of the Imaginary", in: *The Space of Literature*, University of Nebraska Press, Lincoln, 1982, pp. 254-263.

282 *Ibid*, pp. 257-258.

283 Thomas Carl Wall, *Radical Passivity: Levinas Blanchot and Agamben*, State University of New York Press, Albany, 1999, p. 27.

284 Emmanuel Levinas, "Reality and Its Shadow", in: *The Levinas Reader* (edited by Seán Hand), Basil Blackwell, Oxford, 1989, p. 138.

285 *Ibid*, pp. 138-139.

286 According to Levinas, art has an important relationship with dying: "This presentiment of fate in death subsists, as paganism subsists. To be sure, one need only give oneself a constituted duration to remove from death the power to interrupt. Death is then sublated. To situate it in time is precisely to go beyond it, to already find oneself on the other side of the abyss, to have it behind oneself. Death qua nothingness is the death of the other, death for the survivor. The time of dying itself cannot give itself the other

shore. What is unique and poignant in this instant is due to the fact that it cannot pass. In dying, the horizon of the future is given, but the future as a promise of a new present is refused; one is in the interval, forever an interval. The characters of certain tales by Edgar Allan Poe must have found themselves in this empty interval. A threat appears to them in the approach of such an empty interval; no move can be made to retreat from its approach, but this approach can never end. This is the anxiety which in other tales is prolonged like a fear of being buried alive. It is as though death were never dead enough, as though parallel with the duration of the living ran the eternal duration of the interval - the meanwhile." See Emmanuel Levinas, "Reality and Its Shadow", in: *The Levinas Reader* (edited by Seán Hand), Basil Blackwell, Oxford, 1989, pp. 140-141.

287 *Ibid,* p. 142.

288 *Ibid,* pp. 142-143.

289 Maurice Blanchot, "What is the Purpose of Criticism?", in: *Lautreamont and Sade*, Stanford University Press, Stanford, 2004, p. 2.

290 *Ibid,* p. 4.

291 Timothy Clark, *Derrida, Heidegger, Blanchot: Sources of Derrida's Notion and Practice of Literature*, Cambridge University Press, Cambridge, 1992, p. 86.

292 Leslie Hill, *Maurice Blanchot and Fragmentary Writing: A Change of Epoch*, Continuum, London and New York, 2012, p. 17.

293 Emmanuel Levinas, *Existence and Existents*, Kluwer Academic Publishers, Boston and London, 1995, pp. 52-53.

294 *Ibid*, p. 54.

295 Maurice Blanchot, "Literature and the Right to Death", in: *The Work of Fire*, Stanford University Press, Stanford, 1995, p. 327.

296 *Ibid,* p. 327.

297 Rodolphe Gasché, "The Felicities of Paradox", in: Carolyn Bailey Gill (ed.), *Maurice Blanchot: The Demand of Writing,* Routledge, London and New York, 1996, p. 56.

298 Maurice Blanchot, "Literature and the Right to Death", in: *The Work of Fire,* Stanford University Press, Stanford, 1995, p. 329.

299 Emmanuel Levinas, *Existence and Existents,* Kluwer Academic Publishers, Boston and London, 1995, p. 57.

300 *Ibid,* pp. 59-60.

301 *Ibid,* pp. 57-58.

302 *Ibid,* p. 59.

303 *Ibid,* p. 60. In her influential study on Levinas, Jill Robbins explains this link with Lucien Lévy-Bruhl: "The term [participation] comes from the ethnologist Lucien Lévy-Bruhl (1857-1939) who describes primitive mentality's mystic belief in unseen, supernatural forces, its emotional and affective relation to collective representations, which are perceived as having a transitive influence - through 'transference, contact, projection, contamination, defilement, possession.' This belief structure functions concretely in magic and religious practices and 'accounts for the place of dreams, omens, divination, sacrifices, incantations, ritual ceremonies and magic.' Lévy-Bruhl calls the law or logic governing these contradictions *participation*, a way of thinking indifferent to the law of contradiction, 'which finds no difficulty in imagining the identity of the one and the many, the individual and the species, of entities however unlike they may be.' For example, Lévy-Bruhl writes concerning wizards who are believed to turn into crocodiles: 'between the wizard and the crocodile the relation is such that the wizard becomes the crocodile, without, however, being actually fused with him. Considered from the standpoint of the law of contradiction, it must be either one of the two things:

either the wizard and the crocodile make but one, or they are two distinct entities. But prelogical mentality is able to adapt itself to two distinct affirmations at once.' In short, the conceptual structures which characterize participation are utterly heterogenous to our own way of thinking, and constitute, for the evolutionist Lévy-Bruhl, an earlier prelogical stage of modern mentality. See Jill Robbins, *Altered Reading: Levinas and Literature*, The University of Chicago Press, Chicago, 1999, pp. 86-87.

304 Emmanuel Levinas, *Existence and Existents*, Kluwer Academic Publishers, Boston and London, 1995, p. 61.

305 *Ibid*, p. 62.

306 Maurice Blanchot, "Literature and the Right to Death", in: *The Work of Fire*, Stanford University Press, Stanford, 1995, pp. 322-323.

307 John Gregg, *Maurice Blanchot and the Literature of Transgression*, Princeton University Press, Princeton and New Jersey, 1994, p. 50.

308 Maurice Blanchot, "Death as Possibility", in: *The Space of Literature,* University of Nebraska Press, Lincoln, 1989, pp. 93-94.

309 This is what Blanchot writes: "Purposeless passion, unreasonable and vain: this is, on the contrary, what we read upon Kleist's face, and it is this which seems to us imposing -- this passion which seems to reflect the immense passivity of death, which escapes the logic of decisions, which can perfectly well speak but remains secret, mysterious, and indecipherable because it bears no relation to light. Thus in voluntary death it is still extreme passivity that we perceive -- the fact that action here is only the mask of a fascinated dispossession. For this point of view, Arria's impassivity is no longer the sign of the preservation of her mastery, but the sign of an absence, of a hidden disappearance, the shadow of someone impersonal and neutral. Kirilov's feverishness, his instability, his steps which lead nowhere, do not

signify life's agitation or a still vital force; they indicate, rather, that he belongs to a space where no one can rest, and which is in that respect a nocturnal space: no one is welcomed there; there nothing can abide. Nerval, it is said, wandered adrift in the streets before hanging himself. But aimless wandering is already death; it is the mortal error he must finally interrupt by immobilizing himself. Hence the hauntingly repetitive character of suicidal gestures. He who, through clumsiness, has missed his own death, is like a ghost returning only to continue to fire upon his own disappearance. He can only kill himself over and over. This repetition is as frivolous as the eternal and as grave as the imaginary." Maurice Blanchot, "Death as Possibility", in: *The Space of Literature,* University of Nebraska Press, Lincoln, 1989, p. 102.

310 Kevin Hart and Geoffrey H. Hartman write: "...literature for Blanchot indicates our relation with death; more, it discloses that death is itself divided into the negative and the neutral; and this neutral aspect of death - namely, dying - reveals that our response to the world cannot always take the form of possibility or power but is marked by a passivity beyond all usual oppositions of activity and passivity." See Kevin Hart and Geoffrey H. Hartman, "Introduction", in: *The Power of Contestation: Perspectives on Maurice Blanchot*, The Johns Hopkins University Press, Baltimore and London, 2004, p. 6.

311 Emmanuel Levinas, *Totality and Infinity: An Essay on Exteriority*, Martinus Nijhoff Publishers, Boston and London, 1979, pp. 36-37.

312 "The Face, still a thing among things, breaks through the form that nevertheless delimits it. This means concretely: the face speaks to me and thereby invites me to a relation incommensurate with a power exercised, be it enjoyment or knowledge." Emmanuel Levinas, *Totality and Infinity: An Essay on Exteriority*, Martinus Nijhoff Publishers, Boston and London, 1979, p. 198.

313 In "Reality and Its Shadow", Levinas writes: "A being is that which is, that which reveals itself in its truth, and, at the

same time, it resembles itself, is its own image. The original gives itself as though it were at a distance from itself, as though it were withdrawing itself, as though something in a being delayed behind being... The whole of reality bears on its face its own allegory, outside of its revelation and, its truth. In utilizing images art not only reflects, but brings about this allegory. In art allegory is introduced into the world, as truth is accomplished in cognition. These are two contemporary possibilities of being...The discussion over the primacy of art or of nature - does art imitate nature or does natural beauty imitate art? - fails to recognize the simultaneity of truth and image. The notion of shadow thus enables us to situate the economy of resemblance within the general economy of being. Resemblance is not a participation of a being in an idea (the old argument of the third man shows the futility of that); it is the very structure of the sensible as such. The sensible is being insofar as it resembles 'itself, insofar as, outside of its triumphal work of being, it casts a shadow, emits that obscure and elusive essence, that phantom essence which cannot be identified with the essence revealed in truth. There is not first an image - a neutralized vision of the object - which then differs from a sign or symbol because of its resemblance with the original; the neutralization of position in an image is precisely this resemblance." Emmanuel Levinas, "Reality and Its Shadow", in: *The Levinas Reader* (edited by Seán Hand), Basil Blackwell, Oxford, 1989, pp. 135-137.

314   Levinas claims: "The face opens the primordial discourse whose first word is obligation, which no "interiority" permits avoiding." Emmanuel Levinas, *Totality and Infinity: An Essay on Exteriority*, Martinus Nijhoff Publishers, Boston and London, 1979, p. 201.

315   *Ibid*, p. 195.

316   *Ibid*, p. 73. Adriaan Peperzak adds: "In the fourth subsection, "Discourse Found Meaning" (204-9), Levinas shows that speaking is radically different from "the language" ("*die Sprache*") conceived of as an impersonal system or heritage, of which some claim "it speaks." Without the face, there would be neither a beginning in

language nor any signification, for language would not be voiced and addressed by someone to someone." Adriaan Peperzak, *To the Other: An Introduction to the Philosophy of Emmanuel Levinas*, Purdue University Press, West Lafayette, 1993, p. 165.

317 Emmanuel Levinas, *Totality and Infinity: An Essay on Exteriority*, Martinus Nijhoff Publishers, Boston and London, 1979, p. 200.

318 In "Violence and Metaphysics", Derrida criticizes Levinas's insistence on the idea of presence and describes it as Platonic. He also links it with a privileging of speech over writing that is described in Plato's *Phaedrus*. Derrida writes: "The face does not signify, does not present itself as a sign, but expresses itself, offering itself in person, in itself, *kath auto*: 'the thing in itself expresses itself.' To express oneself is to be behind the sign. To be behind the sign: is this not, first of all, to be capable of attending (to) one's speech, to assist it, according to the expression used in the *Phaedrus* as argument against Theuth (or Hermes) - an expression Levinas makes his own on several occasions. Only living speech, in its mastery and magisteriality, is able to assist itself; and only living speech is expression and not a servile sign - on the condition that it is truly speech, 'the creative voice, and not the accomplice voice which is a servant' (E. Jabes). And we know that all the gods of writing (Greece, Egypt, Assyria, Babylonia) have the status of auxiliary gods, servile secretaries of the great god, lunar and clever couriers who occasionally dethrone the king of the gods by dishonourable means. The written and the work are not expressions but signs for Levinas." See Jacques Derrida, "Violence and Metaphysics", in: *Writing and Difference*, Routledge, New York and London, 2002, p. 126. Robert Eaglestone offers a summary of Derrida's main arguments from "Violence and Metaphysics" and also claims that it is possible to read *Otherwise than Being* as a rewriting of *Totality and Infinity* after Derrida's critique. See Robert Eaglestone, *Ethical Criticism: Reading After Levinas*, Edinburgh University Press, Edinburgh, 1997, pp. 130-136. In a long footnote, Joseph Libertson offers a completely different perspective on the relationship between *Totality*

and Infinity and "Violence and Metaphysics." Libertson writes about "Derrida's astonishing incomprehension of Levinas" that stems from the conservative (and traditional) philosophical approach. See Joseph Libertson, *Proximity, Levinas, Blanchot, Bataille and Communication*, Martinus Nijhoff Publishers, The Hague, 1982, pp. 285-286.

319 Robert Eaglestone writes: "The face is fully present for Levinas, a presence that art cannot achieve: this distinction is important in relation to language and the literary artwork. The face is 'this exceptional presentation of self by self, incommensurable with the presentation of realities simply given, always suspect of some swindle.' Artworks here, as in 'Reality and Its Shadow', are swindling and intoxicating, 'where events other than that of the presentation of the original being come to overwhelm or sublimate the pure sincerity of this presentation.' As Levinas has argued, an artwork has nothing to do with original being. He seems here to be following a Nietzschean understanding of the aesthetic as Dionysiac. Poetic activity, 'where influences arise unbeknownst to us out of this nonetheless conscious activity', threatens to envelop the ethical relation and 'beguile it as a rhythm': this concept of 'rhythm' has already appeared in 'Reality and Its Shadow.' However, the ethical relation in language 'dispels the charm of rhythm and prevents the initiative from becoming a role.' Language is 'rupture and commencement, breaking of rhythm which enraptures and transports the interlocutors - prose.' Art is again feasting during a plague, blinding, illusory, and is now understood to be opposed to the expression of the other, to language." Robert Eaglestone, *Ethical Criticism: Reading After Levinas*, Edinburgh University Press, Edinburgh, 1997, pp. 117-118.

320 Emmanuel Levinas, *Totality and Infinity: An Essay on Exteriority*, Martinus Nijhoff Publishers, Boston and London, 1979, p. 70.

321 Emmanuel Levinas, "The Poet's Vision", in: *Proper Names*, Stanford University Press, Stanford, 1996, p. 130.

322 *Ibid*, p. 131.

323 Emmanuel Levinas, "The Other in Proust", in: *Proper Names*, Stanford University Press, Stanford, 1996, p. 103.

324 *Ibid*, p. 104.

325 *Ibid,* p. 100.

326 *Ibid,* p. 102. At the same page, Levinas adds: "It is not the inner event that counts, but the way in which the *I* grasps it and is overcome by it, as if encountering it in someone else. It is this way of taking hold of the event that constitutes the event itself. Hence the life of the psyche takes on an inimitable vibrancy. Behind the moving forces of the soul, it is the quiver in which the *I* grasps itself, the dialogue with the other within the self, the soul of the soul."

327 Blanchot links this passage from *je* to *il* with impersonality and with presence as absence: "Clearly, in me, the power to speak is also linked to my absence from being. I say my name, and it is though I were chanting my own dirge: I separate myself from myself, I am no longer either my presence or my reality, but an objective, impersonal presence, the presence of my name, which goes beyond me and whose stonelike immobility performs exactly the same function for me as a tombstone weighing on a void. When I speak, I deny the existence of what I am saying, but I also deny the existence of the person who is saying it: if my speech reveals being in its nonexistence, it also affirms that this revelation is made on the basis of the nonexistence of the person making it, out of his to remove himself from himself, to be other than his being." Maurice Blanchot, "Literature and the Right to Death", in: *The Work of Fire*, Stanford University Press, Stanford, 1995, p. 324.

328 John Gregg, *Maurice Blanchot and the Literature of Transgression*, Princeton University Press, Princeton and New Jersey, 1994, p. 50.

329 Emmanuel Levinas, "The Other in Proust", in: *Proper Names*, Stanford University Press, Stanford, 1996, p. 105.

330 Jill Robbins, *Altered Reading: Levinas and Literature*, The University of Chicago Press, Chicago, 1999, p. 82.

331 Emmanuel Levinas, *Existence and Existents*, Kluwer Academic Publishers, Boston and London, 1995, p. 58.

332 *Ibid*, p. 58.

333 The influence of Levinas's description of the *il y a* is visible in this passage from "Literature and the Right to Death": "Literature now dispenses with the writer: it is no longer this inspiration at work, this negation asserting itself, this idea inscribed in the world as though it were the absolute perspective of the world in its totality, it is not beyond the world, but neither is it the world itself: it is the presence of things after the world has disappeared, the stubbornness of what remains when everything vanishes and the dumbfoundedness of what appears when nothing exists. That is why it cannot be confused with consciousness, which illuminates things and makes decisions; it is *my* consciousness *without me*, the radiant passivity of mineral substances, the lucidity of the depths of torpor. It is not the night, it is the obsession of the night, which lies awake watching for a chance to surprise itself and because of that is constantly being dissipated. It is not the day, it is the side of the day that day rejected in order to become light. And it is not death either, because it manifests existence without being, existence which remains below existence, like an inexorable affirmation, without beginning or end - death as the impossibility of dying. See Maurice Blanchot, "Literature and the Right to Death", in: *The Work of Fire*, Stanford University Press, Stanford, 1995, p. 328.

334 *Ibid*, p. 337.

335 Maurice Blanchot, "The Outside, the Night", in: *The Space of Literature*, University of Nebraska Press, Lincoln, 1989, p. 163.

336 *Ibid*, 164.

337 *Ibid*, 164.

338 Leo Shestov, "The Last Judgement: Tolstoy's Last Works", in: Ralph E. Matlaw (ed.), *Tolstoy: A Collection of Critical Essays*, Prentice-Hall, New Jersey, 1967, pp. 166-167.

339 N.K. Mikhaylovsky, "'Master and Man' and 'The Death of Ivan Ilych'", in: Edward Wasiolek (ed.), Critical Essays on Tolstoy, G.K. Hall & Co., Boston, 1986, p. 178.

340 Garry Saul Morson, "What Men Quote By: Tolstoy, Wise Sayings, and Moral Tales", in: Donna Tussing Orwin (ed.), *Anniversary Essays on Tolstoy*, Cambridge University Press, Cambridge, 2010, pp. 209-210.

341 Leo Tolstoy, *Master and Man* (translated by Louise and Aylmer Maude), available: http://www.fullbooks.com/Master-and-Man.html [Date Accessed: 12th January 2014].

342 Maurice Blanchot, "The Outside, the Night", in: *The Space of Literature,* University of Nebraska Press, Lincoln, 1989, p. 167.

343 Alain P. Toumayan, *Encountering the Other: The Artwork and the Problem of Difference in Blanchot and Levinas*, Duquesne University Press, Pittsburgh, 2004, p. 163.

344 Joseph Libertson, *Proximity, Levinas, Blanchot, Bataille and Communication*, Martinus Nijhoff Publishers, The Hague, 1982, p. 96.

345 Maurice Blanchot, "The Outside, the Night", in: *The Space of Literature,* University of Nebraska Press, Lincoln, 1989, p. 168.

346 *Ibid*, p. 169.

347 Joseph Libertson, *Proximity, Levinas, Blanchot, Bataille and Communication*, Martinus Nijhoff Publishers, The Hague, 1982, p. 103.

348 Emmanuel Levinas, "Reality and Its Shadow", in: *The Levinas Reader* (edited by Seán Hand), Basil Blackwell, Oxford, 1989, pp. 137-141.

349 *Ibid*, pp. 140-141.

350 Maurice Blanchot, *The Space of Literature,* University of Nebraska Press, Lincoln, 1989, p. 28.

351 In his analysis of Levinas's essay "The Temptation of Temptation", Christopher Fynsk shows that Levinas was aware that "every inspired act, even artistic [...] follows this order of acquiescent engagement wherein commitment precedes articulation of that to which one has committed oneself" (p. 22.). Fynsk also explains that in *Otherwise Than Being* (under the name of "prophetic witnessing") we encounter a clear example of this "temporal inversion" from "The Temptation of Temptation." The basis of "infinite obligation" is temporal paradox that is also, as Blanchot shows us in "Orpheus's Gaze" and in "Encountering the Imaginary", the main feature of literature. See Christopher Fynsk, "Toward the Question of Peace", in: *Last Steps: Maurice Blanchot's Exilic Writings*, Fordham University Press, New York, 2013, pp. 17-33.

352 Emmanuel Levinas, "The Trace of the Other", in: Mark C. Taylor (ed.), *Deconstruction in Context*, The University of Chicago Press, Chicago, 1986, p. 357. The trace is important because it enables us a relation with the radical absence (otherness). In this essay, Levinas describes the trace in the following way: "A trace is not a sign like any other. But every trace also plays the role of a sign; it can be taken for a sign. A detective examines everything in the area where a crime took place, as revealing signs which betoken the voluntary or involuntary work of a criminal; a hunter follows the traces of the game, which reflect the activity and movement of the animal the hunter is after; a historian discovers ancient civilizations which form the horizon of our world on the basis of the vestiges left by their existence. Everything is arranged in an order, where each thing reveals another or is revealed in function of another. But when a trace is thus taken as a sign, it is exceptional

with respect to other signs in that it signifies outside of every intention of signaling and outside of every project of which it would be the aim. When in transactions one 'pays by check' so that there will be a trace of the payment, the trace is inscribed in the very order of the world. But a trace in the strict sense disturbs the order of the world. It occurs by overprinting. Its original signifyingness is sketched out in, for example, the fingerprints left by someone who wanted to wipe away his traces and commit a perfect crime. He who left traces in wiping out his traces did not mean to say or do anything by the traces he left. He disturbed the order in an irreparable way. he has passed absolutely. To *be* qua *leaving a trace* is to pass, to depart, to absolve oneself." *Ibid,* pp. 356-357.

353   *Ibid*, p. 348.

354   *Ibid*, p. 349.

355   Maurice Blanchot, *The Book to Come*, Stanford University Press, Stanford, 2003, pp. 3-4.

356   Alain P. Toumayan, *Encountering the Other: The Artwork and the Problem of Difference in Blanchot and Levinas*, Duquesne University Press, Pittsburgh, 2004, p. 105.

357   Maurice Blanchot, *The Book to Come*, Stanford University Press, Stanford, 2003, p. 7. Blanchot continues: "It is indeed true that it is only in Melville's book that Ahab encounters Moby Dick; but it is also true that this encounter allows Melville to write the book, such an overwhelming, immoderate, and unique encounter that it goes beyond all the levels in which it occurs, all the moments one wants to place it in; it seems to take place well before the book begins, but it is such that it also can take place only once, in the future of the work, in the sea that the work will have become, a limitless ocean." *Ibid*, pp. 7-8.

358   Emmanuel Levinas, "Reality and Its Shadow", in: *The Levinas Reader* (edited by Seán Hand), Basil Blackwell, Oxford, 1989, p. 141.

359 John Gregg, *Maurice Blanchot and the Literature of Transgression*, Princeton University Press, Princeton and New Jersey, 1994, p. 50.

360 Alain P. Toumayan states: "Blanchot employs both the story of Orpheus and the story of Ulysses to construct an encounter with the other that both escapes the intentions of its author and alters the subject without construing the other as power able to alter the subject. Both stories define the work of art as an activity outside of the jurisdiction of individual power and initiative [*fait d'impuissances*], in which, as in the case of Levinasian desire and infinitude, one is invested with something for which one cannot account, and put in the position of thinking more than one can think." Alain P. Toumayan, *Encountering the Other: The Artwork and the Problem of Difference in Blanchot and Levinas*, Duquesne University Press, Pittsburgh, 2004, pp. 112-113.

361 The story of Orpheus recounts his apparent "failure" and the story about Ulysses's encounter with the Sirens is devoted to his apparent "success." Blanchot explains this situation in the following way: "After the Sirens had been conquered by the power of the technique that always tries to play safely with unreal (inspired) powers, Ulysses was still not done with them. They reached him where he did not want to fall and, hidden in the heart of *The Odyssey*, which has become their tomb, they engaged him, him and many others, in this fortunate, unfortunate navigation, which is that of the tale, the song that is not immediate, but narrated, hence made apparently inoffensive: ode becomes episode. See Maurice Blancot, "Encountering the Imaginary", in: *The Book to Come*, Stanford University Press, Stanford, 2003, p. 5.

362 *Ibid,* pp. 3-10.

363 Alain P. Toumayan, *Encountering the Other: The Artwork and the Problem of Difference in Blanchot and Levinas*, Duquesne University Press, Pittsburgh, 2004, p. 105.

364 The temporal inversion that governs Blanchot's retelling of the myth of Orpheus is at work in Ulysses's encounter with the Sirens. In "Encountering the Imaginary", Blanchot calls it "the secret law of the narrative": "To hear the Song of the Sirens, he had to stop being Ulysses and become Homer, but it is only in Homer's narrative that the actual meeting occurs in which Ulysses becomes the one who enters into that relationship with the power of the elements and the voice of the abyss... It is indeed true that it only in Melville's book that Ahab encounters Moby Dick; but it is also true that this encounter alone allows Melville to write the book, such an overwhelming, immoderate and unique encounter that it goes beyond all the levels in which it occurs, all the moments one wants to place it in; it seems to take place only once, in the future of the work, in the sea that the work will have become, a limitless ocean." *Ibid,* pp. 7-8.

365 Lars Iyer, "Blanchot, Narration, and the Event", in: *Postmodern Culture,* vol. 12, no. 3, 2002. available: http://muse.jhu.edu/journals/postmodern_culture/v012/12.3iyer.html [Date Accessed: 24th March 2014].

366 Borges's story where this joining of Ulysses and Homer happens is entitled "The Immortal." Borges warns his reader that the narrated story might seem unreal because it mixes the events of two different men. At the end of the story, this passage from Ulysses (*je*) to Homer (*il*) will will be described as a path toward essential anonymity: "When the end draws near, there no longer remain any remembered images; only words remain. It is not strange that time should have confused the words that once represented me with those that were symbols of the fate of he who accompanied me for so many centuries. I have been Homer; shortly, I shall be No One, like Ulysses; shortly, I shall be all men; I shall be dead." See Jorge Luis Borges, "The Immortal", in: *Labyrinths: Selected Stories and other Writings,* New Directions Publishing Corporation, New York, 1964, p. 120.

367 Lars Iyer, "Blanchot, Narration, and the Event", in: *Postmodern Culture,* vol. 12, no. 3, 2002. available:

http://muse.jhu.edu/journals/postmodern_culture/
v012/12.3iyer.html [Date Accessed: 24th March 2014].

368   Kevin Hart and Geoffrey H. Hartman, "Introduction", in: *The Power of Contestation: Perspectives on Maurice Blanchot*, The Johns Hopkins University Press, Baltimore and London, 2004, p. 6.

369   Blanchot writes: "The writer, then, is one who writes in order to be able to die, and he is one whose power to write comes from an anticipated relation with death. The contradiction subsists, but is seen in a different light. Just as the poet only exists once the poem faces him, only after the poem, as it were -- although it is necessary that first there be a poet in order for there to be a poem -- so one senses that if Kafka goes toward the power of dying through the work which he writes, the work itself is by implication an experience of death which he apparently has to have been through already in order to reach the work and, through the work, death. But one can also sense that the movement which, in the work, is the approach to death, death's space and its use, is not exactly the same movement which would lead the writer to the possibility of dying. One can even suppose that the particularly strange relations between artist and work, which make the work depend on him who is only possible within the work -- one can even suppose that such an anomaly stems from the experience which overpowers the form of time, but stems more profoundly still from the ambiguity of that experience, from its double aspect which Kafka expresses with too much simplicity in the sentences we ascribe to him: *Write to be able to die -- Die to be able to write.*" Maurice Blanchot, "Death as Possibility", in: *The Space of Literature*, University of Nebraska Press, Lincoln, 1989, pp. 93-94.

370   This is especially visible in the discussion about the genre of *Infinitive*. However, what Leslie Hill writes about Blanchot's literary works can also be applied to the work of Sreten Ugričić: "Literature is not an entity coincident with itself and possessed of the purity of self-presence...; it is more like a constant movement of disappearance

and effacement that is perpetually put into crisis by its own lack of stability, identity, or definition. In the end, what Blanchot's novels demonstrate is the fundamental aporia and impossible possibility of literature 'as such'. For literature founds itself only upon the abyss; and whatever literature founds, therefore, including literature itself, is necessarily without foundation." See Leslie Hill, "The (Im)Possibility of Literature", in: *Blanchot – Extreme Contemporary*, Routledge, London and New York, 1997, pp. 68-69.

371 In Blanchot's work the time of time's absence is described in the following way: "It is the time when nothing begins, when initiative is not possible, when, before the affirmation, there is already a return of the affirmation.... The time of time's absence has no present, no presence. This "no present" does not, however, refer back to a past.... The irremediable character of what has no present, of what is not even there as having once been there, says: it never happened, never for a first time, and yet it starts over, again, again, infinitely. It is without end, without beginning. It is without a future. What appears is the being deep within being's absence, which is when there is nothing and which, as soon as there is something, is no longer. For it is as if there were no beings except through the loss of being, when being lacks. The reversal which, in time's absence, points us constantly back to the presence of absence -- but to this presence as absence, to absence as its own affirmation (an affirmation in which nothing is affirmed, in which nothing never ceases to affirm itself with the exhausting insistence of the indefinite)..." See Maurice Blanchot, *The Space of Literature*, University of Nebraska Press, Lincoln, 1982. p. 30.

372 Vivian Liska, "Two Sirens Singing: Literature as Contestation in Maurice Blanchot and Theodor W. Adorno", in: Kevin Hart and Geoffrey H. Hartman (eds.), *The Power of Contestation: Perspectives on Maurice Blanchot*, The Johns Hopkins University Press, Baltimore and London, 2004, pp. 83-84.

373 This is how Blanchot describes the song of the Sirens: "This song, we must remember, was aimed at sailors, men who take risks and feel bold impulses, and it was also a means of navigation: it was a distance, and it revealed the possibility of traveling this distance, of making the song into the movement toward the song, and of making this movement the expression of the greatest desire. Strange navigation, but toward what end? It has always been possible to think that those who approached it did nothing but come near to it, and died because of impatience, because they had prematurely asserted: here it is; here I will cast anchor. According to others, it was on the contrary too late: the goal had already been passed; the enchantment, by an enigmatic promise exposed men to being unfaithful to themselves, to their human song and even to the essence of the song, by awakening the hope and desire for a wonderful beyond, and this beyond represented only a desert, as if the motherland of music were the only place completely deprived of music, a place of aridity and dryness where silence, like noise burned, in one who once had the disposition for it, all passageways to song." See Maurice Blancot, "Encountering the Imaginary", in: *The Book to Come*, Stanford University Press, Stanford, 2003, p. 4.

374 Lars Iyer, "Blanchot, Narration, and the Event", in: *Postmodern Culture,* vol. 12, no. 3, 2002. available: http://muse.jhu.edu/journals/postmodern_culture/v012/12.3iyer.html [Date Accessed: 24th March 2014]. The quotation is modified. Iyer mentions the names of Breton and Nadja, while I am using the names of Alain-Fournier and Yvonne.

375 Emmanuel Levinas, "Reality and Its Shadow", in: *The Levinas Reader* (edited by Seán Hand), Basil Blackwell, Oxford, 1989, p. 132.

376 *Ibid,* p. 132.

377 *Ibid*, pp. 140-141.

378 *Ibid,* p. 142.

379 Emmanuel Levinas, "The Other in Proust", in: *Proper Names*, Stanford University Press, Stanford, 1996, pp. 99-105.

380 *Ibid*, p. 103.

381 Maurice Blanchot, "The Experience of Proust", in: *The Book to Come*, Stanford University Press, Stanford, 2003, pp. 15-16.

382 John Gregg, *Maurice Blanchot and the Literature of Transgression*, Princeton University Press, Princeton and New Jersey, 1994, p. 50.

383 Emmanuel Levinas, "The Trace of the Other", in: Mark C. Taylor (ed.), *Deconstruction in Context*, The University of Chicago Press, Chicago, 1986, p. 348.

BIBLIOGRAPHY

AGAMBEN, G., 2007. *Profanations*. New York: Zone Books.

AGHEANA, I.T., 1982. Borges 'Creator' of Cervantes, Cervantes 'Precursor' of Borges. *Revista de Estudios Hispanicos*, IX, pp. 17-22.

ALAIN-FOURNIER, 2007. *The Lost Estate*. London: Penguin Books.

ALAZRAKI, J., (ed.), 1987. *Critical Essays on Jorge Luis Borges*. Boston: G.K. Hall and Co.

ARISTOTLE, 1922. *The Poetics*. London: Macmillan and Co.

ARISTOTLE, 2004. *Rhetoric*. New York: Dover Publications.

ARISTOTLE, 2007. *On Rhetoric: A Theory of Civic Discourse*. Oxford and New York: Oxford University Press.

ARKELL, D., 1986. *Alain-Fournier: A Brief Life*. Manchester: Carcanet Press Limited.

AUERBACH, E., 2003. *Mimesis: The Representation of Reality in Western Literature*. Princeton: Princeton University Press.

AUSTIN, J.L., 1962. *How to Do Things with Words*. Oxford: Clarendon Press.

BAILEY GILL, C. (ed.), 1996. *Maurice Blanchot: The Demand of Writing*. London and New York: Routledge.

BALDERSTON, D., 1993. *Out of Context: Historical Reference and the Representation of Reality in Borges*. Durham: Duke University Press.

BECKETT, S., 1965. *Proust: And Three Dialogues with Georges Duthuit*. London: Calder Publications Ltd.

BLANCHOT, M., 1981. *The Gaze of Orpheus and Other Literary Essays*. Barrytown and New York: Station Hill Press.

BLANCHOT, M., 1989. *The Space of Literature*. Lincoln: University of Nebraska Press.

BLANCHOT, M., 1993. *Infinite Conversation*. Minneapolis and London: University of Minnesota Press.

BLANCHOT, M., 1995. *The Work of Fire*. Stanford: Stanford University Press.

BLANCHOT, M., 1995. *The Writing of the Disaster*. Lincoln: University of Nebraska Press.

BLANCHOT, M., 1997. *Friendship*. Stanford: Stanford University Press.

BLANCHOT, M., 1999. *The Station Hill Blanchot Reader*. Barrytown: Station Hill.BLANCHOT, M., 2003. *The Book to Come*. Stanford: Stanford University Press.

BLANCHOT, M., 2004. *Lautreamont and Sade*, Stanford: Stanford University Press.

BLEGEN, J., 1972. Writing the Question: About Maurice Blanchot. *Diacritics*, vol. 2, no. 2.

BLOOM, H., (ed.), 1986. *Jorge Luis Borges*, New York: Chelsea House Publishers.

BORGES, J.L., 1964. *Labyrinths: Selected Stories and other Writings*. New York: New Directions Publishing Corporation.

BORGES, J.L., 1970. *The Book of Imaginary Beings*. London: Cape.

BORGES, J.L., 1971. *The Aleph and Other Stories 1933-1969*. New York: Bantam Books Inc.

BORGES, J.L., 1972. *A Universal History of Infamy*. New York: E. P. Dutton & Co.

BORGES, J.L., 1979. *The Book of Sand*. Harmondsworth: Penguin.

BORGES, J.L., 1998. *Collected Fictions*. London and New York: Penguin Books.

BORGES, J.L., 2000. *Selected Non-Fictions*. London and New York: Penguin Books.

BRAVER, L., 2009. *Heidegger's Later Writings: A Reader's Guide,* London and New York:Continuum.

BRUNS G.L., 1989. *Heidegger's Estrangements: Language Truth and Poetry in the Later Writings.* New Haven and London: Yale University Press.

BRUNS G.L., 1997. *Maurice Blanchot: The Refusal of Philosophy.* Baltimore and London: The Johns Hopkins University Press.

BURNETT, J., 1920. *Early Greek Philosophy*. London: A. & C. Black.

CALDERON DE LA BARCA, P., 1998. *Life is a Dream*. London: Nick Hern Books.

CASCARDI, A.J., (ed.) 2002. *The Cambridge Companion to Cervantes*. Cambridge: Cambridge University Press.

CHAMPIGNY, R., 1954. *Portrait of a Symbolist Hero: An Existential Study Based on the Work of Alain-Fournier.* Bloomington: Indiana University Press.

CLARK, T., 1992. *Derrida, Heidegger, Blanchot: Sources of Derrida's Notion and Practice of Literature*. Cambridge: Cambridge University Press.

CLARK, T., 2005. *The Poetics of Singularity: The Counter-Culturalist Turn in Heidegger, Derrida,*

COHEN, J., 2005. *Interrupting Auschwitz: Art, Religion, Philosophy*. New York and London: Continuum.

COHN, D., 1999. *The Distinction of Fiction*. Baltimore and London: The Johns Hopkins University Press.

CONNOR, S., (ed.), 2004. *The Cambridge Companion to Postmodernism*. London and New York: Cambridge University Press, pp. 62-81.

CULLER J., 2000. Philosophy and Literature: The Fortunes of Performative. *Poetics Today*, vol. 21, no. 3.

DE CERVANTES SAAVEDRA, M., 2001. *The Ingenious Hidalgo Don Quixote de la Mancha*. London: Penguin Books.

DE MAN, P., 1979. *Allegories of Reading*. New Haven and London: Yale University Press.

DE MONTAIGNE, M., 2010. *Essais - Livre II*. Guy de Pernon/numlivres.fr.

DERRIDA, J., 1978. *Spurs: On Nietzsche's Styles*. Chicago: The University Of Chicago Press.

DERRIDA, J., 1981. *Dissemination*, Chicago: The University Of Chicago Press.

DERRIDA, J., 1987. *The Truth in Painting*. Chicago: The University of Chicago Press.

DERRIDA, J., 1988. *Limited Inc*. Evanston: Northwestern University Press.

DERRIDA, J., 1992. *Acts of Literature*. New York and London: Routledge.

DERRIDA, J., 2002. *Writing and Difference,* New York and London: Routledge.EAGLESTONE, R., 1997. *Ethical Criticism: Reading After Levinas*. Edinburgh: Edinburgh University Press.

ECHEVARÍA, R.G., (ed.) 2005. *Cervantes's 'Don Quixote': A Casebook*. Oxford: Oxford University Press.

EL SAFFAR, R., (ed.), 1986. *Critical Essays on Cervantes*. Boston: G.K. Hall and Co.

FEHN, A., HOESTEREY, I., TATAR, M., (eds.), 1992. *Neverending Stories: Toward a Critical Narratology*. Princeton: Princeton University Press.

FELMAN, S., 2002. *The Scandal of Speaking Body: Don Juan with J.L. Austin or Seduction in Two Languages*. Stanford: Stanford University Press.

FLAUBERT, G., 1980. *The Letters of Gustave Flaubert: 1830-1857*. Cambridge: Belknap Press.

FOUCAULT, M., 2006. *History of Madness*, London and New York: Routledge.

FREUD, S., 1927. *The Interpretation of Dreams*. New York: MacMillan.

FYNSK, C., 1993. *Heidegger: Thought and Historicity*. Ithaca and London: Cornell University Press.

FYNSK, C.,2013. *Last Steps: Maurice Blanchot's Exilic Writings*. New York: Fordham University Press.

GELVEN, M., 1989. *A Commentary on Heidegger's Being and Time*. DeKalb: Northern Illinois University Press.

GIBSON, R., 1953. *The Quest of Alain-Fournier*. London: Hamish Hamilton.

GIBSON, R., 2005. *The End of Youth: The Life and Work of Alain-Fournier*. Devon: Impress Books Ltd.

GORNER, P., 2007. *Heidegger's Being and Time: An Introduction*. Cambridge: Cambridge University Press.

GREGG, J., 1994. *Maurice Blanchot and the Literature of Transgression*. Princeton and New Jersey: Princeton University Press.

GRUBOR, N., 2005. *Hajdegerova filozofija umetnosti*. Pančevo: Mali Nemo.

GUIOMAR, M., 1964. *Inconscient et imaginaire dans 'Le Grand Meaulnes'*. Paris: Corti.

HAND, S., 2009. *Emmanuel Levinas*. London and New York: Routledge.

HARRIES, K., 2009. *Art Matters: A Critical Commentary on Heidegger's "The Origin of the Work of Art"*. New York: Springer.

HARRIS, N., and SAYNER, J., (eds.), 2008. *The Text and Its Context*. Bern: Peter Lang

AGHART, K., and HARTMANN, G., (eds.). 2004. *The Power of Contestation: Perspectives on Maurice Blanchot*. Baltimore and London: The Johns Hopkins University Press.

HEIDEGGER, M., 1971. *Poetry, Language, Thought*. New York: HarperCollins.

HEIDEGGER, M., 1982. *On the Way to Language*. New York: Harper & Row Publishers Inc.

HEIDEGGER, M., 1996. *Being and Time*. Albany: State University of New York Press.

HEIDEGGER, M., 1998. *Pathmarks*. Cambridge and New York: Cambridge University Press.

HEIDEGGER, M., 2000. *Elucidations of Hölderlin's Poetry*. New York: Humanity Books.

HEIDEGGER, M., 2002. *Off the Beaten Track*. Cambridge: Cambridge University Press.

HILDESHEIMER, W., 1983. *Marbot: A Biography*. London and Melbourne: J. M. Dent & Sons Ltd.

HILDESHEIMER, W., 1983. *Mozart*, London and Melbourne: J. M. Dent & Sons Ltd.

HILL, L., 1997. *Blanchot – Extreme Contemporary*. London and New York: Routledge.

HILL, L., 2012. *Maurice Blanchot and Fragmentary Writing: A Change of Epoch*. London and New York: Continuum.

HILL, L., NELSON, B., and VARDOULAKIS, D., (eds.), 2006. *After Blanchot: Literature, Criticism, Philosophy*. Newark: University of Delaware Press.

HOFFMAN, M.J., and MURPHY, P.D. (eds.), 2005. *Essentials of the Theory of Fiction*. Durham: Duke University Press.

HÖLDERLIN, F., 1988. *Essays and Letters on Theory*. Albany: State University of New York Press.

HURD P., 2007. *Anaxagoras of Clazomenae: Fragments and Testimonia*. Toronto: University of Toronto Press Incorporated.

HUTCHEON, L., 1980. *Narcissistic Narrative: The Metafictional Paradox*. Ontario: Wilfrid Laurier University Press.

HUTCHEON, L., 1988. *A Poetics of Postmodernism: History, Theory, Fiction*. New York and London: Routledge.

ILIĆ, D., 1997. Postoje tri Eudoksa: prvi je ovaj naš. *Reč*, vol. 4, no. 40, pp. 177-180.

ILIĆ, D., 1998. "Čudotvorni" performativ. *Reč*, vol. 5. no. 42, pp. 143-148.

ILIĆ, D., 2008. *Osam i po ogleda iz razumevanja*. Beograd: Fabrika knjiga.

IRWIN, J.T., 1986. Mysteries We Reread, Mysteries of Rereading: Poe, Borges, and Analytic Detective Story. *Modern Language Notes*. pp. 1168-1215.

IYER L., 2002. Blanchot, Narration, and the Event. *Postmodern Culture*, vol. 12, no. 3.

KAFKA, F., 1991. *Blue Octavo Notebooks*. Cambridge: Exact Change.

KIERKEGAARD, S., 2009. *Repetition and Philosophical Crumbs*. Oxford: Oxford University Press.

KOCKELMANS, J.J., (ed.), 1972. *On Heidegger and Language*. Evanston: Northwestern University Press.

KORHONEN, K., (ed.), 2006. *Tropes for the Past: Hayden White and the History/Literature Debate*. Amsterdam and New York: Rodopi.

LEVINAS, E., 1979. *Totality and Infinity: An Essay on Exteriority*. Boston and London: Martinus Nijhoff Publishers.

LEVINAS, E., 1989. *The Levinas Reader*. Oxford: Basil Blackwell.

LEVINAS, E., 1995. *Existence and Existents*. Boston and London: Kluwer Academic Publishers.

LEVINAS, E., 1996. *Proper Names*. Stanford: Stanford University Press.

LIBERTSON, J., 1982. *Proximity, Levinas, Blanchot, Bataille and Communication*. The Hague: Martinus Nijhoff Publishers.

LODGE, D., (ed.) 1972. *20th Century Literary Criticism: A Reader*. London: Longman.

LYOTARD, J., 1988. *The Differend: Phrases in Dispute*. Minneapolis: University of Minnesota Press.

MALLARMÉ, S., 1945. *Œuvres completes*. Paris: Éditions Gallimard.

MATLAW, R.E., (ed.), 1967. *Tolstoy: A Collection of Critical Essays*. New Jersey: Prentice-Hall.

MCHALE, B., 1987. *Postmodernist Fiction*. London and New York: Routledge.

MILIĆ, N., 2001. Od Pjera Menara do Don Kihota, *PH5 - godišnjak za poetička i hermeneutička istraživanja*, pp. 154-214.

MONEGAL, E.R., 1978. *Jorge Luis Borges: A Literary Biography*, New York: E.P. Dutton.

NIETZSCHE, F., 1968. *The Will to Power*. New York: Vintage Books.

NIETZSCHE, F., 2006. *The Nietzsche Reader*. Oxford: Blackwell Publishing Ltd.

NUSSBAUM, M., 1990. *Love's Knowledge: Essays on Philosophy and Literature*. Oxford: University Press, Oxford.

PASCAL, B., 1819. *Œuvres de Blaise Pascal*. Paris: Chez Lefèvre Libraire.

PEPERZAK, A., 1993. *To the Other: An Introduction to the Philosophy of Emmanuel Levinas*. West Lafayette: Purdue University Press.

PLATO, 2002. *Phaedrus*. Oxford and New York: Oxford University Press.

PLATO, 2007. *Ion*, Leiden and Boston: Koninklijke Brill.

PÖGGELER, O., 1987. *Martin Heidegger's Path of Thinking*. New Jersey: Humanities Press International.

POLT, R., 1999. *Heidegger: An Introduction*. New York: Cornell University Press.

RABINOW, P., (ed.), 1984. *The Foucault Reader*, New York: Pantheon Books.

RICHARDSON, W.J., 1967. *Heidegger: Through Phenomenology to Thought*. The Hague: Martinus Nijhoff.

RIVIÈRE, I., 1938. *Images d'Alain-Fournier*. Paris: Emile-Paul.

ROBBINS, J., 1999. *Altered Reading: Levinas and Literature*. Chicago: The University of Chicago Press.

SACERIO-GARI, E., 1980. Towards Pierre Menard. *Modern Language Notes*, vol. 95, no. 2, pp. 460-471.

SANOUILLET, M., and PETERSON, E., (eds.) 1989. *The Writings of Marcel Duchamp*. New York: Da Capo Press.

SCHAEFFER, J., 2010. *Why Fiction?*. Lincoln: University of Nebraska Press.

SCHAPIRO, M., 1994. *Theory and Philosophy of Art: Style, Artist, and Society: Selected papers 4*. New York: George Braziller.

SEARLE, J., 1977. Reiterating the Differences: A Reply to Derrida. *Glyph*, vol. 1.

STENDHAL, 1998. *The Red and the Black: A Chronicle of the Nineteenth Century*, Oxford: Oxford University Press.

STERN, J.P., 1982. Sweet Sin. *London Review of Books*, vol. 4, no. 14.

TAYLOR, M.C., (ed.), 1986. *Deconstruction in Context*. Chicago: The University of Chicago Press.

TOLSTOY, L., *Master and Man*. available: http://www.fullbooks.com/Master-and-Man.html [Date Accessed: 12th January 2014].

TOUMAYAN, A.P., 2004. *Encountering the Other: The Artwork and the Problem of Difference in Blanchot and Levinas*. Pittsburgh: Duquesne University Press.

TRUFFAUT, F., 1978. *Hitchcock*. London: Paladin.

TURNELL, M., 1979. *The Rise of French Novel*. London: Hamish Hamilton.

TUSSING ORWIN, D., (ed.), 2010. *Anniversary Essays on Tolstoy*. Cambridge: Cambridge University Press.

UGRIČIĆ, S., 1993. *Maja i ja i Maja*. Novi Sad: Prometej.

UGRIČIĆ, S., 1997. *Infinitiv*. Beograd: Stubovi kulture.

UGRIČIĆ, S., 1998. O sebi. *Reč*, vol. 5, no. 41, pp. 157-166.

VALÉRY, P., 1958. *The Art of Poetry*. New York: Pantheon Books.

VATTIMO, G., 2008. *Art's Claim to Truth*, New York: Columbia University Press.

VON HERMANN, F., 1994. *Heideggers Philosophie die Kunst*. Frankfurt am Main: Klostermann.WALL, T.C., 1999. *Radical Passivity: Levinas Blanchot and Agamben*. Albany: State University of New York Press.

WARDROPPER, B.W., 2005. *Don Quixote*: Story or History?.*Cervantes's 'Don Quixote': A Casebook,* Oxford: Oxford University Press.

WASIOLEK, E., (ed.), 1986. *Critical Essays on Tolstoy*. Boston: G.K. Hall & Co.

WELLEK, R., and WARREN, A., 1955. *Theory of Literature*. London: Lowe and Brydon.

WHITE, H., 1975. *Metahistory: Historical Imagination in Nineteenth Century Europe*. Baltimore and London: The Johns Hopkins University Press.

WHITE, H., 1978. *Tropics of Discourse*. Baltimore and London: The Johns Hopkins University Press.

WHITE, H., 1990. *The Content of the Form: Narrative Discourse and Historical Representation*. Baltimore and London: The Johns Hopkins University Press.

WRATHALL, M.A., 2010. *Heidegger and Unconcealment: Truth, Language, History*. Cambridge: Cambridge University Press.

ŽIŽEK, S., 2008. *The Sublime Object of Ideology*. London and New York: Verso.

www.ingramcontent.com/pod-product-compliance
Lightning Source LLC
Chambersburg PA
CBHW042042240426
43667CB00048B/2956